Retirement Reconsidered: Economic and Social Roles for Older People

Robert Morris, D.S.W., is the Cardinal Madeiros Lecturer and Senior Fellow at the University of Massachusetts at Boston and Kirstein Professor Emeritus of Brandeis University. He is a Past President of the Gerontological Society of America and a Fellow of the American Association for the Advancement of Science and of the American Public Health Association. In 1987 Dr. Morris was the recipient of the Donald P. Kent Award of the Gerontological Society of America and was presented with an award from the Commonwealth of Massachusetts, University of Massachusetts at Boston, in recognition of lifelong contributions to gerontology and geriatrics in Massachusetts and the nation. He has received research awards from the Ford Foundation, the Veterans Administration, the U.S. Public Health Service, and the National Science Foundation, among others. Dr. Morris has published in all the major gerontological and social welfare journals. His books include *Feasible Planning for Social Change* with Binstock and Rein, *Urban Policy* with Frieden, *Toward a Caring Society,* and, most recently, *Rethinking Social Welfare.* He was the Editor-in-Chief of the 16th edition of the *Encyclopedia of Social Work.*

Scott A. Bass, Ph.D., Associate Professor at the University of Massachusetts at Boston, is the Director of the Gerontology Institute and the gerontology program. He is a Fellow of the Gerontological Society of America and the recipient of the Society's 1985 Ollie Randall Symposium Award. Dr. Bass's research has focused on the state social policy for the elderly and he has written extensively in this area. His first book, which was co-authored, received the 1981 Academic Book of the Year award by *Choice.* Articles by Dr. Bass have appeared in *The Gerontologist, Generations, Educational Gerontology,* and the *New England Journal of Human Services,* as well as other professional journals. Several of the policy papers prepared by Dr. Bass have triggered state legislation or changes in administrative policy. Dr. Bass received a joint doctorate in Psychology and Education in 1976 from the University of Michigan.

Retirement Reconsidered
Economic and Social Roles for Older People

Robert Morris, D.S.W.
Scott A. Bass, Ph.D.

Editors

SPRINGER PUBLISHING COMPANY
New York

Copyright © 1988 by Springer Publishing Company, Inc.

Springer Publishing Company, Inc.
536 Broadway
New York, NY 10012

88 89 90 91 92 / 5 4 3 2 1

LIBRARY OF CONGRESS
Library of Congress Cataloging-in-Publication Data

Retirement reconsidered : economic and social roles for older people/
    Robert Morris, Scott A. Bass, editors.
        p. cm.
    Bibliography: p.
    Includes index.
    ISBN 0-8261-5870-6
    1. Aged—Employement—United States. 2. Aged—United States-
-Economic conditions. 3. Retirement—United States. 4. Aged-
-Employment—Government policy—United States. I. Morris, Robert,
1910-. II. Bass, Scott A.
    HD6280.R43 1988
    305.2'6'0973—dc19   87-36760
                                                                   CIP

Printed in the United States of America

In memory of Frank J. Manning for his vision and leadership in shaping a contemporary view about old age.

Contents

Preface

This volume was stimulated by the Gerontology Institute at the University of Massachusetts at Boston and its associated gerontology program (see Chapter 15 in this volume). Through the university's efforts, graduates have been able to participate in their choice of full-time employment, part-time employment, or volunteer or stipended roles in service to the elderly. The demand for graduates has far outstripped the capacity of the program.

The popularity of the program and the fundamental idea that underlies it—identifying significant social and economic roles for the elderly—led to a series of national symposia mounted by university faculty, first at the national meetings of the American Association for the Advancement of Science and later at the Gerontological Society of America, the Association for Gerontology in Higher Education, and the National Council on the Aging. The response to such public symposia confirmed the belief that the time had arrived for a volume of readings that would examine the societal roles of the healthy able elderly—the majority of older citizens.

This volume explores several dimensions of the possible social and economic roles for the elderly. Many people have contributed to the evolution of these ideas and the many new programs that have since been instituted in Boston. Among them the editors want to acknowledge the great help offered by the University of Massachusetts at Boston from the Chancellor, Robert A. Corrigan; the Provost, Robert A. Greene; and Vice-President Edgar E. Smith. James Jennings, Dean of the College of Public and Community Service, was instrumental in the expansion of programs that involve older people. Outside the university, the late Frank J. Manning, president of the Massachusetts Association of Older Americans, for whom the instructional program is named, was a significant figure in the development of educational opportunities for older learners. His commitment to higher education is being carried on by Elsie Frank, the current president of the Massachusetts Association of Older Americans. Richard Rowland, Secretary of the Massachusetts Executive Office of Elder Affairs, performed a pivotal role in designing the initial structure of the educational program and served as its first director. The growth and funding of these programs to serve older learners was spearheaded by the Massachusetts legislature, with strong leadership by the Senate president, William M. Bulger, and Speaker of the House, George Keverian.

Finally, this book could not have been completed without the ideas and inspiration of the many older learners who entered the gerontology program, studied at the University of Massachusetts at Boston, and forced many around them, including the editors, to reassess and reconsider their capacity to contribute to society. We are grateful for their courage and determination.

In conclusion, we wish to acknowledge the support provided by the gerontology institute in preparing this volume. Particularly, we are indebted to the administrative support provided by Nita Goldstein and the thoughtful copyediting of James O'Brien.

ROBERT MORRIS
SCOTT A. BASS

Contributors

Scott A. Bass, Ph.D., a community psychologist, is the Director of the Gerontology Institute and Gerontology Program at the University of Massachusetts at Boston.

Sally Coberly, Ph.D., is Research Assistant Professor at the Ethel Percy Andrus Gerontology Center, University of Southern California, Los Angeles, California.

Edgar S. Cahn, J.D., Law School, University of Miami, Florida, was the architect of the legal assistance agency system originally funded through the Office of Economic Opportunity.

Yung-Ping Chen, Ph.D., Professor of Economics, is holder of the Frank M. Engle Distinguished Chair in Economic Security Research at the American College, Bryn Mawr, Pennsylvania.

William Crown, Ph.D., an economist, is Senior Research Associate and Lecturer at The Policy Institute on Aging, Brandeis University, Waltham, Massachusetts.

Janice Gibeau, R.N., Ph.D., is Executive Director of the Franklin County Home Care Corporation of Turners Falls, Massachusetts. She holds a social policy degree from the Heller School for Advanced Studies in Social Welfare, Brandeis University.

Gunhilde O. Hagestad, Ph.D., is Professor, Northwestern University, Evanston, Illinois.

Robert B. Hudson, Ph.D., a political scientist, is Professor of Social Welfare Policy at Boston University, Boston, Massachusetts.

E. Douglas Kuhns, an economist, is Assistant Director of Research of the International Association of Machinists and Aerospace Workers, Washington, D.C.

Robert Morris, D.S.W., is Kirstein Professor Emeritus of Social Planning at Brandeis University and Cardinal Medeiros Lecturer at the Gerontology Institute, University of Massachusetts at Boston.

Henry R. Moody, a philosopher, is Director of Academic Affairs at Brookdale Center on Aging, Hunter College, New York.

David A. Peterson, Ph.D., is Director of the Leonard Davis School of Gerontology, Ethel Percy Andrus Gerontology Center, University of Southern California, Los Angeles, California.

Anna M. Rappaport, F.S.A., is Principal at William M. Mercer–Meidinger–Hansen, Inc., Chicago, Illinois.

Peter Plumley, F.S.A., is a consulting actuary, Chicago, Illinois.

George Rohrlich, J.D., Ph.D., is Professor Emeritus of Economics and Social Policy at Temple University, Philadelphia, Pennsylvania.

Frances R. Rothstein, an employment and training consultant to national and local groups on public–private partnerships to promote older worker employment. She was for five years the Research Director of the National Alliance of Business.

Steven Sandell, Ph.D., is Director of the Project on National Employment Policy and Older Americans, National Commission for Employment Policy, Washington, D.C.

Harold L. Sheppard, Ph.D., is Director of the International Exchange Center on Gerontology at the University of South Florida, Tampa, Florida.

RETIREMENT RECONSIDERED: ECONOMIC AND SOCIAL ROLES FOR OLDER PEOPLE

Part I

The Dynamics of Change

1

Toward a New Paradigm About Work and Age

Robert Morris and Scott A. Bass

The late twentieth century is witness to a rapidly maturing American society, the consequences of which are not yet fully realized. For some years the phrase "the graying of America" has been popular, referring to the growing numbers of older citizens; but the phrase does not clarify the major change in the fabric of American society and culture that the concept of maturing entails. For the most part Americans are still influenced by the relative youthfulness of their nation. They share a confidence that the frontiers of opportunity are still wide open and the belief that their destiny will continue to be unique. This helps explain the continuing buoyancy, changeability, and cultural experimentation that have made us the envy of so many in less privileged parts of the world.

This openness to social change and experimentation is seen in our resilience in coping with new patterns of family life, sexual mores, and relationships. But our economic views are slower to change; in this area, static nineteenth-century concepts prevail. Prime examples are the beliefs that the Industrial Revolution made work by older people either unnecessary or undesirable and that by age 60 individual abilities decline too much to fit into a fast-moving world. In reality, however, the abilities and capacities of older people have improved dramatically over the past 100 years. This has created a tension between the popular views about the need for workers and about when people want to or should retire. This tension in the economic sphere, in turn, may propel us into new and unfamiliar forms of economic as well as social relationships with widespread repercussions.

One way of approaching this subject is to consider the common beliefs about who belongs in the labor pool. In the nineteeth century all males from perhaps age 12 to death or decrepitude were considered potential workers, as were young girls and women until marriage. Married women were not encouraged to work. Beginning in the late nineteenth century the labor pool was constricted by child labor laws and the belief that more education was needed in an industrial nation; the pool slowly shrank to those between ages 14 (and then 16, and then 18) and old age. Pensions began to fix the upper end of the pool at around age 65, which fit the physical realities of the times. The consequences were obscured by the vast influx of immigrants who were absorbed into the labor pool. In times of war, when many males were absent from work, women increasingly began to find permanent places in the labor force.

After World War II the components of the labor force settled into the age range 18 or 22 to 65. Up to half of college-aged youth entered college, which became a prerequisite for economic advancement. The labor force was further depleted by the largest standing army in American history: between 2 and 3 million men plus a large number in civilian support positions. An improved economy encouraged many workers to begin retirement as early as age 62 or 60. The labor shortfall was filled by married women entering the workplace in very large numbers.

This oversimplified excursion into the past suggests that our ideas about who belongs in the workforce are quite malleable; they respond to forces we understand only imperfectly and can identify only after the fact. The retirement age has remained relatively fixed, although the physical and intellectual vigor of the elderly has so improved that the physiological and psychological age for removal from an economic role is probably better set at 75 than 65. From a nineteenth-century workforce of males aged 16 to 70 with relatively few women, heavy immigration, and a small standing army, we went to a mid-twentieth-century workforce aged 18 to 62 with many women, a large standing army, and controlled immigration. The world of the early twenty-first century may consist of a workforce made up of adults between the ages of 24 and 70 or 75. In such a context, work for a large number of 65-to-75 year olds is not improbable.

THE FUTURE: A WORLD OF OPPORTUNITY OR OF ALIENATION?

What we do in the twenty-first century will depend as much on social choices as on predetermined economic patterns. These include choices by married women to work or not; government choices about immigration and the size of the armed forces; the desire of able elders to be economically active; and the value placed on more and more education into the 23rd and 24th years. Such choices, of course, will be influenced by such economic factors as the cost of living and the ability to sustain a high level of employment.

This volume explores several aspects of a more mature nation that will determine the future position which older citizens will fill in their society. More specifically, it explores the economic roles that elders can assume and may have to assume. The wealth of nations has always been an important determinant in history, but for the United States, the production of wealth has assumed an importance far overshadowing those other aspects of national life that, in earlier eras, were also of major significance—religion, tradition, inherited class positions, and so forth. An individual or group's position in economic life has become, perhaps, the major source of identity and worth. This identity is often fixed by dollar income, not pride or investment in craftsmanship. And it is in precisely this realm that the rapidly increasing numbers and proportion of older citizens find themselves displaced, either by personal choice or by economic policy.

Whether this exit from the world of work is a step into a new world of undreamed-of opportunity or a step into alienation for a large part of the population cannot yet be definitively determined. But the following chapters review the evidence for creative new roles and new opportunities, based on both the requirements of a changed economy and the social needs of a changed population.

At first glance this seems like a commonplace issue that faces all nations and communities as change works its way through their systems; the fact that change seems to be occurring at an ever more rapid pace need not change the commonplace nature of the events. But a closer examination suggests that the changes that lie ahead will be anything but familiar or commonplace; they may well be in the nature of a slowly building earthquake, which, when it breaks through the traditional crust of daily life, wreaks enormous damage. The possibility of so serious a series of consequences can be seen most easily by comparing what lies ahead with three historical eras when the situation of the aged changed very little.

Classical Times: Labor Required by All

The earliest recorded attitude is that captured in the biblical injunction to honor your father and mother. In later times this injunction has often been translated to mean that each individual has a duty to love and care for his or her parents and by the sixteenth century this personal obligation had been expanded to a public community obligation to care for sick or abandoned or childless elders. But in earlier times the position of the aged was fixed in a pastoral or agrarian society which, when it had urban centers, built them in human scale in which family, clan, and tribal ties and mores were powerful protectors of all members. Except for the powerful nobility, work was required of all, however arduous or however light it might be; an aged and enfeebled elder could still perform essential work in or near the household. When an elder became too ill for even that effort, however, the family ties were likely to reinforce a sense of obligation to care for the elders in their last days. A patriarch's control of land assured both physical care and a vital economic role for the elder.

In Roman times and the Middle Ages the elders often controlled the wealth of a family, and the culture's strong hierarchical structure sustained the authority through most families. On occasions, when this position of authority was abandoned or overturned by force, the results could be tragic. They are described poignantly in *King Lear*, when the old king, having abandoned his authority, is abused by the greed and ambition of his kin.

Middle Ages and Renaissance: Economic and Personal Charity

We know little of the condition of the aged among the larger masses of the Middle Ages. They probably continued to have useful functions to perform on farms, but fewer in the cities. Whatever there was to do, their position was only as secure as their close kin were able to make it. When that failed the church provided alms and institutions for the isolated and sick. The economy of the times had little margin for time-wasting attention to the roles of the elderly; they performed what work there was to do or they begged. Periodic plagues and wars also depleted the population, creating an occasional labor shortage rather than a surplus. Economic life was also transformed. In England, the times were characterized by much upheaval, which left many able-bodied adults periodically without means of self-support and turned them from farm workers to wandering beggars. The Elizabethan Poor Laws were a way to provide some minimal sustenance for the feeble aged and the able-bodied poor, but in ways that confined adults to their parishes. Throughout these centuries the aged for the most part were expected to work or to beg even if work was not available.

Industrial Change: Beginnings of Surplus Labor and Leisure

During the 19th century, the Industrial Revolution gained momentum. While there were mass dislocations of people, and laborers were not treated kindly, the net effect over time was to increase the demand for labor. The aged were not given special attention, except through the Poor Laws and the poorhouses and asylums developed under those laws. This same pattern carried over to America. Respectable American opinion in the nineteenth and early twentieth centuries held that there was work for all who would work, and personal or family charity for those who could not, including the displaced aged. The fact that, periodically at least, there were conditions when labor power was in surplus, when there were more adults than the economy required, was ignored. Work to the end of one's days was an economic and socially imposed standard.

By 1900, Simon Patten, professor of economics at the Wharton School, developed the thesis that America was entering a period when all people's needs could be met with less and less manpower. He anticipated a time when there would be an excess of labor, when working time could be drastically reduced, and when adults would have large amounts of leisure time at their disposal. His concern with this coming situation was focused on how to prepare people psychologically for a constructive social use of the new leisure. In many ways he was a prophet of the view that our 20th-century economy would be one with many "surplus" people, at least in relation to the production of goods.

During most of these centuries, the aged as a group did not play a central role in the evolution of ideas beyond those of the original biblical injunctions: work and family obligations. However, with the twentieth century the capacity of the American economy to produce more goods with less labor was matched by a major change in the demographic nature of its population. Life expectancy grew rapidly as infant mortality declined. Other improvements in health care meant that the elderly became not only more numerous but more healthy, vigorous, and able-bodied. The first policy approach to this evolution was the enactment by many states of old age pension laws and, during the Depression of the 1930s, the national Social Security Act with its provision for almost universal retirement income. Public policy provided an income base to help the no-longer-needed older worker leave the labor force.

CHANGE IN THE LATE TWENTIETH CENTURY

An income-oriented economic approach was welcomed by all at first as solving most problems of old age. But by the 1970s, several probing questions had been raised by quite different interest groups. For advocates of the elderly, the absence of significant roles to which the nonworking, retired aged could move if they wished led to demands that forced retirement at 65 be abandoned. The same groups began to search for alternative meaningful roles for the able aged, especially as retirement incomes encouraged earlier retirement at 62, 60, or even 55. By now, many of the aged were too vigorous to be comfortable doing nothing. This led to rapid growth in education for personal enrichment in retirement and to many new ways to use leisure time, such as by travel and sports. At the same time, the goods-producing dynamism of a consumer society left many significant functions ill attended to. A growing concern with self-gratification produced so strong a dislike for taxation as a way to help the sick and disadvantaged that many public services that characterize a modern industrial society, including health and welfare, began to suffer labor shortages.

To make the contemporary picture even more confused, family functions changed. The driving economy found uses for so many young and middle-aged adult women that the functions once performed by wives at home shifted to restaurants, laundries, and the like, creating a demand for more low-paid workers.

The increase in single-parent working families and families with two working parents increased exponentially the demand for child-care services. However, the older social functions of grandparenting had also been eroded as aged parents established their independent lives apart from their children. This did not produce a break in family psychic and social ties, but it meant less inclination for family members to provide care for children, the sick, and the feeble aged and to perform other household duties as a family obligation. The interaction among these forces is too complex to elaborate here. Suffice it to note that while the aged were no longer so necessary for the goods producing economy, the community and welfare service economy did not directly benefit from the large new surplus labor created by a tradition of early retirement and independent life for the elderly.

By the 1970s economic concerns began to arise about the growing dependency ratio, with the fear that it would create an unbearable burden on the shrinking workforce.

While there is argument about the existence of this dependency shift, its iteration exemplifies the new concern with economic roles for the aged, which matches the concern about the social roles of grandparenting, consumption, or leisure. It captures an interlocking set of concerns about family responsibility, intergenerational obligation, productivity, and taxation; it is reconsidered below at some length.

In the 1980s public perception about the elderly began to shift, especially at the level of national policy making. Retirement with security, even comfort, became a divisive issue in debate over the use of national resources and government budget allocations. More and more the elderly are being viewed from a labor and manpower perspective: those who are made redundant by industry at age 50 or 55 and those who retire voluntarily at age 60 or 65 are seen as surplus labor who may have a role to play if the national economy is not stagnant. But what role? The many unanswered questions that are raised with increasing persistence have the potential for challenging many traditional ways of organizing national and local life.

A few examples can be identified. The threat of intergenerational conflict has arisen as various age groups argue their interests against others—advocates for children, for example, claiming the elderly benefit too generously under present laws. Such conflict, if it really grows, could endanger the sense of community and national solidarity on which public well-being depends. The Social Security Act, foundation for all social provision, was sustained by a consensus now threatened by the conflict.

There is widespread discussion over the best ways to use increased productivity: whether workers should consume more leisure or should work even harder to produce more goods. Workplace patterns are already shifting as new kinds of industry begin to replace heavy industry. Part-time and temporary work is increasing rapidly and in 1986 was estimated to represent 27% of all employment. Such work is often low-paid and insecure, carrying little or no social benefits such as health insurance. Better pay in better jobs demands more years of education or training. The increase in part-time work fits very well the needs and interests of many older and retired workers, but it also means less total annual income for workers so employed. This in turn encourages pressure to redistribute income through higher pay for less work, for everyone regardless of productivity.

The educational system faces a crisis in maintaining its position as the ratio of school and college-aged youth declines for a decade or two. One possible replacement for a dwindling young student body is the new population of elderly students, whose interests and patterns of activity do not fit the conventional educational patterns of most colleges and universities. Interests of the aged are also ambiguous and unsettled, sometimes leaning to cultural self-improvement, sometimes veering to training for a second career.

Finally, the pattern of family relationships and responsibilities seems to be changing as individuals seek to build family ties while at the same time living independent lives. This is especially unclear as policy makers debate the proper boundary for collective and governmental responsibility for children, the sick, and the aged as against family responsibility.

Employment patterns, changing income patterns over the life cycle, the uses of leisure consumption versus goods production, the function of the educational system, and patterns of family relationship are all being shaken up by the maturing of the society both demographically and economically. But this time we seem able to produce material goods without full use of all labor, a situation that did not exist in the past.

This volume is an attempt to explore in depth the work aspect of the role dilemma for the aged in such a mature society. The authors are aware that it is much easier to conceptualize a public issue than it is to act on it in a complex society. Those issues that we explore will not be easy to resolve. A mature society is one that also has its own rigidities of social, political, and economic organization to match the stiffening joints of personal old age. Employers and unions find it most difficult to change patterns of production and employment, especially when so much of that work must now compete with industry in other countries. Attitudes and ways of behaving are deeply ingrained. Even 50 years in which the elderly of an affluent society found it easy to retire from work to leisure is enough time to make it difficult to reconsider the conventional age of retirement as being too early, not too late. The psychological barrier or difficulty arises not only in free-market nations but also in planned economies, where the customary retirement age is already 55 to 60, lower than in the United States.

FUTURE SCENARIOS

Despite these resistances to change, the authors believe that the scale of change that the new demography and the new economy combine to force is so urgent that we must look carefully at the available options. They are limited. We could visualize a world in which more and more people work less and less. That world would force us to confront most directly the meaning of living itself. If work is not needed (the very term may have to be redefined), what do people do with their lives?

Seek hedonistic pleasure? Engage in new active forms of social organization? —but to what ends? Seek to find fulfillment entirely (or nearly so) in family relationships alone? Try to remake the world? —but in what directions? And how will workers react to sharing income with the retired when the few can produce enough goods for all without more labor?

An alternative scenario would read that a surplus of people is temporary, that the labor of most people will be required to maintain the society we define for ourselves, and that this includes the aged who are now retired without work expectation. This approach requires that we consider the potential of technological change and the consequences of the nation's entering more fully than ever a world economy. How will our wages and income be sustained at present levels? Will the new information economy require more low-paying than high-paying jobs? If so, what will the consequences be for the standard of living in the future?

A third scenario, and one we think is most probable, involves a slow redefinition of work and leisure, where dissatisfied able-bodied older individuals place pressure on societal institutions, such as churches, government, schools, family, and corporations, to find flexible ways of accommodating them in meaningful and productive ways. This will involve the identification of labor and tasks that provide personal satisfaction, independence, and flexible use of time. Work will become a matter of choice rather than obligation, although it may become a necessity for the well-being of society. These new roles will emerge after completion of a primary career and may require preparation or training for new careers, which may provide less economic return than a previous career but more personal satisfaction. Such a change in work patterns may involve tension, even conflict, with older people being accused of displacing younger workers or of wage rate "busting" or of unfair appropriation of the benefits of a surplus economy. Nonetheless, the discontent that the elderly often experience in long periods of non-productivity may well combine with the economy's need for constructive use of all man-power resources to crystalize in new collective action to sustain a healthy world economy.

Information Bases for Making Policy Choices

Half a dozen policy issues are the foci around which much debate is being conducted as the maturing American society begins to confront the changes in all its institutions that the new demography of its population is forcing. These changes are in the nature of a low, rolling swell of change, not a sudden sharp shift.

Retirement: The questions about retirement involve both personal and cultural attitudes about withdrawal from work, as well as the formal policies of government and industry that encourage either early retirement or retention in productive work. Practical policy questions such as these arise: age discrimination in the work place; the age at which retirement benefits can be drawn; the generosity of retirement benefits and discharge bonuses; the means of providing medical protection for retirees (by employer extension of medical insurance or by wider national insurance?); whether re-training pro-grams should be designed for older workers as well as for youth and who should finance them. Should education and training concentrate on training older workers for new or second careers or on upgrading skills of the older employed workers to facilitate their retention in jobs they now hold?

Social Benefits: Aside from medical protection, especially for long-term illness, a major issue is presented by women in the workforce. By and large they accumulate less benefits than do their male counter-parts. They retire with less security, or are compelled to continue work longer than men, while at the same time performing household duties for family members without much relief. Can the total of employment and social benefits be better designed for fairness to both men and women?

Intergenerational Equity: The relative improvement in the economic position of the elderly has not eliminated poverty among the aged, but it has raised serious doubts that national resources are being fairly shared between the needy young and the old. The issue directs attention to the larger share of caring for children that still falls on family members. At the heart of this issue is not so the conflict between youth and old age as changing expectations about the responsibilities of government, families, and voluntary associations.

Another dimension is whether the commonly shared problems of youth and age—affordable housing, health care, and income for the most poor—can be handled on any basis that is not categorical and age-dependent.

Leisure Versus Work: Retirement policies of government, of industry, or of individuals involve a tradeoff between work and leisure. It is a matter of policy just how much leisure can be afforded, by society and by individuals.

Labor-Force Requirements: Future decisions concerning the elderly will be influenced by public decision about just how much active manpower society requires at each phase of its evolution. Does economic development require the labor of all its able-bodied, more so than in the past? Will machine technology and economic developments require more manpower (womanpower) or less? Is it in society's interest to reorder the workplace to allow for shared work or part-time work or flexible work schedules and if so, at what level of compensation?

Service Requirements: What changes in the health and welfare services are required by an aging population. The increased demand for medical care is not followed by recognition that long-term social supports are required in increasing volume by a small but growing segment of the older population. Such supports seem to exceed the capacity of families to fill them. How can advance arrangements be made by individuals against this risk, and whence will come the manpower to provide such care? How much of this care must be given in large institutions? And if it is to be given to the elderly where they live, what is necessary to overcome widespread public reluctance to live next to severely disabled people?

Such issues are clearly interrelated, but each can also be approached piece by piece. There are numerous demonstrations and promising ideas afloat, but none has sufficiently broad and wide support or consensus to lead to widespread action by either government or voluntary associations. The foundation evidence for approaching many of these questions is explored in these chapters.

While many of the answers to such questions are speculative, the work option can be examined with some empirical foundation. The following chapters are organized in three sections. Part One lays out the thesis that the third quarter of life (ages 50 to 70) challenges our capacity to absorb in a constructive way the now-retired elders. Rappaport and Plumley lay out the magnitude of the problem and the demographic trends, while Hudson and Moody consider the contradictions that are presented.

Part Two reviews several factors that influence policy choice: the physical and intellectual capacities for work of older people (Peterson & Coberly), and their interests (Sheppard). Sandell reviews best estimates about labor force requirements in the near future. The reality or unreality of the dependency ratio, as a matter of public concern, is examined from differing perspectives by Chen and Crown.

Rothstein and Kuhns review what is known about the attitudes of employers and of trade unions toward work retention of older workers. Hagestad and Gibeau examine the special situation confronting women, who make up so large a proportion of the retired population.

Part Three introduces several broad approaches to the subject: Rohrlich, Bass, and Cahn consider some political, economic, educational, manpower, and cooperative options. The chapter by Cahn is presented as one example of new thinking and experimentation to rebuild community care. Work in the twenty-first century not only will be a sensible role that many of the elderly will desire, but may even be a necessity if the nation is to maintain and improve its level of well-being for all. If we are right, then it is not too early to prepare for the massive changes that lie ahead. Careful planning is needed to avoid the most damaging consequences of a social upheaval of earthquake proportions. But planning must be preceded by a change in thinking, in the paradigm held both by experts and by the public.

2

The Contradictions of an Aging Society: From Zero Sum to Productive Society

Henry R. Moody

PARADOXES OF PRODUCTIVITY

Advocates of greater productivity by older people in an aging society are confronted by a paradox. These advocates urge a new view of late life—a positive view of late life as a time of productivity and social contribution. This view directly contradicts a commonly accepted stereotype of old age as decay and decline (Tibbits, 1979). The stereotype is not only held by the broad public; it serves a crucial ideological purpose in providing an underpinning legitimating social spending on behalf of the elderly in the welfare state. Thus, advocates of greater productivity in old age are faced with the very serious possibility that widespread adoption of their attractive ideal of "positive" old age could well serve to undermine the ideological consensus—the "failure model" of old age (Kalish, 1979)—that has conferred legitimacy on liberal social policies of the welfare state.

In the second place, productivity advocates argue that the conditions for a productive old age—better health, higher levels of education, and flexible opportunities in a service economy—are in fact already at hand (Clark & Barber, 1981). In other words, the vision of an aging society as a productive society is not a utopian dream but a realistic forecast that corresponds to objective historical conditions already coming into being: for example, trends toward the primacy of human capital in a postindustrial economy. Yet this claim seems contradicted by widely known facts. Why, we may wonder, do we not see larger numbers of old people taking on more contributive roles, either as volunteers or in the paid labor force? Why are our major social institutions—corporations, pension funds, training programs, and government social policies—not more responsive to this new opportunity? The simultaneous growth of capacity for productive roles and widespread social needs have so far not called for productive engagement by the aging population. The question of why this has been so remains to be resolved.

The answers to these questions are not clear. But the paradox itself seems inescapable. A recent major collection of essays about the future impact of population aging was titled, significantly, *The Aging Society: Promise and Paradox*, as if to underscore the contradictions inherent in our current situation (Pifer & Bronte, 1986). In recent years, as the American economy has lurched from crisis to crisis, pessimists about future national productivity have called for a reassessment of social policy in favor of greater productivity. On one side, liberals have called for full employment policies, while, on the other side, conservatives have criticized the "revolution of rising entitlements" in the historical evolution of the welfare state (Berkowitz & McQuaid, 1989)[1]. On both the Left and the Right, whether in tax reform, welfare reform, international trade, or educational policy, we see the same themes repeatedly coming to the surface: namely, the need to turn away from sluggish institutional inertia in favor of investment in greater productivity.

This broad shift in policy opinion, in the long run, cannot help but affect how we think about productivity in an aging society. To date, however, surprisingly little attention has been given to policy dilemmas that would be produced by serious attention to productive engagement by the aging population. On the contrary, liberal advocates for the elderly have been on the defensive, generally resisting any pessimistic forecast that might call for spending cuts or serious changes in aging programs. At the same time, liberal defenders of the aged have continued to uphold an image of older people as vulnerable and needy, and therefore, justifiably entitled to benefits: that is, an image of the elderly as consumers, not producers. Portrayed in this way, old people are easily seen as a burden on society, thus unwittingly giving support to pessimistic forecasts about what may happen in the future as this "surplus population" of older people

---

[1] For other historical background, see Gilbert (1984) and Eisenstadt and Ahimeir (1985). On "uncontrollable entitlements" of welfare state spending, see Freeman (1981), Huntington (1975), and Offe (1983).

grows ever larger in size. Ironically, the negative image of old people, as a group, as vulnerable and needy is quickly becoming historically out-of-date. Yet our policy agenda has not changed accordingly. Instead, we are left with deep contradictions in our view of old age that are an index of profound cleavages—"fault lines"—that run across the landscape of social policy throughout the advanced industrialized countries.

Some contradictions highlighted here for American domestic policy in the field of aging are directly tied to questions about productivity in an aging society. First, there is the recent history of falling retirement age combined with rising potential for greater labor productivity in later life. Second, there is the regressive Social Security payroll tax with its burden on the working poor. Third, there is the contradiction between public attitudes of support for present-day social insurance programs combined with declining confidence about the future of those programs. And, fourth, there is the contradiction between objective improvements in the well-being of today's older population and a public image of decline and impoverishment. Let us examine these contradictions briefly.

Retirement

During the post–World War II historical period, when the health and life expectancy of old people have been improving, average retirement age has fallen earlier and earlier. This tendency is an ominous one in terms of the long-run growth of a large dependent population. It is not average life expectancy or even the period of old age that poses a threat, but rather the growing proportion of the lifespan spent in retirement. Over time, the result will be to put more pressure on financing both private pension plans and the Social Security system; this was certainly an element in the crises faced by the system in the late 1970s and then again in 1983 (Estes, 1983; Myles, 1983).

Moreover, this contradiction between rising pension expenditures and falling retirement age is not limited to America. Ann Marie Guillemard has explored in detail similar tendencies since the 1970s in the French labor market and retirement policy (Guillemard, 1983). In France and the United States, as indeed in virtually all of the advanced industrialized countries, we see this same contradiction—enhanced productive capacity (e.g., rising indicators of physical health) combined with declining retirement age and diminished productive contribution to society (Ginzburg, 1983). Whether the pension income of retired persons is understood as a "citizen's wage" or as an earned property right makes little difference from this point of view (Myles, 1984). What we are seeing is the unprecedented growth of a leisured segment of society possessing rising distributive claims on the total wealth of that society in a condition with no collective mechanism, either market-based or government-based, by which productivity gains could offset distributive claims.

Social Security Financing

There is a second set of contradictions closely linked to this trend, but more specific to special historical circumstances of the United States. Unlike those of other countries, the American retirement income system is separately funded by a payroll tax, which is highly regressive in its impact on workers at lower wage levels. In contradiction to the principle of progressive income taxation, the regressive payroll tax falls most heavily on the working poor (Kuttner, 1984). And more than half of American workers now pay more in Social Security taxes than they do in income taxes—in clear contradiction to public principles of equity. Some of the inequity will be reduced by the Tax Reform Act of 1986, but the fundamental contradiction remains.

When we ask if this burden has prompted an incipient tax revolt or intergenerational conflict, the answer is "no". Public opinion polls still show that Americans are willing to pay high taxes to support the elderly. Indeed, social insurance programs are emphatically not perceived as "welfare" programs. They are seen as "legitimate" entitlements and in fact are among the most popular of government benefit programs. Whatever may be the resistance to or feeling about the unfairness of taxes in general, Americans appear not to feel that the payroll tax is unfair. They are much more likely to express antagonism toward the use of tax revenues for "welfare" programs, such as Aid to Families with Dependent Children, or for local school bond issues. This direction taken by the "tax revolt" poses serious dangers of generational equity.

Confidence in the Future

Before passing over the question of public support for Social Security, it is necessary to highlight the contradiction between present support and future confidence. Defenders of old age entitlements are eager to cite public-opinion data showing support for income transfer programs. But when we look to the future, the present aura of good feeling exhibits a disturbing contradiction. Public support for Social Security is not matched by confidence in the stability or future of the system. In fact, younger workers by clear majorities doubt that they themselves will ever collect full Social Security benefits in the future. According to the poll data, confidence in the future of the system tends to be directly proportional to age: older workers believe in the system's future, younger workers do not (Yankelovich, Skelly, & White, 1985). A recent Yankelovich poll on this subject, among supposedly well-informed young urban professionals, revealed that 73% have "little or no confidence" in the Social Security system, and 40% believe that they will likely receive "no payments."

False Consciousness: The Negative Image of Old Age

Finally, public opinion data bring out a further point concerning the "false consciousness" about aging in America today (O'Gorman, 1980). In 1974 and 1981 two comprehensive national surveys were undertaken by Louis Harris and Associates (1981). In that same seven-year period, the condition of older Americans was improving on virtually every indicator measured. Measured by health status, educational level, disposable income, incidence of poverty, life expectancy, psychological morale, and so on, the condition of older people was improving. But in precisely this period, public opinion, among both younger people and older people, perceived the aged as becoming *worse* off over time. Upon more detailed probing, another contradiction emerged. Older people in the Harris survey generally felt that they themselves were doing fine, but other older people, they thought, were in bad shape. This pervasive negative stereotype was shared by both young and old, in direct contradiction to the subjective reports along with all objective indices of well-being.

And the same trend continues unabated, even as the objective condition of the elderly as a group has continued to improve in the Reagan years. In April 1985, a similar survey by the *Los Angeles Times* showed that two-thirds of respondents believed that poverty among the elderly was *increasing*.[2] Yet the 1983 United States census data confirmed a progressive 20-year decline in the poverty rate for those over age 65. Indeed, economic improvement in the population age 65 and older had been so impressive that, by 1983, the poverty rate among the old was no different from the average poverty rate for the

[2]Quoted in the *Wall Street Journal*, December 19, 1985.

rest of the population and, in fact, was far lower than for children as a group. There remain subgroups of older people, such as women and minorities, who still experience serious impoverishment. But these problems should not obscure the dramatic improvements over a 20-year period—improvements that are part of "America's hidden success" (Schwarz, 1983). At the same time, these objective gains in economic advantage and general well-being are directly contradicted by public attitudes toward the aged as a group.

In sum, we have a pattern of contradictions embedded in American attitudes and policies toward the aging. These include the gap between improving productive capacity but diminishing social contribution; the contrast between progressive and regressive principles of taxation; the conflicting attitudes of support for present-day social insurance programs along with pessimism about their future; and, finally, a belief in the declining well-being of the elderly population during the same period when social interventions were improving their objective condition.

Discussion and analysis of these contradictions has proceeded along familiar ideological lines. Conservatives eager to cut benefit programs have cited the broad gains, while liberals, fearful of cuts in programs for the aging, have argued, quite correctly, that substantial subgroups of the elderly (single elderly women, minorities) exhibit serious rates of poverty or other age-related needs, such as long-term care. But this ideological response has failed to illuminate the meaning of the contradictions identified above. Liberals, fearful of conservative attacks on the gains of the welfare state, have resisted acknowledging too openly the gains of the elderly, preferring instead to suppress contradictions or "fault lines" in the present policy structure. Conservatives, interested in dismantling collective provision in all areas, have seized on those contradictions and urged policies of "privatization" based on the premise that the current system is constructed in ways that violate equity or efficiency (Ferrara, 1985).

What both liberals and conservatives, defenders and attackers, of the status quo have failed to do, however, is to provide a coherent analysis of the *historical meaning* of the contradictions apparent in the system. This essay is a preliminary statement of "critical gerontology": an effort at critical assessment of the ideology and institutions of policies on the aging from the perspective of a critical theory of society (Bernstein, 1985). To demonstrate the power of its perspective for contemporary policy analysis, consider as an example an issue of current concern, the so-called generational equity debate.

THE GENERATIONAL EQUITY DEBATE

The vulnerability of old people has been a recurrent theme in modern social policy, and it is one source at least for the idea that the elderly as a group should receive special protection. In fact, in recent American history, the aged, as a group, have been a favored political constituency of the welfare state (Achenbaum, 1982, 1986). Unlike welfare mothers, the unemployed, or minorities, the aged have been regarded as the "worthy poor." Public opinion has repeatedly favored providing support for older people, both income maintenance and health care, even when these were repeatedly denied to other needy groups,such as children or single mothers.

Advocates for the elderly must today face serious questions. Perhaps the most challenging has been raised by the advocates of a concept of "generational equity": that is, the claim that *all* generations and *all* age groups have a right to be treated fairly, that we cannot advocate for increased benefits for the elderly without considering the competing rights and claims of other groups.

Proponents of generational equity fear that present generations of elderly are being unfairly advantaged, while future generations of older people will be less favorably treated at just the time when future generations of younger people will be unduly burdened by supporting them. At the same time, the advocates of generational equity point out that there are serious inequities being experienced by younger Americans, especially by children: for example, the shocking rate of poverty for children under the age of six; the skyrocketing price of housing that has pushed young couples out of the housing market; and the rising burden of Social Security payroll taxes, which, for the working poor, now generally exceed income tax obligations. Their conclusion? Younger workers and children are worse off today than they were a generation ago. Still worse, they point to declining productivity in American industry; to rising federal deficits that mortgage future generations of taxpayers; and to a dismal future for retirement plans, both public and private, as the dependency ratio— the proportion of productive workers to retired person—declines in the future.

What conclusions do the advocates of generational equity recommend? First and foremost, one must recognize that their policy recommendations go beyond policy on the aging and are based on a bipartisan appeal. Many of their recommendations—such as working to reduce the federal deficit, providing more environmental protection, investing more in public education and the needs of children—

will appeal to liberals. Other recommendations—such as cuts in Social Security, pro-family tax policies, and reform of federal civil service retirement policies—will appeal to conservatives. But above all,
the agenda for generational equity is based squarely on the need to
shift toward more emphasis on productivity, savings, and preparation for the future. A left-wing view of intergenerational obligations
emphasizes the need for productivity limited to added news about
collective acts for a common good and differs sharply from both
interest-group liberalism, on the one hand, and neoconservative proponents of productivity through privatization, on the other. The
issues, in other words, concern general economic and social policy
and are not limited solely to benefits for the elderly. There is a danger
that advocates for the elderly may miss this larger context in their
zeal to defend current benefits from any possible cuts. Generational
equity involves at least three different concerns about the future: an
economic concern, an environmental concern, and a demographic
concern.

First, there are the economic concerns—the fear that, as a society,
we are consuming our seed corn and not replacing it. There are many
thoughtful analysts who believe that, beneath the surface prosperity
of the 1980s, there are serious problems being ignored. The economic
concern revolves around trade deficits, budget deficits, low rates of
saving and capital formation, weak productivity gains, and poor
educational preparation of succeeding generations of school children.

Second, there is the environmental concern—the awareness that
our natural resources are being squandered without replacement. It is
significant that the Worldwatch Institute titled its State of the Earth
Report for 1986 *The Children's Fate*. That report concluded that
"although we wish to leave our children a rich inheritance, we are
instead saddling them with an alarming array of debts" (Worldwatch
Institute, 1986).

Third, there is the demographic concern—the coming of an aging
society, where a declining proportion of children is being matched
by declining concern for children, in particular children in poverty.
More ominously, when we look at our practices of work and retirement, health care, retraining, and social services, when we project
these practices into the demography of the future, it is hard to
avoid the conclusion that we are not creating sustainable institutions
that will endure and safeguard future generations, both young and
old.

It is important to realize that what we are now calling the generational equity debate is not something unique or special to the United

States. In advanced industrialized societies all over the globe—in Eastern and Western Europe as well as Japan—policymakers are worried about three things when they think about population aging. First, they are worried about growing costs—the burden of health and pension expenditures for the expanding older population. Second, they are worried about intergenerational competition—how to insure enough spending for educational and human investment in children. And third, they are worried about stagnation—the need to encourage innovation in a postindustrial information economy where a premium is placed on rapid change and creativity, particularly growth in science and technology and where an older population is threatened with obsolescence.

The question for the future is this: How will the liberal coalition, the traditional defenders of the needs of the aging, respond to the new challenge? What seems clear at the moment is that orthodox liberalism—the tradition from Franklin Roosevelt to Walter Mondale—is no longer a satisfactory guide to the future. Somewhere along the line liberals began to separate the idea of economic growth from social welfare (Reich, 1983). Instead of being linked, these two ideas became opposed to one another. Liberal solutions always seemed to involve claims by various interest groups on the public treasury; but little attention was being paid to growth or productivity as a basis for the future. The result was a state of affair Lester Thurow has called the "zero-sum society": a condition in which all attention is paid to *redistributing* resources and which finally leads to a "war of all against all," with each interest group pitted against others competing for a limited pie (Thurow, 1980, 1985). Advocates of the aging who insist that they do not want the needs of the elderly to be pitted against the needs of children are right to resist the competitive outcome. But what solution do they have that can command support beyond an appeal to interest groups and voting blocs, always couched in the language of unlimited human needs? This, in essence, is the crisis of doctrinaire liberalism in a society where the fiscal crisis of the state has become a seemingly permanent state of affairs, where we confront staggering federal deficits as far as the eye can see.

Finally, we need to stress again that, in policy on the aging, we are concerned with an entirely different kind of policy problem from the usual formulation of social policy for vulnerable groups. Neoconservatives are fond of describing the Great Society domestic programs as uniformly a failure: an experiment opening the floodgates of government spending and, moreover, an experiment that was a failure at solving the problems (Murray, 1984). This claim is doubtful to start with but, in any case, no such thesis can be upheld concerning policy on the aging since the 1960s. On the contrary, the heart of today's problem is that, concerning the aged, the liberal agenda has been, to speak ironically, too successful. The reductions in poverty and improvements in health status of older people are dramatic testimony to the effectiveness of social insurance programs, including Medicare. But the limit of those programs is that they are now no longer responsive to the new demographic realities of an aging population. The conflict raised by the tension between success for some and crisis for others demands attention.

A point of departure is provided by Claus Offe in his *Contradictions of the Welfare State* (Offe,1984). Offe develops the familiar Marxist idea that capitalist society contains intrinsic contradictions that are self-destructive for the system as a whole. That is, the system destroys the preconditions for its own existence, as contradictions become intolerable. For example, in Marx's original account, demands for the accumulation of capital are shown to lead to ever greater concentration of capital in the hands of an ever smaller group within the ruling class, while the other classes are progressively impoverished, finally leading to the overthrow of the system.

A different version of the "intrinsic contradiction" thesis is offered by Daniel Bell, in his argument that advanced capitalist economies encourage tendencies toward hedonism and self-augmentation in the cultural sphere (Bell, 1976). The result, argues Bell, is to undermine the discipline and self-restraints needed for capital accumulation and efficient operation of the economic system. Thus, in Bell's sociocultural analysis, as well as in Marx's original version, the political economy of capitalism produces the contradictions that generational-equity debate only publicizes.

This debate brings us to the question of productivity in an aging society. Liberals, characteristically, defend a view of the welfare state that has little room for productivity as a category applicable to the aged population. Liberals have not seen productivity in an aging society as an issue for social theorizing. By contrast, conservatives have repeatedly expressed concern about economic productivity (capital formation, international competitiveness, etc.) (Peterson, 1983). But, like liberals, they treat aging as an item for social welfare considerations alone. From the conservative standpoint, the only thing to be said about policy on the aging is that entitlements should be trimmed and work incentives introduced (e.g., by raising the retirement age).

If new policy alternatives are to be considered, it will be necessary to introduce new theoretical perspectives in which it is possible to make existing contradictions more intelligible.

THE PERSPECTIVE OF CRITICAL THEORY

The generational equity debate and discussion of economic productivity can be analyzed from the perspective of critical theory. I distinguish between three categories of crisis tendencies confronting social policy in general today:

Legitimation Crisis

The "legitimation crisis" refers to the overall loss of government credibility and therefore loss of public support for policies enacted by government. In the American context, the historical origins of the current legitimation crisis can be traced back to the Vietnam War and Watergate, reinforced by the inability of government in the 1970s to contain inflation or respond effectively to foreign and domestic problems. One consequence of that period of turmoil, in the United States and in other industrialized countries, was that conservative governments came to power. From the standpoint of the legitimation crisis, the most important element of this transition was that conservatives, such as the Reagan administration, effectively portrayed government itself as the problem, even when conservatives achieved power. In other words, the leitmotif of legitimation crisis itself is becoming a permanent feature of the political landscape. This does not, in itself, suggest any permanent political realignment or defeat for liberalism. But it does suggest that the terms of the debate have radically changed.

Motivation Crisis

The "motivation crisis" refers to declining confidence in future promises or commitments, accompanied by an unwillingness to sacrifice on behalf of goals required for maintaining the social system into the future. The motivation crisis therefore poses a serious problem for the systemic requirements of advanced industrial society. The motivation crisis contributes to an erosion of psychosocial norms of deferred gratification in favor of present-centered consumption. This contradiction is embedded in the opposing requirements of the economic system itself. On the one hand, consumer buying is needed to maintain economic growth. On the other hand, capital formation and the long-range stability of the system obviously demand at least a minimum degree of constraint on consumption: for example, a necessary rate of savings as opposed to consumer purchasing on credit. But saving for the future in turn requires a form of motivation opposed to the hedonism of individual consumer buying. Thus, individual motives and social system requirements pull in opposing directions, creating a fundamental contradiction in the system.

Fiscal Crisis

The "fiscal crisis of the state" describes the situation where claims on the state's provisions begin to outstrip resources available to meet those claims—a condition that manifests itself in inflation, chronic budget deficits, or some other disruption of long-range economic behavior (O'Connor, 1973). The result is a permanent fiscal crisis, which may erupt into disorder in the monetary system or the international balance of payments. Because of rising demands on the public treasury, the overload erodes the state's capacity to plan and manage economic growth. In the case of policy on the aging, the fiscal crisis is shown in the growing proportion of public budgets, in all industrialized countries, commanded by pension and health costs of the aging population. Some of these costs, such as unfunded pension obligations for municipal workers or civil service and military retirement, are not fully reflected in current accounting procedures— another sign of how the fiscal crisis and motivation crisis are related to one another.

The fiscal crisis of the state reinforces the motivational crisis and the legitimation crisis of Social Security. The fiscal crisis provides an "objective correlative" for private gloom about the future and disbelief in the ability of government to plan and prepare for the future. All three crises raise the temptation of further privatization, where individuals progressively withdraw from government protection in the face of future uncertainty—in turn eroding support for public provision. The popularity of individual retirement accounts (IRA's) among upper-middle-class groups in the United States since the early 1980s is one example of such privatization accompanied by sizable loss of tax revenues: an illustration of how privatization and fiscal crisis reinforce one another.

By analogy to medicine, we can describe a massive depression or civil war as "acute diseases" of the body politic. On the contrary, what we have today is something more akin to a chronic disease—like diabetes or emphysema—that is gradually eroding the health and confidence of the populace. As with chronic disease, the suffering never gets so severe that the patient is prompted to take decisive action that might radically attack the conditions underlying the disease. But, in the long run, the effects of the disease undermine the body politic in far-reaching ways, undermining the recuperative powers that might be mobilized to combat decline. In the case of an aging population, these recuperative powers would include, above all, a shift to policies favoring greater productivity in the future.

CRITICAL THEORY APPLIED TO GERONTOLOGY

Legitimation Crisis

Government benefit programs for the elderly are among the most popular programs supported by the American welfare state. Therefore, it may seem implausible to speak of a legitimation crisis in those same programs. Yet such a legitimation crisis for old age policies is already evident, in part, ironically, because of the public appeals by advocates of the aging to generate political support for their programs in the past. The legitimation crisis for advocacy has two parts. First, there is an *internal* legitimation problem for advocates of the aging: how to assure their credibility in the eyes of the elderly themselves. Advocates of the aging want to speak for the elderly as a whole. They do not wish to emphasize contradiction or competition among subgroups of the elderly.

But the debate over generational equity raises a disturbing specter of divisions among these subgroups, who may have different needs and claims.

Second, there is an *external* legitimation problem: how to preserve support for the legitimacy of public spending on the elderly when past gains have already had an overwhelming positive impact on their welfare. In light of this external legitimation problem, advocates of the aging must be ambivalent about the "good news" of gains made by older people. They of course must celebrate the gains (in order to underscore their own advocacy role in terms of the internal legitimation problem). But at the same time, they must minimize those gains and insist that they are not enough, that problems still remain.

The danger is that if new stereotypes of old people as rich and happy become accepted, then the old will no longer be uniformly seen as the "deserving poor." As legitimacy becomes eroded, old-age advocates run the risk of appearing as just "one more interest group." In that case, power or electoral strength, rather than any moral claim, would become the exclusive factor in political calculations. The result is a contradiction: to maintain the overall unity of the elderly as a group, while acknowledging problems faced by subgroups within the elderly. But this contradiction reflects the deeper contradictions of social class within the older population.

Motivation Crisis

The generational equity debate has called attention to the future of all social insurance programs. Here the debate has reopened a disturbing question, namely: Are we designing sustainable institutions—that is, interage group transfer programs that can endure over generations and command confidence by successor generations? The social insurance transfer programs are not like other government expenditures because they are constructed under assumptions about the long-range future—50 years or more into the future. Here lies the weak link in the system. A motivation crisis arises because the public, particularly young people, no longer have confidence in this long-range future. If Social Security is legitimated as a form of "saving" for my own future, then it must confront serious problems of motivation and confidence in the future.

It is here that a gap opens between individual motivation and the demands of system maintenance: in this case, maintaining the intergenerational transfer payments under Social Security and Medicare. In the conventional rationale for these programs, prior contributions serve to underwrite claims by people to future entitlements—"I paid into the system." For the present, public *support* for Social Security continues to remain high, while public *confidence* in the future of the system is low.

Fiscal Crisis

Current federal deficits are creating serious burdens for future generations. Along with these general economic problems, we must now contemplate new demands arising from population aging, which is occurring in all advanced industrialized countries and is generating strains on health and social welfare systems. Here it is important to distinguish between short-run and long-run strains on those systems. At present, for example, the tax structure of the United States Social

Security system is generating surpluses that fund the federal deficit. Indeed, far from contributing to the federal deficit, Social Security surpluses are actually masking the size of the present deficit. But the federal government budget deficit and large foreign trade deficits combine to create widespread doubt that present expenditure levels can be sustained, let alone assure us about even larger outlays under Social Security expected in the next century.

The crises of legitimation, motivation, and finance are now intertwined. In the face of this, two alternatives are available: on the one hand, a *defensive* response—hold on to what we have got and give no ground to proponents of generational equity; on the other hand, a *constructive* response—to refashion social policies to respond to the contradictions and crisis tendencies evident within the system. It is here that questions about productivity and social contributions by the aging must come to the forefront.

The Political Economy of Aging

In recent years, we have seen the emergence of theoretical perspectives quite different from those associated with the incrementalist, problem-solving style of mainstream social gerontology. I am referring to what can be broadly characterized as the political economy view of aging as a problem of advanced industrial society. This political economy perspective on aging has enormously enriched our understanding of the structural contradictions that have come to characterize policy on the aging in the American welfare state. The writings of Estes and Olson in the United States, and Walker and Guillemard abroad, reveal the contradictions that liberals have preferred to overlook. This perspective underscores the political role of major forces such as corporations, labor markets, capital accumulation, and ideology as these have shaped, not only the development of policy, but the *mystification* of policy in the public mind. Furthermore, by locating specific contradictions of policy on the aging in concrete historical terms, we can now begin to glimpse a way beyond the current impasse of crisis and conflict.

Yet it is just here that the political economy perspective fails to offer the guidance we need. The reason for that failure is that the political economy perspective itself suffers from a crucial, perhaps fatal, ideological deformation that renders it incapable of envisaging a positive resolution for the current crisis. The most serious defect of the political economy perspective is that it remains bound to an

exclusively *redistributive* view of social policy. It fails to take account of
the potential productive or contributive capacities of the growing
numbers of vigorous members of the aging population. What is called
for is a solution that lies outside the zero-sum game of redistributing
consumer goods, whether through the private marketplace or
through the machinery of the state. Neither mode of redistribution
actually enhances productivity or helps channel the new capacities of
the able aging population. On the contrary, as long as we view old
people exclusively as "consumers," as social service "clients," or as
"victims," we consign them to a passive role outside the mainstream
of society. We need to think more imaginatively of old people as
obligated to the common good and as contributors to social purposes
that transcend their own life expectancy. If the generational equity
debate reminds us of this overriding obligation, then it will have
given us a touchstone for assessing social policy proposals for the
aging society of the future.

These policy proposals need to be grounded, on the one hand, in a
critical acknowledgment of contradictions and, on the other, in a
realistic assessment of prospects for concrete change. Both the global
critique and the realism about strategies for action are equally indispensable. One of the best places to begin this exercise is in the area
of publicly funded pension programs, that is, Social Security. There
are those on the Left who have recognized the contradictions in
American policy on the aging in this as in other areas. Awareness of
the problems inherent in a nonfunded public pension system is not
limited to right-wing critics seeking to attack the Social Security system. More recently, on the Left, Robert Kuttner has pointed out that
pay-as-you-go systems seem to invite redistributive disputes among
contending interest-groups: e.g., calls for "generational equity."

Pessimism about the future of an aging society thus results from
the pessimism of redistributive interest-group liberalism tied to the
fiscal crisis of the state. But that pessimistic future is not inevitable,
argues Kuttner. Indeed, he offers as a contrasting case the Swedish
public pension system, which is a funded systems where workers'
contributions are used to purchase bonds for collective industrial
development. Thus the welfare of present and future retirees is tied
to the collective welfare and economic growth of the society as a
whole (Kuttner, 1984). Whether in pension policy, health care, or
social services, a parallel analysis and critique can be offered. Instead
of global pessimism, what we need is a precise delineation of the
contradictions, in ideology as well as social structure, and then the
description of plausible alternatives that give strategic guides for
policy proposals in the future.

Productive Aging and the Zero Sum Society

This brings us back to the question of productivity and the aging society. What is needed today is for the agenda of "productive aging" to find its place in policy proposals about social welfare in an aging society. To understand the strategic and practical political importance of that agenda, we may point to the way that work issues are now beginning to find a place in welfare reform discussion. Few people any more really doubt that work is better than welfare, at least if this is understood to be meaningful, socially productive employment. The real point is that, in welfare-reform debates, the assumptions of the debate have shifted decisively in recent years. The debate is no longer limited to redistributive issues but includes the question of productivity as well. In welfare reform, the issue is no longer whether work, along with training and preparation for work, is to be a part of welfare administration in America. The issue today is how and on what principles preparation for and placement in jobs is to be part of a humane welfare system. Gradually, at least among social policy planners, we seem to be evolving toward a position in which the excess dependency of welfare is no longer seen to be acceptable and also toward a position where, instead of punitive or ideologically polarized proposals, we are experimenting with pragmatic measures such as childcare, transportation allowances, job training, and so on.

It is striking that no similar debate has been occurring or seems about to occur in the field of policy on the aging. Instead, we are treated to pessimistic scenarios of decline on the one hand (e.g., generational equity), or stout defense of the status quo on the other (e.g., interest groups on aging). Even where a few voices have introduced the issue of productive aging, this has not been done in a way that confronts the contradictions of the existing system. On the contrary, easy talk about productivity opens another danger. This is the danger that productivity, the "rising tide that lifts all boats," will be seen as a kind of panacea. In health care policy, there are many who are reluctant to talk about allocation decisions or "rationing" health care and who make the argument that by better efficiency— e.g., squeezing the fat out of the system—we will avoid those kinds of painful, often politically divisive decisions. What we have here is the appealing idea that greater efficiency, or productivity, alone will allow us to avoid having to make clear allocation decisions or decisions about priorities. Fair allocation and distribution choices must join productivity and economic growth in the future to allow us to meet all needs without making divisive choices between children and the elderly.

CONCLUSION: BEYOND THE GRIDLOCKED SOCIETY

This discussion of interest-group politics and ideological deformation, however compelling, could lead us to a conclusion of ineluctable pessimism. Interest groups, including the elderly, will never give up gains in favor of a hypothetical "productivity" that would necessarily involve real losses for some, or, perhaps more seriously, an unraveling of the consensus behind welfare-state spending on behalf of the aged, a unique example of a "deserving" population with political clout as well.

Nonetheless, this pessimistic response would be premature. The success of the 1986 Tax Reform Act, which broke a longstanding logjam of powerful interest groups, is only the most visible example of the power of a determined minority who, for whatever reasons, promote an agenda based on collective productivity rather than gains by special interest groups. We could point to similar successes in the environmental movement, the consumer movement, and other areas where genuine reform has proved possible. To conclude that an aging society must be a "gridlocked society" is certainly premature. But political success along these lines depends on a willingness to confront contradictions in the existing policy system and to break out of an ideological framework that has contaminated even the supposedly "value-free" stance of scientific gerontology.

Proponents of generational equity, along with the political economy school of policy on the aging, have provided valuable contributions to an emerging debate that promises to take on a very different form from the liberal hegemony of the past. In promoting that debate, the ideal of productivity, however contradictory it appears today, must occupy a central role in promoting a more just aging society in the future.

REFERENCES

Achenbaum, W. A. (1982). *Shades of grey*. Boston: Little, Brown.

Achenbaum, W. A. (1986). *Social Security: Visions and revisions*. New York: Cambridge University Press.

Bell, D. (1976). *The cultural contradictions of capitalism*. New York: Basic Books.

Berkowitz, E., & McQuaid, K. (1980). *Creating the welfare state*. New York: Praeger.

Bernstein, R. (1985). *Habermas and modernity*. Cambridge, MA: MIT Press.

Clark, R., & Barber, D., (1981). *Reversing the trend toward early retirement.* Washington, DC: American Enterprise Institute.

Eisenstadt, S. N., & Ahimier, O. (1985). *The welfare state and its aftermath.* Totawa, NJ: Barnes & Noble Books.

Estes, C. (1983). Social Security: The social construction of a crisis. *Millbank Memorial Quarterly*, 61 (3), 445-62.

Ferrara, P. (1985). Social Security: Bad deal for young workers. *Cato Policy Report*, 7(1), 10-13.

Freeman, R. (1981). *The wayward welfare state.* Palo Alto, CA: Hoover Institution Press.

Gilbert, N. (1984). *Capitalism and the welfare state: Dilemmas of social benevolence.* New Haven, CT: Yale University Press.

Ginzburg, E. (1983). The elderly: An international policy perspective. *Millbank Memorial Quarterly, 61*(3), 473-488.

Guillemard, A.-M. (ed.). (1983). *Old age and the welfare state.* London: SAGE

Harris and Associates. (1981). *Aging in the eighties: America in transition.* Washington, DC: National Council on the Aging.

Huntington, S. P. (1975) The democratic distemper. *The Public Interest,* 41(Fall), 9-38.

Kalisih, R. A. (1979). The new agism and the failure models: A polemic. *The Gerontolgist, 19*, 398-402.

Kuttner, R. (1984). *The economic illusion: False choices between prosperity and justice.* Boston: Houghton Mufflin.

Murray, C. (1984). *Losing ground.* New York: Basic Books.

Myles, J. (1983). Conflict, crisis and the future of old age security. *Millbank Memorial Quarterly, 61*(3), 462-472.

Myles J. (1984). *Old age in the welfare state: The political economy of public pensions.* Boston: Little, Brown.

O'Connor, J. (1973). *The fiscal crisis of the state.* New York: St. Martin's.

Offe, C. (1983). Ungovernability: On the renaissance of conservative theories of crisis. In J. Habermas (Ed.), *Observations on the spiritual situation of the age.* Cambridge, MA: MIT Press.

Offe, C. (1984). *Contradictions of the welfare state* (John Keane, Ed.). Cambridge, MA: MIT Press.

O'Gorman, H.J. (1980). False consciousness of kind: Pluralistic ignorance among the aged. *Research on Aging*, 2(1), 105-128.

Peterson, P. (1983, March 17). A reply to critics. *New York Review of Books*, pp. 48-57.

Pifer, A., & Bronte, L. (1986). *The aging society: Promise and paradox.* New York: Norton.

Reich, R. (1983). *The Next American Frontier.* New York: New York Times Books.

Schwarz, J.E. (1983). *America's hidden success: A reassessment of 20 years of public policy.* New York: Norton.

Thurow, L. (1980). *The zero-sum society* New York: Basic Books.

Thurow, L. (1985). *The zero-sum solution: Building a World Class American Economy.* New York: Simon and Shuster.

Tibbits, C. (1979). Can we invalidate negative stereotypes of aging? *The Gerontologist, 4*(3), 10-20.

Worldwatch Institute. (1986). *Annual Report, State of the earth report*. Washington, DC: Worldwatch Institute.

Yankelovich, Skelly, and White, Inc. (1985, August). *A 50-year report card on the Social Security system: Attitudes of the American Public*. Washington, DC: Author.

3

Changing Demographic Profiles in Maturing Societies

Anna M. Rappaport and Peter Plumley

Demographic trends in the United States will have major implications for the future of age at retirement and retirement options. Mortality rates have generally decreased, as have birth rates. As a result, the age mix of the population is shifting upward, and further increases can be expected. The average age at which people retire also has declined to the low sixties. As a result of these trends, if current retirement practices are continued, the balance between workers and retirees will continue to shift, resulting in increasing proportions of retirees and decreasing proportions of workers.

Another set of trends points to a different family composition and economic structure. Divorce and second marriage have become common, and many more women are working outside the home than was the case 15 or 20 years ago. These trends have implications for the aging population because they affect household composition and the likelihood that older persons can get support from family members. Women are most often the ones who provide care for the elderly. The chances that a daughter or daughter-in-law will be available to care for an older person are less today than in the past, and they are likely to be still lower in the future.

Some of these trends have also been experienced by others of the more developed countries. For these countries, mortality rates have also decreased, and in some cases these countries are experiencing lower mortality rates than in the United States. Growth rates are also low, with a consequent change in the population mix.

The less developed countries have different demographic profiles, with higher birth rates and shorter life expectancies. As a result, problems relating to the role of older persons tend to be less significant, at least in terms of the proportion of the population involved.

This chapter will cover the following: (1) the demographic situation in the United States, including trends and how they have developed; (2) demographic characteristics of various segments of the U. S. population; (3) the impact on life expectancy and mortality patterns of a variety of possible medical breakthroughs; (4) a comparison of the situation in the United States with those of other developed industrial and information economies; and (5) some comments on differences between developed and less developed countries.

Throughout, there will be emphasis on understanding how demographic characteristics impact on the labor force and retirement issues. Alternative futures will be considered.

THE DEMOGRAPHIC SITUATION IN THE UNITED STATES

Overview

There are several demographic trends that are of great importance in understanding the work and retirement patterns in the United States. Some of the key trends are:

- Large differences in birth rates and the number of births in different years, with a major bulge, the "baby boom," from 1945 to the early 1960s
- Differences in birth rates by race, with long-term implications for the composition of the population and labor force by race
- Growth in illegitimate births, with a substantial number of these occurring in households that are, and are likely to remain, dependent on public assistance, so that they will have a relatively small role in serving as workers helping to support retirees
- Decreasing mortality rates, particularly at older ages in recent years, so that life expectancy after 65 has been increasing, as has the number of persons over age 80
- Differences in mortality rates between the sexes, so that the older population is very heavily female

- Entry of large numbers of women into the workforce, so that the most common family pattern includes both husband and wife in the labor force
- Increasing divorce rates and the growth in the number of single and single parent households
- More households with unmarried persons of opposite sex sharing living quarters

For each of these trends, data and supporting documentation will be presented, together with the implications.

General Population Trends

Data on a number of variables over the last 80 years show the general shift in population patterns. Birth rates have decreased from 30.1 per thousand in 1910 to about 15.5 in 1983. During the same period, death rates decreased from 14.7 per thousand to 8.6. Infant death rates have dropped from 85.8 per thousand in 1920 to 10.9 in 1983. Divorce rates have risen from 0.9 per thousand in 1910 to 5.0 in 1983.

The population today is one in which the family is more fluid than in the past, and individuals can rely much less on other family members. Many people are geographically mobile and may live far from most of their family. Divorce is common. There are smaller families. For all of these reasons, even as life expectancy increases, those who reach old age are much more likely to have to depend on themselves rather than family members for support and care.

While overall birth rates have been dropping, the trends have not been the same by population segment. Most relevant is the fact that there has been a striking increase in teenage births and births to unmarried women. While some of the births to unmarried women occur in economically stable situations, many are to women who have no adequate personal means of support. These families turn to public assistance and often continue to have children. These mothers do not earn the right to significant Social Security or pension benefits, since they generally do not have any stable long-term employment. The dependency of these families on society as a whole is likely to create increasing pressure on tax dollars and increasing competition between the aged and other groups for scarce resources.

The overall birth rate (births per 1,000 women 15 to 44 years of age) went from 77.5 in 1940 to 116.7 in 1960 then declined to 68.5 in 1980. High, middle, and low projections can be made for the future; in these alternative scenarios, the projected rates for the year 2020 would be, respectively, 80.2, 65.1, or 53.2. In any of these scenarios, birth rates for nonwhites as a category are expected to be higher than for whites, so that the population mix by race can be expected to change.

Mortality Rates and Life Expectancies

The life expectancy data shown in Table 3.1 indicate the effect of decreasing mortality rates. Life expectancy at birth has increased from 46.4 years in 1900 to 69.9 years in 1980 for males, and from 49.0 years to 77.5 years for females. Thus during that period the difference by sex has widened from less than 3 years to more than 7 years. At age 65, the male life expectancy has increased from 11.3 years in 1900 to 14.0 years in 1980, and is projected to increase to 15.6 years by 2040.

For females, life expectancy at 65 has increased from 12.0 years to 18.4 years, and is expected to increase to 20.6 years by 2040.

As expected, these increases in life expectancy have resulted in increases in the average age at death. Table 3.2 shows the trends in average age at death.

Life Expectancies and Expected Periods of Retirement

When the Social Security system was adopted in the 1930s, age 65 was accepted as a standard retirement age in the Untied States. If life expectancies are used to measure expected retirement periods, it can be seen from Table 3.3 that the average length of retirement has

TABLE 3.1   Life Expectancy at Birth and at Age 65

	At birth			At age 65		
Year	Male	Female	Diff.	Male	Female	Diff.
1900	46.4	49.0	2.6	11.3	12.0	0.7
1920	54.5	56.3	1.8	12.3	12.3	0.0
1940	61.4	65.7	4.3	11.9	13.4	1.5
1960	66.7	73.2	6.5	12.9	15.9	3.0
1980	69.9	77.5	7.6	14.0	18.4	4.4
2000 proj.	72.1	79.5	7.4	14.8	19.5	4.7
2020 proj.				15.2	20.1	4.9
2040 proj.				15.6	20.6	5.0

Source: Social Security Administration, Actuarial Study Number 92 (U.S. Senate, 1985).

TABLE 3.2 Average Age at Death—United States

Year	White		All others	
	Males	Females	Males	Females
1900	46.6	48.7	32.5	33.5
1910	48.6	52.0	33.8	37.5
1920	54.4	55.6	45.5	45.2
1930	59.7	63.5	47.3	49.2
1940	62.1	66.6	51.5	54.9
1950	66.5	72.2	59.1	62.9
1960	67.4	74.1	61.1	66.3
1970	68.0	75.6	61.3	69.4
1980	70.7	78.1	65.3	73.6

Source: U.S. Department of Health and Human Services (1982), Vol. II, Section 6, Life Tables.

TABLE 3.3 Age 65 at Retirement

	Male	Female
	Expected period of retirement	
1900	11.3	12.0
1920	12.3	12.3
1940	11.9	13.4
1960	12.9	15.9
1980	14.0	18.4
2000 proj.	14.8	19.5
2020 proj.	15.2	20.1
2040 proj.	15.6	20.6
	Percentage increase since 1940	
1960	8%	19%
1980	18%	37%
2000 proj.	24%	46%
2020 proj.	28%	50%
2040 proj.	31%	54%

increased materially since the adoption of the Social Security system (see Chen, Chapter 5 this volume, for a discussion of "equivalent retirement ages"). The increase in the period after 65 from 1940 to 1980 has been 18% for males and 37% for females. By 2040, the increase since 1940 is projected to be 31% for males and 54% for females.

Age Composition of the Labor Force

The Conference Board data shown in Table 3.4 give projected increases in the labor force by age and sex in the 1980s as compared with the 1970s.

In the 1980s, there will be fewer males under age 25 in the labor force than in the prior decade. Instead, the age mix of the labor force will shift to the middle years. This reflects the ongoing change in the median age of the United States population. After dropping from 30 in 1950 to 28 in 1970, it rose to 30 in 1980. It is projected to rise to 33 by 2000, 38 by 2020, and 42 by 2050 (U.S. Bureau of the Census, 1983).

Labor Force Participation Rates by Sex

Labor force participation rates by sex shown in Table 3.5 indicate small decreases at all ages for males and substantial increases at all ages for females.

The increase in female labor-force participation means that some of the activities previously done in the home must now be provided through purchase in the marketplace. Childcare and care for aging family members are two such activities. The need for care for aging family members will grow more acute as there are more persons over age 65 and as medical science offers the means to keep such people alive longer.

Labor-force participation rates also show the trend to early retirement and the declining labor-force participation at ages over age 65. However, there is some concern that this data may be distorted by

TABLE 3.4   **Projected Changes in Labor Force by Age and Sex (in millions of persons)**

	Ages	1970–1980	1980–1990	Change between periods
Males	under 25	4.1	-1.5	-5.6
	25–54	6.7	8.3	1.6
	55+	0.02	-0.7	-0.7
Females	under 25	3.6	0.3	-3.3
	25–54	9.6	11.1	1.5
	55+	0.8	-0.1	-0.9

Source: Conference Board, (1981).

**TABLE 3.5   Labor Force Participation Rates by Sex
1960 vs. 1980**

Age group	Male rates		Female rates	
	1960	1980	1960	1980
16–19	56.2%	60.7%	39.3%	53.1%
20–24	88.1%	86.0%	46.1%	69.0%
25–34	97.5%	95.3%	36.0%	65.4%
35–44	97.7%	95.5%	43.4%	65.5%
45–54	95.7%	91.2%	49.8%	59.9%
55–64	86.8%	72.3%	37.2%	41.5%
65 +	33.1%	19.1%	10.8%	8.1%
Total	83.3%	77.4%	37.7%	51.6%

Source: U.S. Bureau of the Census (1981). *Statistical Abstract*, p. 381.

two factors: (1) the presence of older persons in the underground economy and (2) the tendency for unemployed older persons who would like work but have trouble finding it to become discouraged and leave the labor force.

Retirement and Life Cycle Patterns

Mary Jones is aged 60, a retired military officer drawing a pension of $12,000 per year and earning $35,000 working as a middle manager in a local bank. Tom Smith is aged 68 and runs a small business from which he earns $5,000 each year; however, the value of the business is increasing. He was a policeman until he reached age 50 and then worked for 10 years as a security officer in a local company. He is drawing Social Security, a police pension, and a pension from the company where he worked. His total retirement is $30,000. Is Mary retired? Is Tom retired?

The traditional life-cycle pattern that underlies defined benefit plan design calls for three periods of life: growing up and education, work until retirement, and then retirement and leisure. In fact, many people have much more varied and complex life cycles. This has been called a cyclical life pattern. Retirement may not be a sudden and total event. Instead, people may have multiple careers, perhaps with interruption between them for leisure and/or more education. Retirement may be more of a gradual process. Retirement benefits are not paid only when the person is not working. Often they are supplemented by wages from other work or earnings from a small business. Likewise, entry into the workforce may be a gradual process, with school and work intertwined over a period of years. There may be serious new periods of education in midlife.

Over the last 30 years, there has been a steady trend toward earlier retirement, at least with regard to employment in large organizations that offer pension plans. However, it is not really known what activity patterns are selected by the early retirees, so that it is not clear to what extent they choose to pursue additional, probably scaled-down, careers. This trend to early retirement is documented by labor force participation rates of males at ages 55 and over.

The trend to early retirement has been reinforced by many early retirement incentive programs, which offer special incentives to employees who retire during a limited period. This has been a major method of dealing with reductions in the workforce.

As mentioned earlier, reductions in mortality rates have increased the male life expectancy at age 65, the normal Social Security retirement age, from 11.9 years in 1940 (soon after Social Security started), to 14.0 years in 1980. When the baby-boom generation ages, there will be a significantly larger percentage of the population over 65 than is the case today. Congress has already taken steps to gradually increase the age for receipt of full Social Security benefits to age 67. It seems inevitable that the meaning of retirement and of retirement ages will have to be reconsidered in light of the changing mortality patterns.

The Impact of Medical Breakthroughs and Life Extension Technology on Mortality and Morbidity

In recent years, there has been a significant reduction in mortality rates, particularly at the older ages. Since 1965, there has been a reduction of about 25% in deaths from cardiovascular disease. Part of this improvement, as well as reductions in rates from other causes, probably is a result of a better understanding of the relationship between health and behavior, which in turn has resulted in improved lifestyles. Much of it, however, is the result of advances in medical technology and a better understanding of the human body.

Improved public health practices were very important earlier in this century in bringing about reductions in mortality, but they have not played a significant role in the United States in the past few years. However, changes in public health practices offer the potential for significant reductions in mortality in the less developed countries.

For the future, as technological advances have an even greater impact on medical research (as seems almost certain to be the case), it is very possible that some major breakthroughs may occur and could bring about significant reductions in mortality, particularly at the older ages. Exactly when and how this will occur is not known; however, some possibilities include:

1. Further major reductions in deaths from heart disease because of a much clearer understanding of what causes it, and the development of medication or encouragement of further behavior changes to prevent or cure it.
2. Major breakthroughs in the effort to develop a cure (or cures) for cancer. Although no such cure is available today, the large amount of medical research that is underway could well result in major breakthroughs in the foreseeable future. This could be particularly true with respect to research involving the body's immune system. Because of the AIDS problem, such research has a high priority at the present time.
3. The slowing of the aging process itself. Although life expectancies have improved tremendously during this century, the maximum lifespan does not appear to have changed materially, remaining at around 110 or so. The development of means to slow the aging process may be a more remote possibility than the other two mentioned above; nevertheless, given the basic medical research that is taking place today, who is to say that such a breakthrough is less of a possibility than was the development of the jet plane, space travel, color television, or the personal computer a few decades ago?

Life expectancy forecasts have been developed using a number of different scenarios with respect to changes in mortality rates. The first of these focuses on the possibility of life extension through a slowing of the aging process, so as to extend the maximum lifespan to ages 120 and 130.

Another scenario assumes that there will be substantial percentage decreases in mortality rates for some of the major causes of death. For example, current mortality rates for heart disease or cancer might decrease by 50%. Or there might be major improvements in mortality rates from all causes, but without any extension of the maximum lifespan.

Table 3.6 compares the life expectancies that would result from these scenarios with current mortality levels for annuitants, using data from Plumley (1986).

TABLE 3.6   Comparison of Male Life Expectancies for Various Mortality Improvement Scenarios

Age in 1985	0	25	45	65	75
Life expectancies					
Basic life expectancy	76.9	53.0	34.0	17.3	10.5
Reduction by cause of death of:					
50% from heart disease	80.5	56.6	37.4	20.2	13.0
50% from cancer	78.1	54.1	35.0	18.0	11.1
50% from heart disease & cancer	82.1	58.1	38.9	21.3	13.9
100% from all except heart & cancer	81.1	56.3	37.0	19.6	12.5
Major improvement from all causes	87.0	62.9	43.5	25.4	17.5
Life extension to age					
120	81.5	57.6	38.6	21.7	14.5
130	85.9	62.1	43.2	26.1	18.6
Increases from basic life expectancy					
Reduction by cause of death of:					
50% from heart disease	3.6	3.6	3.4	2.9	2.5
50% from cancer	1.2	1.1	1.1	0.8	0.6
50% from heart disease & cancer	5.2	5.1	4.9	4.1	3.4
100% from all except heart & cancer	4.1	3.3	3.0	2.4	2.0
Major improvement from all causes	10.1	9.9	9.5	8.2	7.0
Life extension to age					
120	4.5	4.6	4.6	4.5	3.9
130	8.9	9.1	9.2	8.9	8.1

Source: Plumley (1986).

Although these figures are necessarily speculative, future mortality improvement probably will occur either by reductions in death rates from specific causes or from some type of life-extension technology. When it does occur, some significant increases in life expectancies will occur, with resulting further changes in the age distribution of the population.

The differences between the life expectancy figures shown in Table 3.6 and those shown in Tables 3.1 and 3.3 are noteworthy. Table 3.6 shows a basic male life expectancy at age 65 of 17.3 years. The corresponding figure for 1980 shown in Tables 3.1 and 3.3 is 14.0

years. This difference of 3.3 years is primarily due to the fact that the basic life expectancies shown in Table 6 are for annuitants, whereas those shown in Tables 3.1 and 3.3 are for the general population. Since people do not generally purchase annuity contracts if they are not in good health, the annuitants can be expected to have a greater life expectancy than the population as a whole, which of course includes many people in poor health, particularly at the older ages.

The differences between the increases in life expectancies also should be compared. Tables 3.1 and 3.3 show that the life expectancy for a male at age 65 is projected to increase from 14.0 years in 1980 to 15.6 years in 2040, a gain of 1.6 years. On the other hand, Table 3.6 suggests that, if there are major improvements in mortality from heart disease or other major causes of death, the actual improvement in life expectancy at the older ages could be much greater, particularly under the life extension scenario.

While some persons are engaged in research relating to life extension, others are studying how to extend the number of "quality" or productive years of life—that is, the years during which persons are physically and mentally able to be useful and productive.

A related issue, which is getting increasing discussion, is how to determine when an old person is "ill." At the younger ages, illness is relatively clearly defined; however, at the older ages, conditions that would be considered illness at young ages may be viewed as part of the natural process of aging.

The implications of even modest success either in life extension efforts or in extending the number of productive years of life are enormous. Periods of retirement could increase greatly unless age at retirement is changed or retirement is redefined. The types of health care that are needed may change, as well as the period during which substantial health care is needed.

Age and Sex Mix of the Older Population

Older persons are not a homogeneous population. As shown in Table 3.7, one of the most important differences is that instances of chronic health disorders and other limitations on activity are much higher in the population over age 75 than for those aged 65 to 75.

The age mix of the population over age 65 is shifting, with an increasing proportion in the over-75 and over-85 groups. As can be seen from Table 3.7, this has substantial implications for the cost of postretirement medical care. Table 3.8 illustrates the shifting age mix.

TABLE 3.7   **Prevalence of Selected Physical Impairments by Age and Sex, 1979**

| | Number of conditions per 1000 persons | | | |
| | Men | | Women | |
	65–74	75 & over	65–74	75 & over
Visual impairments	85.0	191.1	81.4	175.4
Hearing impairments	290.0	404.9	177.9	363.8
Absence of extremities*	41.4	43.2	12.3	12.3
Paralysis of extremities*	21.4	17.3	22.2	12.1
Deformities or orthopedic impairments of:				
Back	81.8	65.7	114.0	100.9
Upper extremities	35.3	21.1	15.3	31.6
Lower extremities	44.8	55.1	57.0	69.0

*or parts of extremities.
Source: U.S. Senate (1985b).

The distribution of the older population by sex also is changing. As Table 3.1 indicated, the life expectancy of females at birth and at age 65 is significantly greater than for males. Furthermore, this difference is increasing and is projected to continue to increase in the years ahead. The result is that, although about 50% of the under-65 population is female, around 60% of the over-65 and 70% of the over-85 population is female. This male–female imbalance is expected to continue to grow, so that by the year 2000, for example, about 73% of the over–85 population may be female.

This has implications for the economic and family status of the older population. Older females are much more likely to be living alone than are older males. Widowers are much more likely to remarry than are widows. Older females also are much less likely to have substantial retirement income based on their own employment, and continued Social Security spouse benefits are at a lower level than the benefits paid to the worker. Older females who live alone are the people most likely to need long-term care.

COMPARATIVE DEMOGRAPHIC DATA

The same types of trends found in the United States can also be found in industrialized nations generally. All of these countries have experienced increases in life expectancy due to improvements in public

TABLE 3.8 Actual and Projected Growth of Older Population—1900–2040

Year	Total— All ages	Ages 55–64	Ages 65–74	Ages 75–84	Ages 85 +
		Number of persons (in thousands)			
1900	76,303	4,009	2,189	772	123
1920	105,711	6,532	3,464	1,259	210
1940	131,669	10,572	6,375	2,278	365
1960	179,323	15,572	10,997	4,633	929
1980	226,505	21,700	15,578	7,727	2,240
2000 proj.	267,955	23,767	17,677	12,318	4,926
2020 proj.	296,597	40,298	29,855	14,486	7,081
2040 proj.	308,559	34,717	29,272	24,882	12,834
		Percentage of total in age group			
1900		5.3%	2.9%	1.0%	0.2%
1920		6.2%	3.3%	1.2%	0.2%
1940		8.0%	4.8%	1.7%	0.3%
1960		8.7%	6.1%	2.6%	0.5%
1980		9.6%	6.9%	3.4%	1.0%
2000 proj.		8.9%	6.6%	4.6%	1.8%
2020 proj.		13.6%	10.1%	4.9%	2.4%
2040 proj.		11.3%	9.5%	8.1%	4.2%
		Percentage of Age 65 population in age group			
1900			71.0%	25.0%	4.0%
1920			70.2%	25.5%	4.3%
1940			70.7%	25.3%	4.0%
1960			66.4%	28.0%	5.6%
1980			61.0%	30.2%	8.8%
2000 proj.			50.6%	35.3%	14.1%
2020 proj.			58.1%	28.2%	13.8%
2040 proj.			43.7%	37.1%	19.2%

Source: U.S. Senate (1985a).

health and medical technology and changes in the family composition. Table 3.9 shows crude birth rates for the United States and other countries.

These are selected examples, selected to illustrate the differences. All of the more developed countries with industrial and information economies show several characteristics that are quite similar to those of the United States. They include: (1) male life expectancies at birth of 70 years or more, (2) female life expectancies at birth of 76 years or more, (3) significantly longer life expectancies for females than males; and (4) relatively low birth rates.

The issues the United States will face with respect to the age mix of the population will also be found in these other countries. Some will have a relatively high proportion of older persons earlier, largely because they experienced a different historical pattern of births.

In contrast, the less developed countries have much higher birth rates—generally three to four times as high as those of the industrialized countries. They also have much lower life expectancies for both men and women. In some less developed countries, the life expectancy is less for women than for men, whereas the more developed countries all show a substantially greater life expectancy for women than men. Thus issues relating to the age group over age 65 would not appear to be of nearly as much concern in the less developed countries.

The net effect of greater population growth in the less developed countries and the shifting age distribution in the more developed countries is illustrated in Table 3.10.

TABLE 3.9   Growth and Birth Rates and Life Expectancies
             Selected Countries

Country	1984 growth rate (percent)	Crude Birth Rate (per 1,000)	Expectation of life at birth in Years	
			Male	Female
United States	0.9	15	70	78
More developed regions				
Australia	1.3	15–16	71	78
Canada	.9–1.3	15	70	77
France	.4–.5	14–15	70	78
Japan	.5–.6	11–12	73	79
Spain	.4–1.1	12–17	70	76
United Kingdom	−.1–.2	12–13	70	76
Less developed regions				
Afghanistan	2.3	48	41	40
Bangladesh	3.1	48–49	50	47
India	2.1–2.2	34–35	51	50
Pakistan	2.6–2.7	43–44	49	47
Uganda	3.0–3.1	46–50	46	47

Source: U.S. Bureau of the Census, World Population 1984, forthcoming.

TABLE 3.10 World Population Characteristics, 1975–1984, and Projections to 1995

	Actual					Projected	
	1975	1980	1983	1984	1985	1990	1995
Population (in millions)							
World total	4,082	4,451	4,687	4,767	4,846	5,263	5,712
Males	2,045	2,232	2,353	2,393	2,434	2,646	2,873
Females	2,037	2,219	2,334	2,374	2,412	2,617	2,839
More developed regions	1,096	1,136	1,159	1,167	1,174	1,208	1,238
Less developed regions	2,987	3,315	3,528	3,600	3,672	4,055	4,474
Percent distribution of population by age—more developed countries							
Under 5 years old	13.6%	12.2%	12.0%	11.9%	11.8%	11.4%	11.1%
5 to 14 years old	23.5%	23.4%	22.5%	22.2%	21.9%	20.6%	20.0%
50 to 64 years old	57.4%	58.6%	59.8%	60.2%	60.6%	62.1%	62.6%
65 years old +	5.5%	5.8%	5.7%	5.7%	5.7%	5.9%	6.3%
Population characteristics							
Median age	21.6	22.4	22.9	23.1	23.3	24.2	25.3
Population per square mile	78	85	89	91	92	100	109

Source: U.S. Bureau of the Census, World Population 1984, forthcoming, and unpublished data.

Labor force characteristics seen in Tables 3.11, 3.12, and 3.13 show that within the more developed countries there are some differences that reflect the differences in culture.

As Table 3.13 shows, major increases in female labor force participation are found in the United States, Canada, Sweden, and the United Kingdom. France shows a much smaller increase. Italy and Germany show flat female labor participation, and Japan shows a small decline in female labor force participation. The percentage of the labor force that is female has also increased in the United States, Canada, and Sweden, and to a lesser extent in France and the United Kingdom. This data demonstrate that while there is much commonality in the patterns of birth and death rates, there is much more

TABLE 3.11   Labor Force Participation Rates

Country	Year					
	1960	1970	1975	1980	1982	1983
United States	90.5%	85.4%	84.7%	84.7%	84.3%	
Canada	91.1%	84.7%	86.2%	86.3%	84.9%	
France	95.5%	87.8%	84.4%	82.5%	80.4%	
Germany, F.R.	94.4%	92.5%	87.0%	83.4%	81.2%	
Italy	95.3%	86.8%	84.2%	82.9%	81.8%	
Japan	92.2%	89.4%	89.7%	89.0%	89.1%	
Sweden	98.5%	88.8%	89.2%	87.8%	86.3%	
United Kingdom	98.1%	94.3%	92.2%	90.8%	90.4%	

Source: U.S. Bureau of the Census (1984).

TABLE 3.12   Female Labor Force Participation Rates

Country	Year					
	1960	1970	1975	1980	1982	1983
	Female participation rates					
United States	42.6%	48.9%	53.2%	59.7%	61.4%	
Canada	33.7%	43.2%	50.0%	57.2%	58.9%	
France	45.4%	47.5%	49.9%	52.5%	52.9%	
Germany, F.R.	49.2%	48.1%	49.6%	50.0%	49.8%	
Italy	39.6%	33.5%	34.6%	39.8%	40.3%	
Japan	60.1%	55.4%	51.7%	54.9%	55.9%	
Sweden	50.1%	59.4%	67.6%	74.1%	75.9%	
United Kingdom	46.1%	50.8%	55.3%	58.7%	57.7%	

Source: U.S. Bureau of the Census (1984).

TABLE 3.13   Females as Percent of Total Labor Force

Country	Year					
	1960	1970	1975	1980	1982	1983
United States	36.7%	39.1%	41.9%	42.8%	43.0%	
Canada	33.3%	36.5%	40.0%	41.0%	41.5%	
France	35.4%	37.1%	40.1%	39.3%	39.3%	
Germany, F.R.	35.9%	37.2%	38.1%	38.3%	38.4%	
Italy	26.8%	28.0%	33.4%	33.8%	34.2%	
Japan	39.3%	37.3%	38.7%	39.0%	39.5%	
Sweden	39.5%	42.5%	45.2%	46.3%	46.6%	
United Kingdom	35.3%	37.7%	39.5%	39.1%	39.6%	

Participation rates based on labor force of all ages as percent of population 15–64 years old
Source: U.S. Bureau of the Census (1984).

variation with respect to female labor force participation, and probably also family structure.

Table 3.14 demonstrates that male retirement ages have been dropping in all of the countries shown. The female data are inconclusive because of the changes in labor-force participation. Decreases in participation are found both at ages 55 to 64 and at ages 65 and over. There is considerable variation by country in labor force participation rates in both of these age ranges.

Labor-force participation rates by age group show increases in the female rate in the 25-to-54 age group for all of the countries; however, the level of difference varies greatly. Canada has had a particularly large increase—from 39.8% in 1970 to 65.1% in 1983—whereas Germany and Japan have had much smaller increases.

ALTERNATIVE FUTURES

Futures can be defined in terms of a number of different characteristics. Among these are: (1) birth rates, (2) rates of mortality and life expectancies, (3) definition of retirement and retirement ages, (4) types of family structure, and (5) the proportion of the adult, nonretirement age families that are dependent on public assistance.

Different scenarios for the well-being and options of older persons can be constructed by considering various combinations of these forces. Some are quite optimistic, while others are very discouraging

TABLE 3.14 Labor Force Participation Rates by Sex and Age Group—Selected Countries

	Ages 25–54		Ages 55–64		Ages 65 & Over	
Country	1970	1983	1970	1983	1970	1983
Male Participation Rates						
United States	94.8%	93.0%	80.7%	68.8%	27.5%	16.8%
Canada	96.2%	93.8%	84.2%	72.3%	22.6%	13.0%
France	96.8%	96.0%	75.4%	53.7%	19.5%	5.4%
Germany, F.R.	97.1%	90.9%	82.2%	62.3%	19.9%	5.8%
Japan	97.3%	97.1%	86.6%	84.7%	49.4%	38.9%
Sweden	94.8%	95.0%	85.4%	77.1%	28.9%	12.0%
United Kingdom	97.8%	95.9%	91.3%	76.8%	20.2%	8.1%
Female Participation Rates						
United States	49.7%	67.0%	42.2%	41.2%	9.0%	7.3%
Canada	39.8%	65.1%	29.8%	33.7%	5.0%	4.6%
France	50.1%	67.0%	40.0%	32.7%	8.6%	2.2%
Germany, F.R.	47.6%	54.7%	29.9%	26.0%	6.5%	2.8%
Japan	55.1%	59.5%	44.4%	46.1%	17.9%	16.1%
Sweden	64.2%	87.0%	44.5%	59.7%	8.7%	4.1%
United Kingdom	53.2%	63.4%	39.3%	37.0%	6.4%	3.5%
Total Participation Rates						
United States	71.8%	79.8%	60.4%	54.1%	16.0%	11.1%
Canada	67.9%	79.4%	56.7%	52.1%	13.0%	8.3%
France	73.5%	81.6%	56.8%	42.7%	12.8%	3.5%
Germany, F.R.	71.8%	73.2%	52.0%	41.1%	11.7%	3.8%
Japan	75.7%	78.3%	64.1%	63.7%	31.8%	25.6%
Sweden	79.8%	91.0%	64.6%	68.2%	18.0%	7.7%
United Kingdom	75.5%	79.6%	63.9%	56.2%	11.7%	5.3%

Participation rates represent percent of population of each specified group in labor force.

Source: Organization for Economic Cooperation and Development, Paris, France, Historical Statistics, 1960–1982, 1984; and Labor Force Statistics, annual.

because they reflect a high proportion of nonproductive individuals competing for the same resources. Development of such scenarios is seen as an important step in the development of retirement-related public policy. Some examples are shown in the comparison in Table 3.15.

Further research and model building are needed to develop and quantify the types of scenarios presented in Table 3.15. However, an

TABLE 3.15 Future Scenarios

Attribute	Scenario *A*	Scenario *B*	Scenario *C*
Mortality	Large decreases	Large decreases	Same as present
Retirement ages	Same as present	Increased 5 years	Same as present
Family patterns	Weak	Weak	Weak
Birth rates	Low	Low	Increased
Retirement options available	Few	Many	Few
Population supported by public assistance	Increased	Reduced	Same as present

examination of the characteristics of the scenarios will indicate that Scenario *A* is very troubling. In it, dependency ratios will rise and few options have been developed. It is one in which there is likely to be increased conflict between different groups competing for the same resources. On the other hand, Scenario *B* is much more optimistic: the increase in retirement ages and development of options is good for the population and has reduced the dependency ratio. Likewise, the public assistance population has been reduced, further reducing the strains on the same resources. The differences between *A* and *B* may well be achievable by differences in public policy. Finally, Scenario *C* falls between Scenarios *A* and *B* in desirability. It will be more costly than the present because of the shifting demographics.

IMPLICATIONS FOR U.S. POLICY

U.S. public policy needs to recognize the implications of the aging of the population and the heavily female mix within the older population. In that regard, there are a number of areas of concern. The two principal problems are retirement ages (and the definition of retirement) and provision of adequate medical care.

Retirement Age Issues

In large companies with good benefits, we expect people to retire early, often at ages 60 to 62. However, some employers experience much older retirement ages. For example, data for a nonprofit organization with several hundred employees show an average retirement age of 67 to 68. In public pension plans, many people retire at earlier ages. Some police and fire systems allow retirement before age 50. Military personnel also retire at very early ages. Social Security retirement ages today are generally 62 to 65.

Currently, age 65 is the age for full Social Security benefits. Under current legislation, this will move gradually to age 67. As discussed earlier, life expectancies at age 65 are about 14 years for men (up from 11.9 years in 1940) and 18.5 years for women (up from 13.4 in 1940). Thus the expected period of retirement for a 65-year-old retiree has increased 18% for men and 37% for women. Women are more likely to live alone than men, so that their needs may be more complex. They are more likely than men ultimately to require long-term care. Yet retirement ages have dropped, so that the increases in the average number of years after retirement are much larger, probably on the order of 40% to 50%.

Early retirement has been a convenient method of dealing with the need to reduce workforces in recent years, and it has been economically feasible since the number of older people was not very great compared to the number of younger people. Large companies often favor early retirement and today are willing to offer generous benefits to make early retirement attractive. However, an overall retirement age of 55 or 60 is certainly not necessary because of any widespread physical or mental inability to perform work by people in this age group.

The traditional life cycle pattern that underlies much human resource and government policy calls for three periods of life, as noted above: growing up and education, work until retirement, and retirement and leisure. In fact, many people have much more varied and complex life cycles. Retirement may not be a sudden and total event, and people may have multiple careers. Older persons are not a homogeneous population. Not only are there many differences among individuals, but the age mix of the over-65 population is shifting so that more individuals are in the over-75 and over-85 groups. Instances of activity limitation and limiting chronic disorders are much higher in the population over 75.

As discussed earlier, the age distribution of the population will be radically different when the baby boomers reach 65. Then we can expect one retiree for every two workers if retirements follow the pattern of most people retiring at ages 62 to 65.

In the long run, higher retirement ages seem to be inevitable. It is essential that the issue of optimal retirement ages be addressed and that public policy be developed that will make sense in light of the demographics and workforce needs of the future.

Postretirement Medical Benefits

It seems that an acute crisis is coming in postretirement medical-benefits. Today, a substantial majority of larger employers have such plans, but there is a delicate balance governing employers' decisions about what benefits to provide. Current and recent events are forcing that balance to shift so that postretirement medical benefits plans will be much less attractive to employers in the future than in the past.

Medicare pays less than half of the bills of the retired over-65 population and nothing for younger retirees. Medical costs are a major expense for retirees. The government has been cutting back on Medicare, and proposals for further cutbacks are under discussion.

Public policy is serving to discourage employers from offering these benefits. The net effect of the current funding situation, potential accounting rules, and legal uncertainties is to create large amounts of risk for employers sponsoring these plans, risks not expected when the plans were adopted. .

Policy makers need to deal with a fundamental issue: Should employers be encouraged to offer these benefits? If the answer is yes, then changes are needed to stabilize the environment and make prefunding attractive. Two changes that would be helpful are permitting voluntary prefunding and allowing pension plan surpluses to be used to help pay for these benefits.

If the answer is "no," and if Medicare benefits are not to be increased, then the cost in the form of increased Medicaid benefits needs to be considered, or, alternatively, we need to be prepared to face a situation in which more people cannot get care because of lack of financing.

Skills Maintenance

Skills maintenance is necessary for job security, particularly for the older worker, and can be seen as an avenue to multiple work and retirement options. Training for a new career also supports multiple options. Takeovers and mergers are a threat to job security.

Human capital is a major form of wealth in the information society. Job security and the need for lifelong education go hand in hand. Job security must be viewed in terms of both current jobs and future options. This is the critical financial security issue of the future. Lewis J. Perelman states:

> Despite the frenzied attention given to childhood education in the past three years, the most crucial unmet learning needs are those of adults. More than three-fourths of America's workers in 2001 will be people who are already adults today. A fifth of the current adult population is functionally illiterate and another fifth is only marginally literate. On the other hand, 15% or more of today's workers are overeducated or over-qualified in that their knowledge and skills no longer fit the requirements of a changing economy. The majority of workers at all levels need substantial retraining every five to eight years, regardless of whether they change careers or stay in existing jobs. (Perelman, 1986, p. 13)

The best job security comes from having skills that are useful in the current job market. Few people get substantial retraining in the five- to eight-year time cycle suggested by Perelman.

Many older workers who have been seen as unproductive in the last few years probably had not kept skills up to date, so that they were not as familiar with new ideas and technology as some of the younger workers. Pension benefits are not effective in promoting security if skills become obsolete and the individual is made unemployable long before retirement age. Dealing with this issue will require a joint effort on the part of employers and employees. The cost of not dealing with it is likely to be felt in productivity and unemployment. This is a public policy issue that really has not been addressed on a broad scale.

CONCLUSIONS

Demographic events that have already occurred point to an inevitable change in the age mix of the population. The events, when considered with the methods of support for that population and the family structures in our society, make it very important for public policy makers and those concerned with financial security systems to carefully study and understand the situation, and to consider new social patterns that will service well the emerging needs of the population.

There are several specific needs for public policy development. First, flexibility in retirement ages and options would be very helpful in giving those people who want to remain longer in the paid labor force the opportunity to do so. Employers should be encouraged to develop those options. If individuals are to be productive longer, education and skills maintenance throughout their middle years is critically important. Public policy should encourage such education and should encourage both employers and individuals to embark on such programs.

In the long run retirement ages will probably have to increase. Midlife education is important to making this work well. Public policy should be preparing people for this.

Governmental funding for medical care for older Americans is being cut back. More attention is needed today to the entire spectrum of medical care alternatives for older persons and the sources of financing. The present situation may well lead to disaster for many older Americans. Public policy today is discouraging to employers who want to offer continued medical coverage to employees. This should be reexamined and public policy modified so that it encourages employers to offer such coverage and makes it attractive to them. Long-term care in the United States is not financed by any regular insurance or medical care payment schemes. The single older person is most likely to need such care. Public policy is needed to develop alternatives to the nursing home and to put in place better mechanisms for financing nursing home care. Medical IRAs have been suggested, as has a tax-sheltered individual savings vehicle to encourage people to save for medical care in retirement. These programs need to be explored further to determine whether they offer a partial solution to the financing of medical care for older Americans.

The policy issues are different, country to country. The underlying issues are common, but the context within which they emerge is different, and the problems and options are different. As highlighted above, in the United States the major issues are retirement options and ages, medical care and its financing, and lifelong skills maintenance. The issue of retirement is one that is linked to industrial and information economies, where the workplace is separate from the home. The more developed countries all face issues related to appropriate retirement policies. Whether the less developed countries will face such issues in the future is not known. This will depend on the form of their economies and the life options that have developed over time.

REFERENCES

The Conference Board. (1981, September). *Economic road maps*. New York: Author.

Perelman, L. J. (1986, March-April). Learning our lesson: Why school is out. *The Futurist*, p. 13.

Plumley, P. (1986). Unpublished committee report on life expectancies. Itasca, IL: Society of Actuaries.

U.S. Bureau of the Census. (1983). *Current population report: Projections of the population of the United States by age, sex, and race, 1983–2080* (Series P-25, No. 952). Washington, DC: U.S. Government Printing Office.

U.S. Bureau of the Census. (1981). *Statistical abstract of the United States*. Washington, DC: U.S. Government Printing Office.

U.S. Bureau of the Census. (1984). *Statistical abstract of the United States*. Washington, DC: U.S. Government Printing Office.

U.S. Bureau of the Census. (1984). World Population, forthcoming, Washington, DC: U.S. Government Printing Office.

U.S. Department of Health and Human Services. (1982). *Vital statistics of the United States*. Washington, DC: U.S. Government Printing Office.

U.S. Senate Special Committee on Aging. (1985a). *America in transition*. Washington, DC: U.S. Government Printing Office.

U.S. Senate Special Committee on Aging (1985b). *Health and extended work life*. Washington, DC: U.S. Government Printing Office.

4

Politics and the New Old

Robert B. Hudson

The issue of how to conceptualize, label, and subdivide the aged has been a thorny one for some years within the gerontological community. The heterogeneity of the older population has grown as fast as the population itself, and the current generation of gerontologists has taken pride in pointing to the diversity and richness of America's elders. Concepts such as the productive or able elderly have the merit of addressing the diversity question and its consequences directly, putting questions of rights and responsibilities in full view. Nowhere have the multiple images of aging relating to the idea of the able elderly been put in sharper relief than in Douglas Nelson's (1982) superb essay in the Neugarten volume *Age or Need?* Writing of the aging advocacy movement, Nelson notes the conflicting images used to characterize older Americans

> as dependent or independent, as appropriately retired or inappropriately excluded from work; as isolated or socially integrated; as frail or vigorous; as impoverished or affluent; as deserving of special status or subject to arbitrary discrimination; as ill or well, and so on. (p.139)

The concept of the able elderly captures the existence of a growing number of older persons who are integrated, vigorous, affluent, subject to discrimination, and well. They are here, they are new, and what, if anything, should they and others do about it?

POLITICAL POTENTIAL OF THE ABLE ELDERLY

Nowhere will the import of this group be greater than in the world of politics. Subjective group identification for this population would be based on positive mental and physical status, considerable economic independence, and the search for roles that can assure ongoing and efficacious engagement with society at large. Because each of these attributes is correlated with political activity and involvement, this population aggregate of able elders has the potential for becoming an influential political grouping. These so-called able elders are a bridge between the younger and older, the healthier and the more frail, the employed and the retired. Therein lie both the empirical and normative dilemmas of whether able elders will and should become a more distinct political entity.

Development of a clearer political identity has consequences for both the persons involved and the larger society. The emergence of this group could well result—as able elders and their advocates contend—in massively undertapped resources being applied to serving families, communities, and older individuals themselves. But it is also critical to recognize that the extent to which collective identity and contributions emerge is a function of social and economic forces every bit as much as it is of individual preference. The contributions these able elders may wish to make can—under foreseeable circumstances —become the obligations that society wishes to impose on them. What able older people choose to do and how larger social forces work to channel (or disregard) their abilities will depend on a number of cohort characteristics and period conditions. Political mobilization of the able elderly will likely be tied to their collective sense of being discriminated against or rejected by employers, community leaders, and politicians, among others. In this potential struggle between group autonomy and societal demands, able elders will want to choose their strategies and label with care.

In a narrower political vein, it is important to consider the particular interests and concerns around which able elders might coalesce. Of concern in this regard is that if able elders emerge as another special interest, what is the interest and what individuals and needs does it address? Older persons and their organizations have, of course, been very active in the political arena over the past quarter century. What makes the continuation of these efforts under the guise of the able elderly potentially troubling is that, almost by definition, older persons with current and pressing needs have been factored out of the group and therefore (in the interest-group model) out of the claim to benefits. If, as proponents contend, the able elderly will be devoting considerable political effort to securing benefits for all older persons, especially the frail, the wisdom of fostering a political separation between the able and less able elderly is subject to question.

Thus one can conclude that the overall older population and its advocates should continue to be a major political presence without endorsing the idea of breaking out the able portion of this population from its remainder. Further discussion of this issue awaits consideration of what the political attributes of the able elderly may be in the years ahead.

BARRIERS TO ABLE-AGED IDENTIFICATION

Three questions posed some years ago by political scientist Robert Dahl (1958) in the context of the "elitist–pluralist" debate are useful here for considering the potential salience and influence of the able elderly. Dahl's three questions to those positing the presence of a dominant elite in the United States, modified for present purposes, are as follow:

- Are the able elderly an identifiable group that seeks to further itself in the political world?
- Is there agreement within the group as to what it wants through government for itself or others?
- Is what the able elderly want different from what other groups and individuals in the political arena want?

There are a number of individual roles and broader sets of life circumstances that could augment identity and cohesion among able elders. Common patterns of work and retirement, similarities in health status, and shared concerns about family roles and needs could potentially enhance group consciousness. These failing, able elders might be shown to have common sets of concerns and expectations about the events, vulnerabilities, and protections that await them at very advanced age. The group's definitional property of "able" need not suggest that "un or less able" is necessarily far off or that the group itself is not partially made up of individuals whose life situation is already to some degree precarious. Shared identity could, as well, result from a common need and desire to channel ability, role changes, and time into new productive capacities. Voluntarism, lobbying, or new economic and social tasks could foster a greater common identity.

Concerns, expectations, and roles such as these can contribute to common political identity, but a more decisive political presence for the able elderly would require the emergence of a more constrained age consciousness or subculture identification (Rose, 1965). Currently there is little evidence that such a pattern of relatively exclusive shared values has developed, but we should pay heed to the cautioning of Cutler, Pierce, and Steckenrider (1984) that age consciousness itself may be a cohort phenomenon.

While selected circumstances could foster greater political identity and cohesion among the able elderly, separate identities and relatively low levels of current need suggest more modest developments in this direction. Most obvious are the countervailing effects of class, ethnicity, sex, and other personal characteristics. Given the millions of persons in the objective group classification, population variation approaches that of the citizenry at large. This certainly holds for political participation and orientations where the within-group variation at any point in time runs close and parallel to that of the general population (Campbell & Strate, 1981; Hudson & Strate, 1985).

It is possible to argue, of course, that by factoring out the less able old (definitionally or otherwise) population heterogeneity is reduced—and in a manner functional to political participation. There are, however, data indicating that it is more the characteristics associated with the less able elderly that are associated with subjective age identification. Widowhood, declining sense of competence, impaired health status, and financial decline have each been tied to increased age identity, whereas the positive responses one would associate with the able old have been negatively related to such identity (Cutler, 1973; Linn & Hunter, 1979; Peters, 1971). In a more directly political vein, "old-age identifiers" among the elderly have been shown to be less politically involved than nonidentifiers (Miller, Gurin, & Gurin, 1980). On the other hand, there is a greater sense of efficacy among the younger (and presumably more able) old than the very old.

In addition to the within-group differences among the old, there are between-group similarities between the young and old that mitigate against a distinct and influential role for the able elderly. Older persons' political values, orientations, sense of efficacy and trust, political participation, and even most specific issue positions are very much in line with those of younger persons. There are, of course, variations—some reasonably significant—but population characteristics other than age account for more of older persons' positions and activities than does age alone.

THE ABLE ELDERLY OVER TIME

Conceivably, consciousness will grow around able older persons seeing themselves as something of a political and economic "sandwich generation" caught between the demands of a frailer generation ahead of it and the pressures of a "command generation" (Williamson, Evans, & Powell, 1982) immediately behind it. Without being needlessly reductionist, it is important to note again that the able elderly identification itself eliminates from "the old" both a significant number of very old or less able elderly and a smaller number of younger old who are also socially or economically vulnerable. This abstract factoring-out process, should it transpire politically, could clearly heighten the group consciousness of this unquestionably growing number of people appropriately deemed able and old. As with the political emergence of any other population grouping, the political rise of the able old will be very much a function of the cohorts, classes, and conditions around them. Should some combination of economic difficulty, budgetary constraints, and age imbalances in the population emerge simultaneously—a distinct possibility to many, 25 years hence—the combined sense of relative deprivation and external pressure would serve, among other things, to heighten group identity.

This pattern would contrast very considerably with the period from 1950 to 1980, when unprecedented public benefits could be made available to the elderly, able and less able alike, in the absence of strong political identity among the aged. In no account of the major age-related policy enactments of the period—Medicare (see Marmor, 1970), Medicaid (Vladeck, 1980), Supplemental Security Income (Burke & Burke, 1974), Social Security (Derthick, 1979), Age Discrimination in Employment (Schuck, 1980)—has age-based consciousness or age-based lobbying been posited as central to legislative passage. Program expansion during the period occurred as a result of economic growth and the assumptions and expectations that were bound up in welfare state politics more generally. Political success and political identity are very separate phenomena, as may eventually be shown by contrasting the events circa 1965 to 1980 with those circa 2010 to 2025.

Of particular importance to this discussion is that where age or date of birth does account for variations between younger and older populations, it often can be laid more to cohort than to life-cycle or aging effects. This, in turn, introduces a longitudinal dimension, which is absolutely essential to assessing the future role of the able elderly.

Who the able elderly are, how they are defined, their potential needs and contributions, and, most importantly, their place in society will be in continual flux. Better educated cohorts of the able elderly will see and act in the world differently than less well educated cohorts; able older women will demand and assume roles that might not suit either their mothers or daughters; and relatively large cohorts of objectively defined able elders will face pressures and make demands noticeably different from relatively small "golden" cohorts, like the one comprising people (especially men) born between the mid-1930s and mid-1940s. The overarching issue here is captured by Bengtson, Cutler, Mangen, and Marshall, who observe that "age-strata are cross-cut by the flow of successive cohorts, (1985, p. 329)." This is simply to say that the same age clustering can see itself and be seen very differently in the circumstances of different historical periods.

Over time, demographic, social, and economic trends will unavoidably lead to major shifts in what might be termed "the social construction of the able elderly" (Estes, 1979). As has happened before (Graebner, 1981), an industrial economy in need of human resources will modify its labor policies to encourage labor force participation among those who might well be called the able elderly. It might, as well, force participation among the not-so-able elderly through further disability policy restrictions, pension plan modifications, and so forth. In turn, the economic system, however managed, will force or induce such individuals out of the labor force as conditions warrant.

Similarly, in times of governmental budget constraints, one can fully expect able older persons being called on by government and others to assume responsibility for health and other forms of care for the less able in their families and communities. The able elderly would also be called on increasingly to look after their own needs, either current or future. In none of this can any stability or certainty be expected as to how economic, social, and political forces prevailing at different times may choose to define ability.

For the able elderly, social and economic pressures will cut two ways. Intensive social demands could easily enhance a sense of in-group solidarity as a collective sense of discrimination, burden, and obligation leads able elders to see themselves scapegoated (Binstock, 1983) with an intensity not yet seen. Under such circumstances, the able elderly could be transformed quite easily from a potential to an actual group.

However, the very pressures that could help generate group solidarity among the able old are the same ones that will make policy or other forms of "success" difficult for the able old to accomplish. Multiple demands for limited resources—governmental or other—will limit the degrees of freedom enjoyed by the able old and require levels of cohesion and mobilization this group has not yet demonstrated. The degree to which able elders choose to come together for their own benefit, as opposed to being forced to come together for their own protection, will be an important process to watch and understand. So, too, will be seeing what issues generate group solidarity and the group's success in seeing their positions adopted.

POLITICAL AGENDAS OF AND FOR THE ABLE ELDERLY

The recent emergence of the able elderly is a major development both because of the size and growth of this population and because only now are many able elders and others in the larger society grappling with who they are, what they want, and what might be expected of them. Having addressed the range of circumstances that might make the able elderly more of a self- and socially defined group, we turn now to some political and policy implications of fostering a new and separate identification.

There are a number of concerns associated with constructing and legitimizing a new population defined as the able old. A first concern centers on reification and labeling. Whatever working definition of the able old might be arrived at, it will bring with it serious ramifications for social and policy purposes. Working assumptions of the able old will be forthcoming on both an overt and covert basis, with problems ranging from new stereotypes to formal misclassification following closely behind. Invidious comparisons, categorizing, sorting, and discrimination that could occur in government, the workplace, the hospital (among both workers and patients), housing complexes, and senior centers, among other settings, are almost nightmarish to consider.

If formalization of the able elderly concept may hold problems for the less able old, it could—in the name of creating opportunities—create additional problems for those who may very properly be considered able. In the area of employment, the able-elderly concept brings into sharp relief the disjuncture between desires to eliminate mandatory retirement and to take early retirement. Individuals and groups proclaiming ability and independence must be prepared—and many may wish—to face the consequences should economic and budgetary conditions dictate higher rates of employment among this population segment. In the areas of income support and medical care, the improved educational and economic status associated with the able elderly will generate new proposals around the self-financing or private financing of pension and health benefits. In the social services, the able elderly concept could lead to stricter and tighter rule making around the targeting-of-services concept, resulting in the imposition of more means-tested and needs-tested standards.

More generally, the able elderly concept contributes to and is affected by three major contemporary governmental and societal trends: privatization, decentralization, and informalization. Each of these has been noted separately by numerous commentators, but there are broad implications, especially for the able old, when they are taken together. In politics and social welfare, privatization connotes reduced reliance on government, decentralization suggests a reduced role for Washington, and informalization envisages a turning away from rules, regulations, and administrative structures in favor of reliance on family, neighborhood, and community ties.

In the case of the able elderly, privatization suggests increased utilization of such financing mechanisms as Individual Retirement Accounts, long-term care insurance, continuing-care residential options, and equity and other forms of asset conversion. Decentralization will place greater responsibility on states and localities both to define community needs and to provide resources. Informalization will have particular consequences for the able old, calling upon them to arrange, provide, supervise, and monitor services to family and community members.

In short, it is not difficult to see that the concept of the able old is fully consonant with this tripartite set of social and political values. The danger lies in the concept of the able old being fostered in places and times where it is not reflective of existing population characteristics. The present danger is for the poor, frail, and isolated, who risk being further segregated; the future danger awaits today's able old who, for whatever reason, do not display sufficient foresight.

The notion of the able elderly must not be applied with a simplicity that exacerbates its two most troublesome features: its logically separating out and relegating to a totally dependent status the remainder of the older population, and its implicit cross-sectional and static definition. In either of these ways the concept of the able old can prove problematic for the able and frail alike, putting the one in a socially stereotyped role and placing potentially excessive burdens on the other.

The potential of making the frail elderly a socially residual category, while elevating the able elderly into a role associated more with the mainstream, leads to a concluding comment about the relative place of class and citizenship in the contemporary American welfare state.

As cogently argued by Myles (1984), the major welfare state development affecting the elderly over the past 50 years has been the evolution of old-age assistance into the retirement wage. Borrowing from Marshall (1963), Myles explores the ongoing tension between class and citizenship as bases of social organization and how that tension has led to a paradoxical joining of the capitalist economy and the protective state. The contradictions but mutual coexistence of economic liberalism and political democracy helped generate a welfare state that has been long enduring, multifunctional, and remarkably similar across time and nations. Claims for resources came to be made in part on the grounds of citizenship, beyond those based on class, through the wage system.

The hybrid result in the case of public pensions is that today they meet the test neither of equity (relationship to contributions, or the wage system) nor of equality (relationship to other citizens). However, the balance between the tensions of class and citizenship in the 30-year period following World War II shifted in the direction of the latter. These citizenship pressures during a period of remarkable economic growth helped generate what Myles terms "the citizen's wage"—the share of the social product workers were able to lay claim to as a deferred wage "over and above any claims they may have possessed in their capacity as wage earners" (1984, p. 25).

As these macrolevel institutions and overall economic growth helped generate the expanded welfare state, they also helped give birth to the elderly as a political constituency. Over time, the elderly (and their families) came to see cause and common ground in a citizenship role around pensions and allied concerns although they had often been found redundant or undervalued in their capacity as workers. However, as Myles and others have observed, countertrends have emerged over the past decade, shifting the institutional balance more toward class and away from citizenship and democracy. Supporting evidence is found in contemporary budgetary, demographic, and economic analyses, but also very much in the earlier noted trends toward privatization, decentralization, and informalization.

Politically, these trends threaten the institutional base of the contemporary welfare state as it benefits the elderly. A shift away from citizenship toward class as the basis of social organization impinges on each of the factors that can be cited as contributing to the development of today's age-related social policies (Hudson & Strate, 1985): the presumed legitimacy of allocations to the old on the basis of age; the involvement of key elites in focusing on the elderly to inaugurate and expand social programs; the set of expectations and assumptions generating the pattern of expansion by increments; and the standing and agendas of the organized aging in the corridors of government.

CONCLUSIONS

However one evaluates these new realities, the concept of the able elderly appears as a creature of its times. Not only are there demonstrably more able elders, but their abilities, independence, and preferences can associate them more with the forces of liberalism and class than with democracy and citizenship. Able elders can produce commercially, they can contribute to their communities, and they can help their families. All of this they can do in the context of the market and the community, and only secondarily need they turn to the polity and government.

Because of these contemporary trends it is incumbent upon those calling for explicit recognition of the personal needs and social utility of able elders to consider carefully the various consequences of such formal institutional recognition. In the first instance, greater cognizance needs to be taken of the implications for those who now are or will be frail and poor. More fundamental is the need to consider what should be the rationale for old-age benefits in the coming period marked by the presence of able elders. The logic of the situation suggests targeting and means-testing for those deemed unable to provide for themselves, although many persons concerned with the potential "rolelessness" of the third quarter of life do not endorse that position. Those who would see able elders assume a more conscious presence in American society do, however, need to make clear their thinking about the bases of old-age benefits in the years ahead. On the strong assumption that gerontologists and others concerned with this new population are neither promoting massive means-testing on the one hand nor endorsing notions of social citizenship on the other, there remains a need to have a clearer sense of what the eligibility criteria should be.

Assessment of the renewed place of the market is very much a function of values, perspectives, and stakes. The incontrovertible point from this presentation is that the able-elders concept is or can be made part of the larger period occurrences discussed here. The connection can be made openly political, as it was by the organizers of the 1981 White House Conference on Aging, or it can be in the form of able elders being involved in any number of productive and worthwhile roles. But the ascendance of able elders as a self-identified and socially promoted population will also contribute to an erosion of social citizenship and the citizen's wage based upon it. There is a real danger that, in celebrating the rise of the able elderly, we will allow institutional commitments to the old as citizens to be transformed into residual programs for the very old as social outliers.

This is a revised version of a paper presented to the 1985 Ollie Randall Symposium of the Gerontological Society of America. The original version was published in *The Gerontologist* under the title "The Rise of the Able Elderly: Implications for the State."

REFERENCES

Bengtson, V., Cutler, N., Mangen, D., & Marshall, V. (1985). Generations, cohorts, and relations between age groups. In R. Binstock & E. Shanas (Eds.), *Handbook of aging and the social sciences* (pp. 130–150). New York: Van Nostrand Reinhold.

Binstock, R. (1983). The aged as scapegoat. *The Gerontologist, 23,* 136–143.

Burke, V., & Burke, V. (1974). *Nixon's good deed.* New York: Columbia University Press.

Campbell, J., & Strate, J. (1981). Are old people conservative? *The Gerontologist, 21,* 580–591.

Cutler, N., Pierce, R., & Steckenrider, J. (1984). How golden is the future? *Generations, 9,* 38–43.

Cutler, S. (1973). Perceived prestige loss and political attitudes among the aged. *The Gerontologist, 14,* 68–75

Dahl, R. A. (1958). A critique of the ruling elite model. *American Political Science Review, 52,* 463–469.

Derthick, M. (1979). *Policymaking for Social Security.* Washington, DC: Brookings Institution.

Estes, C. (1979). *The aging enterprise.* San Francisco: Jossey-Bass.

Graebner, W. (1981). *A history of retirement*. New Haven, CT: Yale University Press.

Hudson, R., & Binstock, R. (1985). Aging and political systems. In R. Binstock & E. Shanas (Eds.), *Handbook of aging and the social sciences* (pp. 369-400). New York: Van Nostrand Reinhold.

Linn, M., & Hunter, K. (1979). Perception of age in the elderly. *Journal of Gerontology, 34*, 46–52.

Marmor, T. (1970). *The politics of Medicare*. London: Routledge & Kegan Paul.

Marshall, T. (1963). *Class, citizenship, and social development*. Garden City, NY: Doubleday.

Miller, A., Gurin, P., & Gurin, G. (1980). Age consciousness and political mobilization of older Americans. *The Gerontologist, 20*, 691–700.

Myles, J. (1984). *Old age in the welfare state*. Boston: Little Brown.

Nelson, D. (1982). Alternative images of old age as the bases for policy. In B. Neugarten (Ed.), *Age or need?* (pp. 131–169). Beverly Hills, CA: Sage.

Peters, G. (1971). Self-conceptions of the aged, age identification, and aging. *The Gerontologist, 11*, 69–73.

Rose, A. (1965). Group consciousness among the aging. In A. Rose & W. Peterson (Eds.), *Older people and their social world*. Philadelphia: Davis.

Schuck, P. (1980). The graying of civil rights law. *Public Interest, 60*, 69–93.

Vladeck, B. (1980). *Unloving care*. New York: Basic Books.

Williamson, J., Evans, L., & Powell, L., (1982). *The politics of aging*. Springfield, IL: Thomas.

Part II

Factors Influencing Choices About New Policies

5

Making Assets Out
of Tomorrow's Elderly

Yung-Ping Chen

Population aging is defined as the growth over time of the proportion of old persons, according to some chronological age, in the total population. The aging of the population raises many issues for individuals, families, and society: social-political-economic, biological-psychological-engineering-medical, ethical-moral-religious-legal, all of which bear on the quality of life in its many dimensions. Economic security in old age is one rubric under which many of these issues and possible solutions may be discussed.

As the population continues to grow older, some have pessimistically predicted a future in which income transfers between generations will likely provoke an "age class war": the young will revolt against having to contribute increasingly more under the Social Security system, for example) for the benefit of the old. This proposition, though seemingly plausible, views the old as liabilities. It is possible that society could make assets out of tomorrow's elderly.

OLD AGE DEPENDENCY RATIOS

Whether the old are cared for within the family or by society, the number of old persons relative to the working population is an important ratio. In the family context, the more children there are, the less each child has to contribute to the cost of supporting old parents. In society at large, as long as the number of persons in the workforce grows faster than those who are no longer working, the share per worker of the cost of providing for the old population will be lower. The comparison of the old population to the working population is the so-called old-age dependency ratio.

Because of declining birth rates and increasing longevity, the old-age dependency ratio in the United States has been increasing and is projected to continue increasing at very high rates in the twenty-first century. But dependency ratios based solely on population size in selected age groups do not show the effects on support costs of such related demographic and economic factors as incidence of disability, actual retirement ages, number of females in the workforce, changes in family structure, labor force participation rates, unemployment rates, inflation rates, productivity rates, mortality and fertility rates, and immigration levels. (For critical evaluations of the concept of the dependency ratio, see, for example, Adamchak & Friedman, 1983; Advisory Council on Social Security, 1979; Crown, 1985; National Council on the Aging, 1982.) Despite their imperfections, however, such crude measures of dependency are useful for the purposes of this chapter. At the very least, they point out directions of change over the past and in the future.

As shown in Table 5.1, the old-age dependency ratio (based on age 65 at retirement) increased from 10.6 to 16.4 (a rise of over 50%) from 1940 to 1960 (and rose to 18.1 in 1980) and is expected to increase to 38.9 (more than double the 1980 figure) by 2060. Put another way, in 1940 there were about 11 elderly persons for every 100 persons of working age; in 1960, about 16; in 1980, about 18; and in 2060, according to the projections, about 39. It is the dramatic increase in the old-age dependency ratio in the twenty-first century that has prompted the theme of the age class war.

It is important to note, however, that the total dependency ratio, which includes young-age as well as old-age dependency, is not expected to rise nearly as dramatically. In the year 2000 it should be almost exactly the same as in 1940, and even as it rises after that, it is not expected to reach the level it was at in 1960.

This is explained by the fact that, although increasing longevity is also a factor, population aging results primarily from declining birth rates. As fewer children are born, the age structure of the population changes: the young become a smaller, and the old a larger, part of the population. Therefore, as the old-age dependency ratio increases, there will be a lower young-age dependency ratio. The total dependency ratio, the sum of young-age and old-age dependency, need not necessarily rise; at least there is some offset between the two

TABLE 5.1 Dependency Ratios in the United States in Selected Years, 1940–2060, Based on Age 65 at Retirement[a]

Year	Young-age dependency ratio[b]	Old-age dependency ratio[c]	Total dependency ratio[d]
1940	48.5	10.6	59.1
1950	51.0	13.1	64.1
1960	65.1	16.4	81.5
1970	60.7	17.1	77.8
1980	45.9	18.1	64.0
1990	41.0	20.2	61.2
2000	38.6	20.9	59.5
2020	37.1	29.5	66.6
2040	38.1	38.7	76.8
2060	38.3	38.9	77.2

[a]Calculations based on Social Security Area Population as of July 1 in each year under Alternative II estimates (intermediate set of assumptions) used for the 1985 *OASDI Trustees Report,* provided by the Office of the Actuary, Social Security Administration, November 1985.
[b]Young-age dependency ratio compares the population under age 18 to the population between ages 18 and 64.
[c]Old-age dependency ratio compares the population aged 65 and over to the population between ages 18 and 64.
[d]Total dependency ratio sums young-age and old-age dependency ratios.

categories of dependency. (See Rappaport & Plumley, Chapter 3, this volume, on population trends and Crown, Chapter 6, this volume, on total dependency ratios.)

Equivalent Retirement Ages

The projected magnitude of population aging is based on a definition of old age or retirement commencing at age 65. This age at retirement, not changed since the inception of the Social Security Act, will be raised in the future. According to the Social Security Amendments of 1983, the normal retirement age will be gradually raised to 67 from 65 in two stages: (1) increasing the age for full benefits by two months a year from 2003 through 2008 so that a retirement age of 66 will be effective for those attaining age 62 in 2005–2016, and (2) increasing the age for full benefits by two months a year from 2022 through 2027 so that the provision would be fully effective for those attaining age 62 in 2022 (67 in 2027).

In recent years there has been considerable interest in the question of whether the normal retirement age of 65, in effect since Social Security benefits were first paid in 1940, should be raised. One of the major arguments for raising the retirement age is that life expectancy at age 65 has been increasing over the years and is expected to continue its increase in the future. (See Table 3.3 in Chapter 3, this volume, for the increase since 1900 in the expected period of retirement.) Assuming agreement on such an increase, the question of by how much will arise. Many would consider it unfair to expect that all the years of life expectancy gained since 1940 should be spent working. At the same time, it is probably unreasonable to expect that all the additional years in life expectancy should be spent in leisure.

How could mortality gains be equitably distributed between working years and retirement years? While there are various methods for computing equivalent retirement ages, figures in Table 5.2 are based on a measure that defines the equivalent retirement age for a given year as the age at which the ratio of the retirement-life expectancy (i.e., the expectation of life at age of retirement) to the working-life expectancy (i.e., the number of years between age 20 and the normal retirement age) is equal to that for age 65 in the base year of 1940 (see Myers, 1985). Under this measure, a retirement age in 1985 that would be equivalent to age 65 in 1940 is 69 years and 2 months; the equivalent age in the year 2000 is 70 years and 7 months. For the distant future, a retirement age of 73 years and 1 month in the year 2060 will be equivalent to age 65 in 1940.

TABLE 5.2   Retirement Age (in Years, Months) in Selected Years, 1940–2060 Equivalent to Age 65 in 1940[a]

Year	Age
1940	65:00
1960	67:00
1980	68:10
2000	70:07
2020	71:05
2040	72:03
2060	73:01

[a]Retirement age is defined as life expectancy at retirement divided by years in labor force where entry into labor force is assumed to be age 20. Calculations based on the latest historical and projected U.S. mortality rates, provided by the Office of the Actuary, Social Security Administration, November 1985.

Based on equivalent retirement ages in Table 5.2, the young-age and old-age dependency ratios have been recalculated and shown in Table 5.3 for 1985 to 2060. Young age is still defined as under age 18 in all years. Old age, however, is variably defined. In 1940, it was 65 and over, while beginning in 2045, it is 73 and over. For all intervening years, the start of old age increases according to equivalent retirement age calculations presented in Table 5.2. Consequently, since working age is defined as the population between young age and old age, as old age is defined variably, so is the working-age population.

Under equivalent retirement age computations, the old-age dependency ratio increases from 13.3 in 1985 to 21.5 (instead of 38.9, as shown in Table 5.1) in the year 2060. In contrast to the figures in Table 5.1, Table 5.3 shows that, under equivalent retirement age computations, there were a little over 13 elderly persons for every 100 persons of working age in 1985, and about the same magnitude is estimated for the year 2000. This proportion rises to about 16 in 2020, nearly 24 in 2040 and then declines to about 21 in the period from 2040 to 2060. There is a 62% increase in the old-age dependency ratio from 1985 to 2060. This increase is still significant, but not nearly so extreme when compared to the 106% increase shown in Table 1, under the invariant retirement age of 65.

The computations for equivalent retirement ages presented in

TABLE 5.3 **Dependency Ratios in the United States in Selected Years, 1985–2060 Based on Equivalent Retirement Ages**[a]

Year	Young-age dependency ratio[b]	Old-age dependency ratio[c]	Total (%)
1985	40.5	13.3	53.8
2000	36.3	13.5	49.8
2020	33.4	16.4	49.8
2040	34.0	23.7	57.7
2060	33.5	21.5	55.0

[a]Calculations based on Social Security Area Population as of July 1 in each year under Alternative II estimates (intermediate set of assumptions) used for the 1985 *OASDI Trustees Report*, courtesy of the Office of the Actuary, Social Security Administration, November 1985.
[b]Young age is defined as 0–17 ages in all years.
[c]Old age is variably defined as 65 and over in 1940; 73 and over beginning in 2045. For years 1945 to 2040, the start of old age increases according to equivalent retirement age calculations.

Table 5.2 take into account mortality, but not morbidity, experience. In other words, they only adjust for the expected length of life spent in retirement due to improved longevity but ignore the question of whether the extra life is spent in more or less good health. One reason for ignoring that question is that the incidence of morbidity is much more difficult to quantify than that of mortality. Another reason is that when mortality improves, morbidity also tends to improve. In the words of the Social Security actuaries:

> For example, increased use of health care facilities can mean alternatively: (1) people are less healthy and use the facilities because they need treatment; (2) people are equally healthy, but use the facilities because of the availability of insurance benefits and government assistance; (3) people are more healthy and use the facilities to maintain their better health; and (4) any combination of the above. Another reason for ignoring morbidity is that we believe that mortality and morbidity are correlated. (Bayo & Faber, 1981, p. 6)

Furthermore, there is evidence that during the last 20 years or so there has been some improvement in the health status of the elderly. On the basis of a comprehensive analysis of data from the national Health Interview Survey (HIS), Erdman B. Palmore reported consistent and substantial improvements in the relative health among the aged in the 20-year period from 1961 to 1981 (Palmore, 1986). HIS data has been collected in a continuing nationwide probability sample of households (representing about 120,000 persons, and approximately 95% of those over age 65) in the civilian noninstitutionalized population in the United States. The HIS is regarded as one of the most comprehensive and detailed health surveys. Its seven indicators of illness and disability are days of restricted activity, days of bed disability, injuries, acute conditions, visual impairments, severe visual impairments, and hearing impairments.

Table 5.4 is taken from Palmore, who showed the values of the seven indicators averaged over five-year periods in order to reduce the effect of short-term fluctuations and allow the long-term secular trends to emerge. The last column shows the percentage change from the base period, 1961 to 1965, to the last period, 1976 to 1981. Specifically, for each of the seven indicators, he calculated the ratios of the average for persons aged 65 and over divided by the average for persons of all ages. These ratios indicate health status among the aged relative to that among all persons. Because HIS data is based on self-reports or reports of other household members, which are subject to errors of recall and other subjective factors, and because of certain

TABLE 5.4   Relative Health of Persons 65+ in the United States, 1961–81 (Ratio of persons 65+to all persons)

Health Indicators	Years				
	1961–65	1966–70	1971–75	1976–81	1961–81
Days of restricted activity[1]	2.33	2.23	2.15	2.11	–10%
Days of bed disability[2]	2.34	2.18	2.09	2.05	–12%
Injuries per 100 persons[3]	.69	.63	.62	.60	–13%
Acute conditions per 100 persons[4]	.59	.53	.48	.50	–15%
% Visual impairments[5]	4.93	NA	4.32	4.09	–17%
% Severe visual impairments[6]	7.45	NA	7.23	6.74	–10%
% Hearing impairments[7]	4.70	NA	5.54	3.84	–18%

NA = Data not available.

[1]*Days of restricted activity.* This is the number of days per person per year in which a person reduced his or her usual activity for the whole day because of an illness or an injury. Persons who have permanently reduced their usual activities because of a chronic condition might not report any restricted activity days during the previous two week period (the interval used in the questionnaire).

[2]*Days of bed disability.* This is the number of days per person per year that a person stays in bed for all or most of the day because of a specific illness or injury.

[3]*Injuries.* This is the number of injuries per 100 persons per year. Injuries are those conditions classified in the International Classification of Diseases code numbers N800–N999; they include fractures, lacerations, contusions, burns, effects of exposure, adverse reactions to medical procedures, and poisonings.

[4]*Acute conditions.* This is the number of acute conditions per 100 persons last year. An acute condition is one that has lasted less than three months and that has involved either medical attention or restricted activity, but is not included in the list of conditions that are always classified as chronic regardless of time of onset.

[5]*Visual impairments.* This is the percentage of persons with any visual impairment that causes vision problems in one or both eyes even when wearing glasses.

[6]*Severe visual impairment.* This is the percentage of persons with visual impairments so severe that they cannot read newspaper print with either eye even when wearing glasses.

[7]*Hearing impairments.* This is the percentage of persons who are deaf in one or both ears, have ringing in the ears, use a hearing aid, or have any other hearing trouble.

Source: Palmore (1986).

developments such as epidemics, economic recessions, and changes in methodology of the HIS, which affect all ages in any given period of time, Palmore used ratios of health status among those over 65 to those among all persons in order to remove these factors in trend analysis.

Using ratios, Palmore demonstrated consistent and substantial declines in all indicators of illness and disability, with each indicator showing a decline during each of the intervals, with only one exception.

This discussion of equivalent retirement ages is not intended to define away the problem of old-age dependency. Rather, it is meant to suggest and stimulate new directions of thought to make assets out of the elderly of the future. There are both theoretical and practical reasons for channeling public and private policies to incorporate the concept of equivalent retirement ages. In so doing, society could lower the economic and emotional costs associated with (1) economic security provisions for the greatly increased number of the retired and the possible intergenerational conflicts or frictions due to rising income transfers and (2) foregone production by the increasing number of the able elderly and the attendant feeling of uselessness and dependency on the part of these persons.

The concept of equivalent retirement ages should not be strictly interpreted to advocate postponement of age of retirement on a mandatory basis; applications of this concept include institutional arrangements for flexible retirement ages.

Dependency Ratios and Costs

As we saw in Tables 5.1 and 5.3, the total dependency ratio is not expected to change dramatically, but its composition will change. With fewer young dependents and more old dependents, there could be just a shift of, but not necessarily an increase in, the cost of supporting all of them. There will be less spent for the young and more spent for the old. Simply put, the shift means buying less baby food but more Geritol, building fewer schools but more retirement homes. It is more complicated than that, however. At present, society aids its elderly members through government-sponsored programs primarily at the federal level, while the young are served at the state and local levels with such public goods as education. This suggests a future shifting of responsibility among the various levels of government in the support of society's dependent members. Moreover, society currently supports its young dependents mainly through private family resources and its elderly under programs sponsored by government. This suggests a change in the funding patterns between private- and public-sector activities to accommodate the shift in the mix of young and old dependents. Some regard the shift of responsibility among governmental levels and the change in funding between private and public activities as difficult institutional problems. It is well to remember, however, that society's institutions are made by men and women as they respond to change.

Others contend that the nature of the respective expenditures is different: support for the young is an investment expected to yield a future return when they become workers, but support for the old is not an investment for the future. This point of view has validity, but it would hardly be realistic to see the old purely as a burden on society, for they can be, and often are, an asset or a resource to society. The young, the middle-aged, and the old have much to learn from one another, and they each have much to give in return.

Still others argue that it is much more costly to care for the old than for the young. There is a belief that the average cost of the aged dependent is approximately three times that of the young dependent. For 1975, it was estimated that $3,701 was spent under government programs for each aged person, whereas only $1,215 was spent per young dependent (Sheppard & Rix, 1977). This three-to-one cost relationship was estimated by dividing the population age 65 and over into the estimated total government program expenditures for the aged, and by dividing the population under age 18 into the estimated total government program expenditures for the young population.

This method of deriving the comparative costs is inadequate, as pointed out by the Consultant Panel of Actuaries and Economists of the 1979 Advisory Council on Social Security:

> The above procedure for arriving at the average cost per dependent produces what should be properly called the "per *assumed dependent* cost" in contrast to the "per *actual recipient* cost." The per assumed dependent cost is a definitional one, because all persons in a given age category, such as aged or young, are included in the denominator which is divided into the program expenditures in the numerator. By contrast, the alternate measure of per actual recipient cost is an appropriate measure, since it counts only those in the dependent age group who actually receive program expenditures. The assumed dependent cost approach conceptually under-estimates the support cost for those young persons who receive benefits under government programs because relatively more among the young than among the old do not receive benefits and yet in

the calculation all persons are included by definition as if they were recipients. (Advisory Council on Social Security, 1979, p. 283) [emphasis added].

The cost per actual recipient is difficult to obtain, however, for several reasons, including the lack of recipient data for many government programs, in-kind programs such as public housing, and the fact that some persons are multiple recipients of several government programs.

LABOR-FORCE NEEDS FOR THE ELDERLY

To the extent that population aging results from declining birth rates, there will be a smaller labor force in the traditional ages, because fewer babies born will imply a relatively smaller potential pool of future workers.

The inverse of the dependency ratio is what may be called the *supporter index*. The term "supporter index" should not be confused with the "support ratio," which has been used synonymously with the dependency ratio in, for example, the report co-authored by the U.S. Senate Special Committee on Aging (1986). The supporter index is the ratio of the population aged 20 to 64 (who are considered potential supporters) to the population aged 19 and younger and 65 and older (potential dependents). Like the dependency ratio, the supporter index is a crude measure, but it does highlight the directions of change.

As shown by extrapolation from Table 5.5, the supporter index is expected to reach 1.54 in the year 2010. The larger the supporter index is, the greater is the potential number of workers to support the dependents. The increase in the supporter index results from the baby boom in the mid-1940s to mid-1960s. This index begins to fall after 2010, and precipitously so after 2020, when it is estimated to be 1.36, to under 1.20 from 2030 to 2060. Low and declining fertility rates from the 1970s and beyond explain this downward trend as baby boomers retire.

When the number of potential supporters relative to potential dependents declines, society may need to call upon the old to remain in, or to reenter, the workforce in order to provide labor resources. (See Sandell, Chapter 7, this volume.) Such an additional source of labor will be a benefit to the young, and to the middle-aged as well. Further, to the extent that population aging arises out of the prolongation of life, there may be better health in old age, and hence the old may desire to work longer. Economically and emotionally, voluntary postponement of retirement will be beneficial to the old themselves, and their continued active contributions to production will also benefit the young and the middle-aged.

The suggestion of delayed retirement invites the criticism that it will leave little or no room at the top and that younger persons will have to cope with slower promotions. In the context of declining supporter indexes, however, to the extent that later retirement takes place, it will (should) take place in the period 20 to 30 years after about 2010, when the workforce aged 20 to 64 will be declining in absolute numbers by as much as 6 million, according to current estimates (Table 5.5).

Another issue concerning the possibility of postponing retirement is that it runs counter to early retirement trends evident in recent decades. (See Table 3.3, Chapter 3, this volume.) The decision by individuals to continue working or retire and the decision on the part of employers to retain older workers or induce them to leave employment are governed by complex forces. Physical, psychological, and economic reasons may lead a person to decide on early retirement. Declining health and tiring of work have led many to retire early. Sufficient economic incentives are a strong factor as well (Employee Benefit Research Institute, 1986). As for the employers, labor-market conditions, the state of the economy, and productivity considerations

TABLE 5.5 Supporter Index in the United States in Selected Years, 1960–2060[a]

Year	Potential supporters (in thousands)	Potential dependents (in thousands)	Supporter index
1940	81,406	56,091	1.45
1960	98,689	90,255	1.09
1980	134,850	101,034	1.33
2000	165,728	111,414	1.49
2020	177,210	130,535	1.36
2040	174,997	148,313	1.18
2060	178,449	152,202	1.17

[a]Supporter index is the ratio of potential supporters (population aged 20–64) to potential dependents (population aged 0–19 plus population aged 65 and over).
Source: Wade (1985).

are factors determining their employment policy. Other things being equal, it would appear that labor force participation by older persons could be encouraged by job redesign, job reassignment, and other modifications to the work environment. The following illustrative practices would be helpful: creating alternate work patterns (such as flex time; part-time work, including part-day, part-week, part-year, or alternating days, weeks, or months; job sharing; a compressed work week, such as a three-day or four-day week; cottage industry); phasing out retirement, which includes rehearsal retirement and sabbaticals; preparing and training for second or third careers; and volunteer work (Buchmann, 1983). In addition, a morale-lifting managerial climate within an organization and a prosperous economy are favorable environmental factors conducive to remaining in the workforce.

Role of Productivity and Fringe Benefits

Even if the total cost of supporting both young and old dependents is higher because of population aging, there is no presumption that the burden as a percent of their earnings on the working population will be necessarily higher; for the financial capacity of workers depends upon their levels of earnings, which in turn are affected by their productivity.

Productivity is generally measured by the ratio of the total value of production (the gross national product) to the total number of hours paid. For future cost projections, the Board of Trustees of Old-Age, Survivors, and Disability Insurance Trust Funds (1985) offers four alternatives based on different sets of demographic and economic assumptions. With regard to productivity, the trustees assumed in their 1985 report an annual rate of increase in productivity of 1.67% under alternative I, 2.35% under alternative II-A, 2.05% under alternative II-B, and 1.75% under alternative III. In other words, the trustees' assumptions ranged from an optimistic annual rate of increase of 2.67% to the pessimistic 1.75%. Alternative II-B is regarded by the trustees as the "best guess" projection of cost over the 75-year period. The 2.05% annual rate of productivity advancement was chosen in light of the following analysis.

Productivity for the total U.S. economy during the 30-year period from 1953 to 1983 rose at an annual rate of 1.97%; for the 20-year period from 1953 to 1973, 2.46%; for the 10 years between 1973 and 1983, 1.00%. In the words of a study by the Social Security Administration:

> Our assumptions of future productivity increases . . . reflect our belief
> that the very bad experience of the past 10 years does not foretell the
> future. Several conditions have prevailed over the past 10 years, signifi-
> cantly affecting productivity, which will not generally exist in the future.
> These include the rapid acceleration of production costs related to new
> environmental and safety regulations, highly significant increases in the
> cost of energy, a great influx of new, inexperienced workers as more
> women choose to enter (reenter) the labor force at the same time that the
> baby boom generation reached working age, and rapidly aging plant and
> equipment.
>
> However, we also do not believe that productivity of the long-term
> future will return to the high post–World War II levels of the 1950s and
> 1960s. Only our optimistic assumption (alternative I) reflects productivity
> increases of that level. The assumed ultimate productivity increase for
> the intermediate (alternative II-B) set is about the same level as the
> average for 1953–83. (Goss, Glanz, & An, 1985)

With the annual rate of productivity advancement assumed at
2.05%, the "necessary" ultimate combined employer–employee
payroll rate (the tax rate beginning in 1990) for Social Security
(OASDI) is scheduled at 12.4% under the intermediate alternative II-B
(best guess) set of assumptions, as against the 11.4% actually in the
law. Should there be an additional productivity increase of 0.2%, the
"necessary" ultimate payroll tax rate could be lowered to about 12.1%
if the additional gain in productivity is fully translated into increases
in earnings subject to payroll taxes. (This point is based on discussions in Board of Trustees, 1985.)

Over the long run, increases in total compensation to workers are
possible only if productivity grows. For wage and salary workers,
however, total employee compensation includes fringe benefits in
addition to cash pay. Over the years, the ratio of cash wages to
compensation has declined, because fringe benefits have grown faster than wages. The percentage of total compensation paid in cash
has declined from almost 96% in 1940 to 90% in 1970 and 82.3% in
1985.

The cost of Social Security in a given year is generally expressed as
a percentage of the taxable payroll in that year. For all practical
purposes, the taxable payroll can be thought of as analogous to the
cash component of the employee compensation and self-employment
earnings subject to payroll taxes.

A given level of Social Security expenditures will be represented by
a higher percentage on taxable payroll if the taxable payroll declines
relatively, as when cash pay becomes a smaller part of total compensation.

Significant about the projected future payroll tax rates is the assumption of a continuous decline in the ratio of cash pay to total compensation. The assumed decline is at the annual compound rate of 0.3% under alternative II-B for the 75-year period from 1985 to 2060, lowering the proportion of cash pay from 82.3% in 1985 to 65.9% in 2060. According to this assumption, as fringe benefits grow, the taxable payroll shrinks, relatively, as cash pay becomes a smaller proportion of total compensation. Consequently, a given percentage of the taxable payroll will represent a steadily shrinking percentage of total cash compensation. At the same time, with lowered covered earnings (due to cash pay as a smaller proportion of total compensation) Social Security benefits will also be somewhat lower. (For more discussion of this and other topics, see Chen, 1981; Wilkins, Gresch, & Glanz, 1982.)

The "necessary" ultimate tax rate of 12.4% reflects the relative shrinkage of taxable payroll to total compensation at the annual compound rate of 0.3% for the next 75 years. Alternatively, fringe benefits level off at a plateau in which they merely keep pace with cash pay (so that the proportion of cash pay to total compensation will remain at the same level in the future as it is today), the "necessary" ultimate tax rate will be 12.0%, not 12.4%.

In addition, should there be an additional productivity increase of 0.2%, which may not be a totally unrealistic assumption, the "necessary" ultimate tax rate will be further reduced to 11.7%. By comparison, the present payroll tax rate is 11.4%.

The above exercise was not meant to be polemical. The point is to stress that, despite population aging that calls for a rise in Social Security benefit payments, the increase in the payroll tax rate is not as substantial as the raw numbers, such as the increase from 11.4% to 12.4%, would suggest. A recognition of this fact will reduce the perception of the aged population as liabilities and thus will cast this segment of the population in a better financial light for society.

SUMMARY

Population aging has created the concern, or even fear, that the projected number of elderly persons in the future will represent a crushing burden on the working population. This view treats the elderly as liabilities. It is the thesis of this chapter that we could make assets out of tomorrow's elderly.

Declining fertility and improving mortality have combined to pro-

Lower birth rates mean a smaller number of
ιich reduces the dependency cost, but also a
which lowers the number of persons in the
pporters. Gains in longevity result in a larger
ɔns if old age is defined to begin at 65 in the
creased morbidity may accompany increased
xtent the elderly of the future could remain in
ι to compensate for the relatively smaller labor
age groups. Changes in the work environ-
prerequisites for keeping older persons in the

challenge of an aging population, society also
ate and public institutions for the care and
support of dependents in response to the changing mix of young and
old dependents.

Finally, economic growth is the fountain of economic security.
Society must endeavor to enhance productivity, with faster improvements in productivity, if the financial burden on the working
population is to be lessened in terms of the percentage of their
earnings devoted to the cost of caring for society's dependents.

This paper is revised from presentation at the Ollie Randall Symposium, 38th Annual
Scientific Meeting, Gerontological Society of America, New Orleans, Louisiana,
November 23, 1985. The author gratefully acknowledges, without implicating them in
the views expressed herein, helpful discussions with Francisco R. Bayo, Stephen C.
Goss, and Alice Wade, all from the Office of the Actuary, Social Security Administra-
tion, Baltimore, Maryland, and with Robert J. Myers, formerly Chief Actuary, Social
Security Administration, 1947–1970.

REFERENCES

Adamchak, D., & Friedman, E. (1983). Societal aging and generational de-
pendency relationships. *Research on Aging, 5,* 319–338.
Advisory Council on Social Security. (1979). *Social Security financing and bene-
fits.* Social Security Administration, U.S. Department of Health and Hu-
man Services. Washington, DC: U.S. Government Printing Office.
Bayo, F., & Faber, J. (1981) *Equivalent retirement ages: 1940–2050.* Actuarial
Note Number 105, Social Security Administration, U.S. Department of
Health and Human Services (SSA Pub. No. 11–11500). Washington, DC:
U.S. Government Printing Office.
Board of Trustees (1985, April 1). *Federal Old-Age and Survivors Insurance and
Disability Insurance Trust Funds: 1985 annual report.* House Document
99-46, 99th Cong., 1st Sess., April 1, 1985. Washington, DC: U.S. Gov-
ernment Printing Office.

Buchmann, A. (1983). Maximizing post-retirement labor market opportunities. In H. Parnes (Ed.), *Policy issues in work and retirement* (pp. 109–158). Kalamazoo, MI: W.E. Upjohn Institute for Employment Research.

Chen, Y-P. (1981). The growth of fringe benefits: Implications for Social Security. *Monthly Labor Review, 104,* 3–10.

Crown, W. (1985). Some thoughts on reformulating the dependency ratio. *The Gerontologist, 25,* 166–171.

Employee Benefit Research Institute (1986). *Economic incentives for retirement in the public and private sectors.* (Issue Brief No. 57. Washington, DC: Employment Benefit Research Institute.

Goss, S., Glanz, M., & An, S. (1985). *Economic projections for OASDI cost and income estimates, 1984.* Actuarial Study No. 94, Social Security Administration, U.S. Department of Health and Human Services (SSA Pub. No. 11-11541). Washington, DC: U.S. Government Printing Office.

Myers, R. (1985). *Social Security,* Homewood, MD: Richard D. Irwin, Inc. for McCahan Foundation.

National Council on the Aging (1982). *Aging in North America: Projections and policies.* Washington, DC: National Council on Aging.

Palmore, E. (1986). Trends in the health of the aged. *The Gerontologist, 26,* 298–302.

Sheppard, H., & Rix, S. (1977) *The graying of working America.* New York: The Free Press.

U.S. Senate Special Committee on Aging and the American Association of Retired Persons, the Federal Council on the Aging, and the Administration on Aging. (1986). *Aging America: Trends and projections* (1985–86 edition) (1986-498-116-814/42395). Washington, DC: U.S. Government Printing Office.

Wade, A. H. (1985, October). *Social Security area population projections, 1985.* Actuarial Study No. 95, Office of the Actuary, Social Security Administration, U.S. Department of Health and Human Services (SSA Pub. No. 11-11542). Washington, DC: U.S. Government Printing Office.

Wilkens, J., Gresch, R., & Glanag, M. (1982). *Growth in financial benefits.* Actuarial Note 113 (Publication 11-11500). Washington, DC: Social Security Administration, U.S. Department of health & Human Services.

6

The Prospective Burden of an Aging Population

William Crown

In the late 1970s and early 1980s the Social Security system experienced several short-run funding "crises." As a consequence, widespread concern developed regarding the ability of the economy to support an aging population. Most experts agree, however, that the 1983 Social Security amendments solved the program's short-run financing problems; the retirement and disability trust funds are now projected to run substantial surpluses through 2020 (e.g., Munnell & Blais, 1984; U.S. General Accounting Office, 1986).

Yet despite this seemingly optimistic outlook, many researchers, pension planners, and policy makers remain concerned about the ability of the economy to support an aging population. This concern is usually expressed in terms of projected increases in the number of "dependent" persons who must be supported by each person in the labor force.

If one equates being dependent with being elderly, the source of concern about the future burden of an aging population is obvious. The proportion of the population aged 65 and over will almost double by the middle of the next century (see Rappaport & Plumley, Chapter 3, this volume, for a demographic overview). Moreover, the population aged 75 and over is growing at an even faster rate. In 1980, about 4% of the population was aged 75 and over; by 2050, this will increase nearly threefold to approximately 12%. Changes of this magnitude in the age structure of the population deserve close scrutiny. But do they necessarily imply an increased support burden for future workers? The answer to this question depends mainly on future rates of economic growth and on which segments of the population we consider to be dependent.

DEPENDENCY RATIOS

A common method for assessing the economic implications of an aging population is to calculate dependency ratios. As the name implies, dependency ratios involve calculating the ratio of "dependent" to "productive" members of society. Like all summary statistics, however, dependency ratios can be used to support almost any conclusion about the future burden of an aging population. In the most misleading studies, the dependency ratio is defined to be the ratio of the older population (i.e., those aged 65 and over) to the population of labor force age (i.e., those aged 18 to 64). Studies using this *aged* dependency ratio invariably conclude that the aging of the population will result in an increased "burden" on members of the labor force. An example of the conclusions reached by this type of dependency ratio study is provided by Torrey (1982, p. 164).

> Historically, there has been an implicit social contract that the working generations will help support the retired and disabled generations either privately or publicly. But the contract may have to be renegotiated if the future size of the retired and disabled more than doubles relative to the size of the working age generation.

A less misleading approach is to calculate *total* dependency ratios. This approach recognizes that the elderly are not the only population segment with limited participation in the labor force. In particular, total dependency ratios recognize that children as a group also have limited involvement in the labor force. Studies using total dependency ratios uniformly indicate that the increased burden from population aging is *more than offset* by a corresponding decline in the younger population (e.g., Cowgill, 1981).

Although less biased than dependency ratios focusing only on the older population, total dependency ratios have been criticized for relying on the assumption that all persons of labor force age work and support all those in other age groups, who are classified as dependents (e.g., Clark & Spengler, 1980; Cowgill, 1981; Rix & Fischer, 1981; Schulz, 1980). Such an assumption is clearly invalid. Many older persons and younger persons participate in the labor force, while many persons of labor force age do not.

Several studies have gone beyond strictly demographic dependency ratios to take account of the labor-force participation rates of different groups (Adamchak & Friedman, 1983; Crown, 1985; De-Vita, 1981; Rosenblum, 1976). All of these studies using *labor force* dependency ratios have concluded that the total burden on the labor force will be lower in the future than that experienced in recent decades. Nevertheless, uncertainties remain regarding the use of dependency ratio calculations as a basis for policy formation.

For example, a major limitation of the dependency ratio approach is the assumption that the per capita costs of supporting alternative groups of dependent persons are identical. Actually, this is not a limitation of dependency ratio analysis but rather a reflection of data availability. Crown (1985) has suggested a methodology for calculating dependency ratios that would allow the straightforward incorporation of such cost differentials. However, these cost differentials are extremely difficult to estimate.

THE RELATIVE COSTS OF YOUNGER AND OLDER PERSONS

The difficulty of constructing estimates of the relative costs of children and the elderly is reflected in the small number of studies that have been conducted. Moreover, analysts have come to widely divergent conclusions regarding the costs of supporting younger versus older dependents. Looking only at government expenditures, Clark and Spengler (1978) concluded that these expenditures were three times greater for older dependents than for children in the United States. However, taking account of all expenditures, Wander (1978) found that in West Germany the costs of supporting children to age 20 were one-fourth to one-third higher than the costs of supporting persons 60 years old for the rest of their lives. Finally, Dixon & Thane (1984) found that in Australia average *government* outlays on the aged were about twice those on the younger population in 1980–1981.

From the above discussion, it is clear that estimating the relative costs of supporting alternative groups of dependent persons is fraught with problems. One of the most difficult problems—and the main reason for the variance in the cost estimates made by different analysts—is the need to take account of both private and public support mechanisms. This is a necessary step for assessing the true costs of shifting from youth to old-age dependency.

Although it is widely recognized that families provide most of the support for younger dependents, the support that families provide for aged dependents is not generally acknowledged. Moreover, even if one assumes that support for younger dependents is provided completely through private sources while support for older dependents is provided completely through public sources, declining youth dependency will enable economic resources to be freed for potential support of the aged.

THE FISCAL "BURDEN" OF POPULATION AGING

Several studies have examined the implications of population aging for the proportion of the federal budget and/or GNP that is allocated to older persons. Torrey (1982) notes that the federal budget share devoted to programs for the elderly has increased from 2% in 1940 to 25% today. Such increases clearly raise concerns about the ability of the federal government to continue to provide the same level of real per capita benefits as the population ages. In fact, most estimates indicate that the budget share devoted to the older population will rise to between 40% and 50% by 2025 (Califano, 1978; Clark & Menefee, 1981; Torrey, 1982; U.S. Senate, 1984). Expenditures on the elderly as a percentage of GNP, however, are projected to increase much less dramatically—to between 4% and 11% (e.g., Califano, 1978; Clark & Menefee, 1981).

In fact, the factors that determined the past growth in spending on the elderly are quite different from those expected to influence future spending growth (Clark & Menefee, 1981; U.S. Senate, 1984). Until recently, rising public expenditures on the elderly were due mainly to the maturation of Social Security and federal pension programs. In addition, legislated benefit increases (especially the 1972 Social Security amendments) substantially raised income transfers to the elderly in the 1970s and early 1980s. For the next 20 years, however, retirement income expenditures as a percentage of the federal budget and GNP are expected to decline; current expenditure shares will not be reached until around 2030 (U.S. Senate, 1984).

Between now and the retirement of the baby boomers, beginning around 2015, spending growth on the older population will come largely from rising health care costs. Overall, however, the share of the federal budget allocated to the elderly should remain fairly stable until the advent of the baby boomers' retirement, because rising health care costs should be offset by the relative decline in retirement income expenditures.

These projections, in combination with the issues raised by the demographic transition from child dependency to aged dependency, suggest that the major issue of supporting future dependents may not be the ability of the economy to provide the support, but rather the politics of transferring the resources from the private to the public sector.

Despite the difficulties of estimating the costs of supporting alternative dependent groups in the population, it is possible to answer a somewhat different question: How much could the *real* costs of supporting dependents in some future period increase relative to those of some base year, before the real burden on society would be higher than it has been historically?

ESTIMATION OF RELATIVE COSTS

To begin, we disaggregate the total labor force dependency ratio into a series of additive age-based components (see Crown, 1985), using population projections from the U.S. Bureau of the Census and projections of labor force participation rates from the Bureau of Labor Statistics (Crown, 1985). These estimates are shown in Figure 6.1. The reader may note that the youth and aged dependency ratios do not add up to the total dependency ratio in Figure 6.1. This is because dependents of labor force age are excluded in order to highlight the trends in youth and aged dependency.

It is clear from Figure 6.1 that the decline in youth dependency over the period from 1960 to 2000 dominates the moderate rise in aged dependency over the same period. However, between 2000 and 2040 the decline in youth dependency will level off, while the rise in aged dependency will accelerate. Around the year 2040, we will shift from being a youth-dominated society to a society that is dominated (albeit slightly) by aged dependents. Beyond 2040, the aged, youth, and total dependency ratios will remain virtually unchanged. The important point is that even in the year 2050 the total dependency ratio will be far lower than it was in recent decades. For example, in 1960—at the height of child dependency associated with the baby boom—the dependency ratio was 1.6, implying that each member of the labor force supported 1.6 dependents. In 2050—at the future height of aged dependency associated with the baby boom—the dependency ratio is

projected to decline to about 1.0, implying that there will be only one
dependent per worker.

Of course, it is not necessarily true that the real burden of support
will decline about 38% between 1960 and 2050—that will depend on
the relative cost of supporting younger and older persons. Unfortunately, estimating such costs becomes very involved when one
attempts to take account of both private and public transfers.

Nevertheless, it is possible to calculate how large future support
costs could become relative to the cost of some base year before a net
burden would be placed on society. We have already noted that in
2050 the dependency ratio is projected to be approximately 38% less
than it was in 1960. This suggests that the per capita cost of supporting each dependent person in 2050 could be about 38% greater than
the corresponding cost in 1960 before a net burden would be incurred
by society. However, this is an *underestimate* of the degree to which

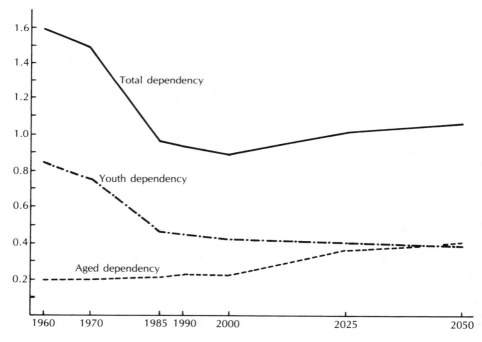

FIGURE 6.1 Decomposition of the Total Dependency Ratio (1960–2050).

Source: Calculations based on middle series population projections of the U.S. Bureau
of the Census and middle series labor force rate projections of the U.S. Bureau of Labor
Statistics. (Fullerton, 1980).

relative support costs could increase. To the extent that real economic growth occurs over this time period, there is the potential to allocate some of this growth to dependent members of society. To see how dependency costs and economic growth are related, let us consider an example.

In 1960 about 109 million persons were not in the labor force. Let COST1960 represent the real cost of supporting each of these dependent persons. Then the total real cost of supporting all of the dependents in 1960 was 109,100,000 − COST1960. Similarly, we can project that there will be about 159 million persons outside the labor force in 2050 (Fullerton, 1980). If we designate COST2050 to be the real cost of supporting each dependent person in 2050, then the total cost of supporting all dependents in 2050 will be 158,529,000 − COST2050.

However, relating the support costs to the size of the labor force (as is traditionally done) ignores increases in productivity and economic growth. Real economic growth averaged 3.3% between 1960 and 1985. Assuming the same rate of growth between 1985 and 2050, we can ask: How many times greater could the real support costs be in 2050 relative to those in 1960, before the real support burden would be as high in 2050 as in 1960?

To find the answer, we need to solve the following equation:

$$\frac{109{,}110{,}000 \times \text{COST1960}}{\text{GNP1960}} = \frac{15{,}852{,}900 \times \text{COST2050}}{\text{GNP2050}}$$

However, GNP2050 is equal to GNP1960 multiplied by the compounded rate of economic growth:

$$\text{GNP2050} = \text{GNP1960} \times (1.033)^{90}$$

Substituting for GNP2050 in the initial equation yields:

$$\frac{109{,}110{,}000 \times \text{COST1960}}{\text{GNP1960}} = \frac{158{,}529{,}000 \times \text{COST2050}}{\text{GNP1960} - (1.033)^{90}}$$

Rearranging terms and simplifying yields:

$$12.79 = \frac{\text{COST2050}}{\text{COST1960}}$$

This means that taking account of economic growth, the real cost of supporting each dependent in 2050 could be almost 13 times the corresponding cost in 1960 before the real support burden would be as great as it was in 1960.

SENSITIVITY ANALYSIS

Future Economic Growth and Labor Force Participation Rates

Of course, the above results represent only a "best guess" based on midrange assumptions regarding future rates of population growth, labor force participation, and economic growth. Variations in these rates and the years chosen for comparison can drastically alter one's conclusions about the future burden of supporting dependent members of society. Table 6.1 illustrates how the "break-even" ratio of real support costs in 2050 relative to those in 1960 would vary under several different assumptions of real economic growth. The sensitivity of the support cost ratio to assumptions about alternative economic growth rates is immediately apparent. For example, if the real rate of economic growth averaged 2.0% over the period from 1985 to 2050, the real costs of supporting each dependent person in 2050 could be 5.6 times higher than they were in 1960 without any in-

TABLE 6.1   Cost Ratios Associated with Alternative Rates of Economic Growth[a]

Real economic growth rate, 1985 to 2050 (percent)	$\dfrac{\text{COST2050}}{\text{COST1960}}$
1.0	2.96
2.0	5.61
3.0	10.59
3.3	12.79
4.0	19.84
5.0	36.95

[a]These cost ratios represent the multiple by which the real per capita costs of supporting dependent persons in 2050 could increase over the corresponding costs in 1960 without imposing an increased burden on society.
Source: Author's calculations based upon the middle series population projections of the U.S. Bureau of the Census (1982) and the middle series labor force participation rate projections of the U.S. Bureau of Labor Statistics (Fullerton, 1980).

creased burden to society. The margin for cost increases could be more than twice as great if the economy grows by 3.3% per year between 1985 and 2050. And, if the future rate of real economic growth averages 5% per year, the corresponding real cost ratio could be 36.9 before society would incur a higher economic burden. (In addition, see Chen, Chapter 5, this volume for a discussion of the effects of productivity increases.)

It is clear that there is an exponentially increasing relationship between real economic growth rates and the allowable ratio of real support costs. As a consequence, marginal increases in economic growth rates help relieve the economic burden of population aging much more than marginal decreases in growth rates intensify the burden.

Of course, the burden of supporting future dependent members of society will also be a function of labor force participation rates. Declines in labor force participation raise the burden of supporting future dependents by increasing the size of the dependent population while, at the same time, reducing the number of workers supporting this population.

Conversely, increases in labor force participation decrease the burden of future support costs. If we assume, for the moment, that economic growth and labor force participation are independent phenomena, it is possible to examine how economic growth and labor force participation could interact to affect the burden of future support costs.[1] This interaction is shown in Table 6.2. It is immediately obvious from Table 6.2 that the break-even ratios of real support costs in 2050 relative to those in 1960 are much less sensitive to changes in labor force participation than to changes in real economic growth.

Choice of Comparison Years

The results of the support cost analyses presented above will also be influenced by the choice of base year and future year to be compared. In the above calculations, 1960 was chosen as the base year because it had the highest dependency ratio in recent decades (i.e., since 1950). As such, it represents an appropriate marker of the dependency "burden" that society has been able to support in the past. Similarly, 2050 was chosen as the future year for comparison because most

[1]This is obviously a major simplification. It represents the case where capital is fully mobile and can be freely substituted for labor when labor force participation rates decline.

TABLE 6.2   Cost Ratios Associated with Alternative Rates of Real
            Economic Growth and Labor-Force Participation[a] (percent)

	1.0	2.0	3.0	3.3	4.0	5.0
Projections of labor-force participation						
Low	2.79	5.28	9.97	12.05	18.69	34.81
Medium	2.96	5.61	10.59	12.79	19.84	36.95
High	3.17	6.02	11.35	13.71	21.27	39.62

[a] These cost ratios represent the multiple by which the real per capita costs of supporting dependent persons in 2050 could increase over the corresponding costs in 1960 without imposing an increased burden on society.

Source: Author's calculations based upon the middle series population projection of the U.S. Bureau of the Census (1982) and the labor force participation rate projections of the U.S. Bureau of Labor Statistics (Fullerton, 1980).

experts agree that this is the year when the elderly will constitute the highest percentage of the total population.

Nevertheless, other choices of comparison years are equally justifiable. For example, rather than selecting 1960 as the base year, one could use the *average* dependency ratio for 1950 to 1980 as an indicator of the dependency burden that society has grown accustomed to supporting in recent decades. Similarly, noting that the total dependency ratio increases only marginally after 2025, one could justify the choice of 2025 as the future year for comparison. What effect would these alternative choices of comparison years have on the support cost ratios?

The historical dependency ratios for 1950 to 1980 and the middle-range dependency ratio projected for 2025 are shown in Table 6.3. Between 1950 and 1980, the dependency ratio averaged 1.37. (This is a weighted average, found by summing the total dependents over 1950–1980 and dividing by the total labor force over 1950–1980.) The dependency ratio for 2025 is projected to be about 1.10—roughly comparable to the support burden in 1980 and much lower than the ratio experienced from 1950 to 1970. Given the similarity of the dependency ratios for 1980 and 2025, it is useful to examine how much per capita support costs could increase by 2025 before society would bear a heavier burden than it supported in 1980.

Real growth in GNP averaged 3.4% from 1950 to 1980. If we assume this same growth rate for 1980 to 2025 and apply the methodology discussed above, real per capita support costs in 2025 could be 3.4 times those in 1980 without increasing the real burden on society.

TABLE 6.3   Historical and Projected Dependency Ratios, 1950–2025

Year	Labor force (thousands)	Population (thousands)	Dependent population (thousands)	Dependency ratio
1950	62,208	151,326	89,118	1.43
1960	69,628	179,323	109,695	1.58
1970	82,771	203,302	120,531	1.46
1980	106,940	226,546	119,606	1.12
2025	143,648	301,024	157,376	1.10
2050	150,323	308,852	158,529	1.05

Sources: Historical data: U.S. Bureau of Labor Statistics (1983, p. 12) and U.S. Bureau of the Census (1984, p. 6).Projections based on middle series population projections of the U.S. Bureau of the Census (1982) and the middle series labor force participation rate projections of the U.S. Bureau of Labor Statistics (Fullerton, 1985).

This implies that if the dependency ratios in two periods are roughly equivalent, real support costs can increase at the same rate as real GNP without any real increase in the support burden. Note, however, that the allowable increase in support costs from 1960 to 2025 (assuming 3.3% real growth in GNP) is much higher than that for 1980 to 2050.

This is the case for two reasons. First, the dependency ratio for 1960 (1.58) is much higher than that for 1980 (1.12), while the dependency ratios for 2025 and 2050 are roughly comparable. This has the effect of reducing the projected future improvements in the total labor force dependency ratio. The major reason for the difference in the estimates in the two periods, however, comes from the reduction in the number of years over which real GNP growth is assumed to occur. For the period 1960 to 2050, real growth occurs for 90 years; from 1980 to 2025, real growth occurs for only 45 years. Thus, the *rate* of the real economic growth and the *period* over which it occurs are the major determinants of society's ability to support dependent segments of the population.

ALTERNATIVE PROJECTIONS FOR FUTURE GNP

Unfortunately, experts disagree about the future path of GNP growth. For example, the Bureau of Labor Statistics (Su, 1985) projects real GNP growth of 3.0% through 1990 and 2.8% for 1990 to 1995. Similarly, in their base-case simulations, Olsen, Caton, and

Duffy (1981) estimate that real GNP growth will average 2.5% through 2005. These estimates assume that labor productivity will increase in future years because of the projected relative growth in the proportion of experienced workers in the labor force. In contrast, the Macroeconomic-Demographic Model of the National Institute on Aging (1984) projects real GNP growth of 1.6% from 1980 to 2010 and only 0.8% growth from 2010 to 2055. The reason for the slower projected growth rate over 2010–2055 is an estimated decline in the total number of hours worked that partly offsets projected productivity increases in the labor force.

POLICY IMPLICATIONS OF WORK/LEISURE TRADEOFFS

Economic growth can arise from many sources: technological change, increased investment, and increases in the quality and/or quantity of labor. But whatever its source, economic growth generally implies rising compensation levels for those in the labor force. Economists suggest that this reflects the fact that workers are being paid in accordance with increases in their marginal productivity. Although it is certainly true that not all workers are paid in accordance with their marginal productivity, there has been a strong relationship between economic growth and productivity increases over the past several decades.

Obviously, when productivity levels are rising, if each worker continues to work the same number of hours, the total output of the economy will rise. However, over the past few decades there has been a tendency to forgo some of this *potential* output and consume more leisure instead. The resulting backward bending supply curve of labor is depicted in Figure 6.2. At wage level w_1 workers will supply h_1 hours of labor; at w_2 they will supply h_2; but at w_3 they will supply h_3 hours.

The important point in all of this is that decisions on the part of society to "consume" increased leisure imply reducing potential output (Kreps & Spengler, 1966)—and thus influence the ability to support future dependents. But this is not all. The degree to which potential output is reduced depends on *when* the leisure is consumed. Figure 6.3 demonstrates the relationship between economic output and average hours worked for a labor force of a given size. (See Chen, Chapter 5, this volume, for further discussion of dependency.)

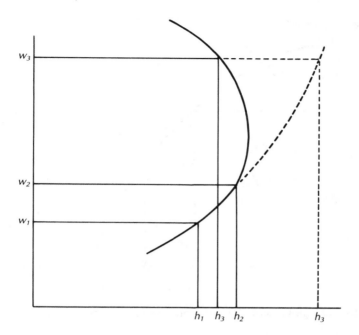

FIGURE 6.2   The backward bending supply curve of labor.

If the average workweek was h_1 (say, 40 hours/week), then output would be equal to q_1. However, if the average workweek declined to h_2 (say, 35 hours/week), output would decline to q_2. This sort of tradeoff between hours worked and potential output is what one would expect from the theory of a backward bending supply curve of labor and was the pattern evident during much of the past century.

In the past three decades, however, a new pattern of leisure consumption has emerged. This pattern is that of early retirement. It is now widely recognized that the labor-force participation of older men has declined dramatically over the past 35 years. For example, in 1950 about half the men aged 65 and over were in the labor force. By 1960, however, the labor force participation rate of elderly men had dropped to 33%; by 1970, it was 25%; and in the last quarter of 1984 only 16.5% of older men were working (U.S. Senate, 1984). Moreover, the decline in labor-force participation rates is evident even among men in their fifties. In 1960, 88% of males aged 55 to 59 were working; by 1984, only 64% were in the labor force. (See Sheppard, Chapter 9, this volume, for differing life satisfaction between early retirers and work continuers.)

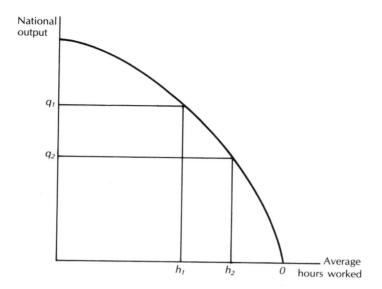

FIGURE 6.3   Movement along the production possibilities frontier.

Interestingly, the declining labor force participation rates of older men have been partially offset by *increases* in the labor force participation rates of women aged 55 to 64. In 1950, 25% of women aged 55 to 64 were in the labor force. By the mid-1960s this proportion had risen to 41% and was relatively stable for almost two decades (Schulz, 1985, p. 51). The labor force participation rates of women aged 65 and over fluctuated at around 10% during the 1950s and 1960s before gradually declining to a little over 7% in 1984.

Yet despite increases in the labor market activity of women aged 55 to 64, labor force participation rates for older persons as a whole have dropped steadily since the 1950s. In 1950, 27% of the population 65 and over were in the labor force; by 1982, this had declined to about 12%. What are the implications of these trends for the ability of the economy to support an aging population?

Early retirement represents the increased consumption of leisure by shortening the period of time spent in the labor force (that is, the duration of the worklife). As illustrated in Figure 6.4, this pattern of leisure consumption may have very different implications for economic growth and, consequently, the "burden" of supporting the future dependent population. Suppose the economy is originally operating with a labor force of 140 million workers. These workers average h_1 hours per week, and q_1 units of output are produced. Now

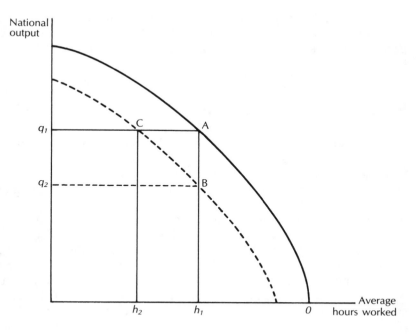

FIGURE 6.4 Inward shift of the production possibilities frontier.

suppose that due to early retirement the labor force shrinks to 130 million workers. This shifts the production possibility frontier toward the origin. Thus, if workers continue to work the same number of hours, output will fall to q_2. In order for output to remain at its old level, average hours must increase to h_2.

Early retirement therefore implies an increasing support burden for future members of the labor force—seemingly in contrast to our earlier conclusions based on the dependency ratio. However, these two sets of conclusions are not as contradictory as they first appear. The dependency ratio calculations presented earlier included projections of future labor force participation rates made by the Bureau of Labor Statistics. Thus these calculations partially take account of the influence of declining labor force participation rates on the "burden" of an aging population. As indicated in Table 6.2, if labor force participation rates are higher than the midrange projections, the projected burden will be lower, and vice versa. This is consistent with the work/leisure theory. However, the results presented in Table 6.2 do not directly capture the impact of early retirement on potential output, because the calculations assume independence between labor force participation rates and real growth in GNP. Much work remains to be done in examining the interrelationships between labor force participation, economic growth, and the "burden" of population aging.

SUMMARY AND CONCLUSIONS

This chapter represents an attempt to enlighten discussion about the future burden of supporting dependent segments of our population—especially the discussion couched in terms of dependency ratio analysis (e.g., Adamchak & Friedman, 1983; Clark & Spengler, 1980; Crown, 1985). The main focus of the chapter was to examine how the future dependency burden may be affected by alternative rates of labor force participation and real economic growth. The discussion attempted to deal with the inherent difficulties of measuring and projecting the costs of supporting different groups of dependent persons, particularly children and the elderly. Estimates were presented of the growth in real support costs that could occur by some future year before a real increase in economic burden would be placed on society. Such estimates were made possible by the explicit introduction of economic growth into a dependency ratio framework.

The results indicate that the future support burden is more sensitive to future economic growth than to changes in labor force participation or demographic shifts. Moreover, even under very conservative assumptions about future economic growth, real per capita support costs for dependent persons in the future could be several times historical rates before any increased burden would be placed on society.

Historically, of course, only a fraction of our economic growth has been allocated to dependent members of society, and this is likely to be true in the future as well. Nevertheless, it seems clear that the aged will not constitute an unbearable burden for society in the coming decades. Rather, the choices will be as they always have been—how best to allocate economic resources among competing segments of society.

REFERENCES

Adamchak, D., & Friedman, E. (1983). Societal aging and generational dependency relationships: Problems of measurement and conceptualization. *Research on Aging, 5*, 319–338.

Califano, J. (1978, July). The aging of America: Questions for the four genera-tion society. *The Annals of the American Academy of Political and Social Science, 438,* 97–107.

Clark, R., & Menefee, J. (1981). Federal expenditures for the elderly: Past and future. *The Gerontologist, 21*(2), 132–137.

Clark, R., & Spengler, J. (1978). Changing demography and dependency costs: The implications of future dependency ratios and their composi-tion. In B. Herzog (Ed.), *Aging and income: Programs and prospects for the elderly.* New York: Human Service Press.

Clark, R., & Spengler, J. (1980). *The economics of individual and population aging.* Cambridge, England: Cambridge University Press.

Cowgill, D. (1981, April). *Can we afford our aging population?* Paper presented at conference on Economics of Aging: Kansas City, MO.

Crown, W. (1985). Some thoughts on reformulating the dependency ratio. *The Gerontologist, 25*(2), 166–171.

DeVita, C. (1981, November). *Measuring dependency in the U.S. and Canada.* Paper presented at the 34th annual meeting of the Gerontological Society of America, Toronto, Ontario.

Dixon, D., & Thane, C. (1984). The relative costs to government of the young and the old. *Australian Quarterly, 56*(1), 41–52.

Fullerton, H. (1980). The 1995 labor force: A first look. *Monthly Labor Review, 103*(12), 48–58.

Fullerton, H. (1985). The 1995 labor force: BLS' latest projections. *Monthly Labor Review, 108*(11), 17–25.

Kreps, J., & Spengler, J. (1966). The leisure component of economic growth. In National Commission on Technology, Automation, and Economic Progress, *The employment impact of technological change,* Appendix to Vol. II (pp. 353–389). Washington, DC: U.S. Government Printing Office.

Munnell, A., & Blais, N. (1984, September). Do we want large Social Security Surpluses? *New England Economic Review,* pp. 5–21.

National Institute on Aging. (1984). *Macroeconomic-demographic model.* (Publication No. 84–2492) Washington, DC : U.S. Department of Health and Human Services, National Institute on Aging.

Olsen, L., Caton, C., & Duffy, M. (1981) *The elderly and the future economy.* Lexington, MA: Lexington Books, D.C. Heath and Company.

Rix, S., & Fischer, P. (1981). *Retirement age policy: An international perspective.* Washington, DC: American Institute for Research.

Rosenblum, M. (1976). *The future path of labor force participation and its impact on retirement policy.* Washington, DC: American Institute for Research.

Schulz, J. (1980). *The economics of aging.* Belmont, CA: Wadsworth.

Schulz, J. (1985). *The economics of aging (29th edition).* Belmont, CA: Wads-worth.

Su, B. (1985). The economic outlook to 1995: New assumptions and pro-jections. *Monthly Labor Review, 108*(11), 3–16.

Torrey, B. (1980). Demographic Shifts and Projections: Implications for pen-sion systems. Chap. 4, appendices to Presidents Commission on Pension Policy. Washington, DC: The Commission.

Torrey, B. (1982). Guns vs. canes: The fiscal implications of an aging population. *American Economic Review, 72*(2), 309–313.

U.S. Bureau of the Census. (1982). Projections of the population of the United States: 1982 to 2050 (advance report), *Current Population Reports*, (Series p–25, No. 922). Washington, DC: U.S. Government Printing Office.

U.S. Bureau of the Census. (1984). *Statistical abstract of the United States: 1985.* Washington, DC: U.S. Government Printing Office.

U.S. Bureau of Labor Statistics. (1983). *Handbook of labor statistics.* Washington, DC: U.S. Government Printing Office.

U.S. General Accounting Office. (1986). *Social Security: Past projections and future financing concerns.* Washington, DC: U.S. Government Printing Office.

U.S. Senate, Special Committee on Aging. (1984). *Developments in aging: 1983* (Vol 1). Washington, DC: U.S. Government Printing Office.

Wander, H. (1978). ZPG now: The lesson from Europe. In T. Espenshade & W. Serow (Eds.), *The economic consequences of slowing population growth.* New York: Academic Press.

7

The Labor Force by the Year 2000 and Employment Policy for Older Workers

Steven Sandell

Employment prospects for older workers in the year 2000 are an area of speculation. While the exact nature of employment opportunities is difficult to predict, the loss of jobs by some older workers is a certainty in a dynamic economy. It would be counterproductive for the nation to attempt, in advance, to keep jobs that could be done substantially more cheaply or efficiently by technologically advanced equipment or by producers with foresight. By the same token, it would be irresponsible not to provide training opportunities, new jobs, and income support for older American in need.

This chapter first examines labor force trends and presents specific occupational and industrial projections for the end of the century. Then older workers' employment problems are examined to provide a basis for policies to improve their employment prospects.

POPULATION AND LABOR FORCE TRENDS

Over the past century, labor force participation rates among persons aged 65 and over have declined as more people could afford to retire and retirement became socially acceptable. (See Rappaport & Plumley, Chapter 3, this volume, for statistics on longevity and on labor force participation among older persons). Recently, labor force participation of persons aged 55 to 64 has also declined. Because of this reduced participation and the effects of the baby boom, the proportion of the labor force that is over 45 has been declining since 1960. It will only begin to rise again after 1990, as the increased numbers in the over-45 population offsets the lower labor force participation rates in that age group.

The relative importance of older persons (defined as 55 and over) in the labor force will decline through the remainder of the century. Regardless of popular conceptions to the contrary, it is important to remember two points. First, the rise in the average age of workers is due to the aging of the baby boom group and not to an increase in the size of the group commonly identified as older workers (those over 55). Second, the population is not the labor force. The proportion of the population over 55 is affected by the dramatic increases in longevity for persons beyond their 65th birthdays. Since most people over 65 are not working, this population increase is not affecting the composition of the labor force.

While the reasons for the declining labor force participation of older persons are the subject of a vast literature, it is important to note that the reduction is primarily due to voluntary decisions by older persons. The increased affluence of older Americans, often channeled through public and private pension benefits, is perhaps the most important factor behind this trend. The current pattern of retirement before age 65 is a product of the general affordability of retirement, individual desires, and social acceptance of retirement. Dramatic declines in labor force participation occur at age 62 and again at age 65 because of eligibility for Social Security and pension benefits.

There is little reason, if current pension benefit structures remain in place, to expect dramatic change in retirement ages. The real value of retirement benefits may be less for the baby boom generation than for people retiring during the remainder of this century. Retirement ages may rise slightly. But only if the current pattern of long-term attachment to a particular employer disintegrates—and with it the concomitant pattern of increased salaries and pensions with longevity—will there be a dramatic change in retirement patterns. Only if there is more flexibility in the labor market, something that may be nascent, will there be more people working later in life.

Table 7.1 compares the industrial distribution of all persons and those 65 and older. Although the pattern for both groups is generally similar, some differences exist. For example, only 3% of all workers, compared to 9% of workers above age 65, were in agriculture. The age patterns reflect retirement patterns by industry as well as the job openings existing when people first entered the job market. Retire-

TABLE 7.1 Employment by Industry, 1981

Industry	65 and over	All ages
All industries (in thousands of persons)	3,119	107,348
Distribution (in percents)	100.0	100.0
Agriculture	9.2	3.0
Mining	0.4	1.0
Construction	3.8	6.4
Manufacturing—durables	6.1	13.4
Manufacturing—nondurables	5.6	8.8
Transportation	3.2	6.3
Trade—wholesale and retail	23.6	20.5
Finance, insurance, and real estate	6.1	5.9
Services	37.8	29.5
Public administration	4.2	5.2

Source: Congressional Budget Office (1982).

ment patterns, in turn, reflect the availability of jobs and pension arrangements.

Projections of the industrial and occupational distribution for the turn of the century are presented in Tables 7.2 and 7.3, respectively. The best projections available, from the Bureau of Labor Statistics, are for 1995 (see Personick, 1985; Silvestri & Lukasiewicz, 1985). These are compared with the actual industrial and occupational distributions for 1984. The differences seem to be minor.

A CONTEXT FOR PUBLIC POLICY TOWARD OLDER WORKERS

Comparing the current pattern of older workers' employment to projections of the industrial and occupational structure of the future economy is of little value for predicting older workers' employment problems at the turn of the century. Older workers, even if they lose their jobs, will be able to adjust if the economy is strong and the jobs are available, the workers have transferable skills, and age discrimination is prevented. Prior knowledge of exactly what the jobs will be and who will hold them is not possible for either private planning or public policy.

While it is important to dispel some of the crisis atmosphere surrounding the discussion of older workers' employment and the fu-

TABLE 7.2   Employment by Major Industrial Sector, 1984 and 1995

| | Employment (in thousands) | | Percent distribution | |
	1984	1995[a]	1984	1995
Total	106,841	122,760	100.0	100.0
Agriculture	3,293	3,059	3.1	2.5
Nonagriculture	103,548	119,700	96.9	97.5
Government	15,984	17,144	15.0	14.0
Federal	2,807	2,800	2.6	2.3
State and Local	13,177	14,344	12.3	11.7
Private	87,564	102,556	82.0	83.5
Mining	651	631	.6	.5
Construction	5,920	6,636	5.5	5.4
Manufacturing	19,779	21,124	18.5	17.2
Durable	11,744	13,216	11.0	6.4
Nondurable	8,035	7,908	7.5	6.4
Transportation, Communication, and Public utilities	5,500	6,304	5.1	5.1
Trade	24,290	28,272	22.7	23.0
Finance, insurance, and real estate	6,296	7,397	5.9	6.0
Services	23,886	31,170	22.4	25.4
Private households	1,242	1,023	1.2	.8

[a]Projection
Source: Personick (1985).

ture of retirement, there are real problems and a need for new policy directions (Sandell, 1987). If in the next century the nation is to use older worker's skills and experience effectively, the development of new retirement and employment policies must begin today.

Although knowledge of specific industrial and occupational opportunities for older workers in the year 2000 is neither possible to project nor by itself important information for developing policies, it is essential to establish a context for discussing the problems and important policy issues concerning older workers. To understand the problems as well as the policy solutions in the area of the older worker, it is useful to keep in mind some prototypical older workers.

- There are average persons, mainstream individuals whose earnings normally increase over their working years, peaking in their fifties and leveling off at the end of their working lives, prior to an anticipated period of retirement.

TABLE 7.3 Employment by Broad Occupational Group, 1984 and 1995

Occupation	Number (in thousands)		Percent	
	1984	1995[a]	1984	1995
Total Employment	106,843	122,760	100.0	100.0
Executive administrative and managerial workers	11,274	13,762	10.6	11.2
Professional workers	12,805	15,578	12.0	12.7
Technicians and related support workers	3,206	4,119	3.0	3.4
Salesworkers	11,173	13,393	10.5	10.9
Administrative support workers, including clerical	18,716	20,499	17.5	16.7
Private household workers	993	811	.9	.7
Service workers, except private household workers	15,589	18,917	14.6	15.4
Precision production, craft and repair works	12,176	13,601	11.4	11.1
Operators fabricators and laborers	17,357	18,634	16.2	15.2
Farming, forestry, and fishing workers	3,554	3,447	3.3	2.8

[a]Projection
Source: Silvestri & Lukasiewicz (1985).

- Average persons can experience unanticipated midlife events, such as major health or disability problems or the loss of a long-held job, that disrupt the average pattern.
- There are disadvantaged people who may have struggled all their lives. They have histories of intermittent employment and low earnings and often have severe labor market problems as they reach old age.

Policies to improve the employment prospects of older Americans must be geared to their specific backgrounds and needs. Since many of the chapters in this volume deal with the needs of mainstream individuals, I will emphasize the situation of older persons with particular employment problems.

The most serious employment problems are faced by older persons who are seeking work. Older workers with jobs often receive above-average pay. In considering policies to alleviate the employment problems of older displaced workers, as well as other unemployed older workers, several conclusions from recent research should be emphasized (see National Commission for Employment Policy, 1985; Sandell, 1985).

First, older workers are significantly less likely than younger workers to lose their jobs or become displaced. Although workers 45 and over are about 31% of the labor force, they are only about 20% of job losers. Greater seniority probably affords older workers protection against dislocation or job loss in general compared to their younger counterparts. However, when job loss does occur, the results can be devastating, sometimes making the difference between economic hardship and a secure retirement.

Second, the consequences of job loss are more serious for older workers than younger ones in specific ways. Older workers stay unemployed longer; they experience a greater drop in pay when they find a new job; and they are more likely to leave the labor market altogether.

Third, while age discrimination is an important cause of these problems, other factors contribute significantly. Characteristics such as education and previous work experience are related to the employment consequences of losing one's job. For example, the fact that older men have, on average, lower education and poorer health than younger men makes the average duration of their job search longer. The greater drop in pay for older workers who lose their jobs is largely due to their greater loss of seniority and firm-specific skills, which were useful on the old job but which the new employers are not willing to pay for (Shapiro & Sandell, 1987). For example, workers who were aged 60 when they lost their jobs averaged more than 11 years of job tenure; these workers experienced an average wage loss of 6%. Workers who were 45 to 49 averaged 6 years of job tenure when they lost their jobs; their wages fell by an average of 3%.

The fourth important finding is that drops in pay, duration of unemployment, and the likelihood of premature retirement are greater when there are adverse conditions in the local and national economy. Regional decline probably causes more severe problems than industry or occupation alone for dislocated workers seeking new work at wages comparable to those of their previous job. In other words, if the local economy is relatively strong and unemployment rates are generally low, dislocated workers are more likely to find new work with other employers at comparable wages. This is especially true if the worker's industry is basically healthy locally and it is only the worker's employer that is having difficulty.

A fifth finding is the documentation of the important relationships among job loss, labor-market conditions, and induced retirement (Shapiro & Sandell, 1984). Older job losers are much more likely to retire than are older workers of the same age who have not lost their jobs. For example, when the national unemployment rate was 6%, almost 30% of 60-year-old male job losers retired; by contrast, less than 10% of all males aged 60 who were still employed retired at that time.

High unemployment rates disproportionately increase the number of older job losers who retire early. For example, although an estimated 18% of all 60-year-old male job losers retire when the economy is at 4% unemployment, almost one-half (44%) of 60-year-old job losers retire when the economy is at 8% unemployment. Moreover, once retired, these workers tend to stay retired.

Although this retirement may be considered voluntary in the sense that workers prefer retirement to searching for or accepting jobs, the retirement is induced by economic conditions. The workers would not have retired if they had not lost their jobs or if conditions had proved more propitious for finding a new one. As a result, job loss and high unemployment have significant long-term costs for the economy—not just the loss of potentially productive workers, but also increased Social Security, private pension, and other payments.

CONCLUSIONS AND RECOMMENDATIONS

In the tradeoffs that inevitably must be made in developing national economic policy, federal policy makers should recognize the often hidden, but substantial, long-term costs to the economy and to older individuals that result from induced retirement caused by high unemployment (see also Kuhns, Chapter 11, this volume). The federal government should establish a new priority for employment in the development of its overall economic policies.

Three additional conclusions are useful in policy planning for the year 2000 (Sandell, 1985):

1. It is undeniable that age discrimination exists in the labor market and that vigorous enforcement of the Age Discrimination in Employment Act by the Equal Employment Opportunity Commission is essential.

2. Many of the labor market problems of older Americans—job losers or not—are grounded in causes other than age discrimination. So even if age discrimination were completely eliminated from the

labor market, many older workers would continue to experience employment problems.

3. Employment policies and programs must treat these other important causes of labor market problems directly.

Although employer actions are critical to improving the employment situation of older workers, many older workers have a need for training and other services that cannot be adequately addressed by employers alone. Thus government has an important training and employment role to play. As a general rule, older workers can be successfully served by existing public job and training programs as long as proper attention is paid to older individuals' needs.

Comprehensive Employment Training Act (CETA) programs were generally successful in training and placing older workers in private sector employment. Although older eligible persons were less likely to participate in CETA than younger adults, a substantial part of the difference is accounted for by factors other than age, such as the fact that many older eligible individuals were retired and had no interest in taking further training for employment. The experience of older workers who are served under the Job Training Partnership Act (JTPA) can also be successful.

Older workers who lose their jobs often face special difficulties. Training programs, such as those funded under JTPA, should provide special assistance to older job losers, with an emphasis on systematic assessment of their strengths in terms of job experience and long-developed skills, so that training can be provided to minimize loss of wages in new employment. Older workers who are eligible and desire training should be given equitable access to JTPA regular training programs (Title II) and to those established for displaced workers under Title III.

Many older job losers wish to work part-time or in new occupations. They often have experience, skills, and talents that go unused because they have difficulty finding appropriate work. Specialized placement services for older workers have proved to be successful in a number of areas of the country.

There are many examples of employer programs and age-neutral personnel practices that other companies can adapt to combat age discrimination and to increase employment opportunities for older workers, especially those who are approaching conventional retirement age (see Rothstein, Chapter 10, this volume). Employer actions that simultaneously meet company-specific business needs and the training and employment needs of older workers are critical to the improvement of their employment opportunities. Federal agencies such as the Department of Labor and the Administration on Aging, as well as state and local governments, should promote the adoption of innovative employer-sponsored programs and practices for older workers through the dissemination of information on successful efforts in this area.

In the next century some older workers, especially those who lose their jobs, will have serious labor market problems. However, government and the private sector can institute policies that will not only help older workers, but will benefit those businesses that hire them.

REFERENCES

Congressional Budget Office. (1982). *Work and retirement: Options for continued employment of older workers*. Washington, DC: U.S. Government Printing Office.

National Commission for Employment Policy. (1985). *Older workers: Prospects, problems and policies*. Washington, DC: U.S. Government Printing Office.

Personick, V. A. (1985). A second look at industry output and employment trends through 1995. *Monthly Labor Review, 108*(11), 26–41.

Sandell, S. H. (1985, July 24). Statement on displaced older workers. In *Hearing before the Select Committee on Aging, House of Representatives, U.S. Congress* (Comm. Pub. No. 99–528). Washington, DC: U.S. Government Printing Office.

Sandell, S. H. (Ed.). (1987). *The problem isn't age: Work and older Americans*. New York: Praeger.

Shapiro, D., & Sandell, S. H. (1984, December). *Economic conditions, job loss and induced retirement*. Paper presented at the Industrial Relations Research Association Meeting, Dallas, TX.

Shapiro, D., & Sandell, S. H. (1987). Older job losers' reduced pay: Age discrimination and other explanations. In S. H. Sandell (Ed.), *The problem isn't age: Work and older Americans* (pp. 37–51). New York: Praeger.

Silvestri, G., & Lukasiewicz, J. M. (1985) Occupational employment projections: The 1984–95 outlook. *Monthly Labor Review, 108*(11), 42–53.

8

The Older Worker: Myths and Realities

David A. Peterson and Sally Coberly

Interest in the older worker is growing rapidly. The most recent stimulation of this interest came from the passage of the 1978 amendments to the Age Discrimination in Employment Act, which raised the mandatory retirement age to 70 for most workers. This has attracted the attention of unions, corporations, and the educational community. Even though it has had a rather minor effect on the workforce in the short run, its potential results require careful consideration since it changes the employer-employee relationship as well as affecting previous attitudes about older workers and the ways in which company policies inhibit or enhance effective utilization of older employees on the job.

Employers have also been concerned about the changing age structure of the labor force and the impact that reduced numbers of younger workers may have on their operations. Some are already turning to older workers as a new source of labor for entry-level jobs previously filled by youth.

Faced with a short-term funding crisis in Social Security in the 1980s and projections of longer-range problems associated with the retirement of the post–World War II baby boom generation, policy makers have also turned their attention to the older worker, primarily with an eye to removing barriers to worklife extension for older persons who are willing and able to work longer. The 1983 amendments to the Social Security Act reflected policy makers' views they favored on-time or delayed retirement. As a result, normal retirement age will gradually increase to age 67 in 2027.

Finally, corporations and unions continue to express commitment to discovering the most effective and productive use of the workforce. As a result, they raise important and difficult questions about the best role of the older worker and the most beneficial policies for both the individual and the employer.

For these reasons and others, interest is directed to older workers as we seek insight into their most effective participation in the future world of work. Retirement has become very common in this nation. It has led to the belief that after age 62 or 65 or 70, the individual is no longer capable of effective job performance and therefore chooses to give up gainful employment. This may be the case for some individuals, but certainly not for most. However, this belief about older workers has encouraged corporations and unions to establish policies that remove individuals from the workforce on the basis of age; it has resulted in both wasted potential and economic loss.

It is this policy on which our interest is focused. The purpose of this chapter is to assess the viability of the older worker and to provide some data that may clarify the employment implications of age-related changes. Four major points will be addressed: labor force participation of older workers; current stereotypes and myths about the older worker; individual variability in the older population; and data on the realities of the older person as a worker. A few comments on the strengths of the older worker will conclude the chapter.

LABOR FORCE PARTICIPATION

After age 54, the percentage of individuals in the labor force declines steadily, so that in 1984 only 16.3% of men and 7.5% of women older than 65 were employed (U.S. Department of Labor, 1985). (See Rappaport & Plumley, Chapter 3, this volume, for more data on population characteristics and labor force participation.)

Even while the participation of women in the labor force has increased dramatically, the percentage of women over 65 who are in the labor force has not increased (Sheppard, 1978), indicating no desire on the part of most women for employment after normal retirement age.

At the same time, an increasing number of men are retiring before age 65. In 1950, 86% of men aged 55 to 64 were in the workforce. By 1984, this figure had dropped to 68.5%. Today, the median retirement age for men in the private sector who receive a pension is 62 (U.S. General Accounting Office, 1985). Do people retire because they are unproductive, ill, tired, or obsolete, or do employers lose their best workers because of the attractiveness of retirement and the bias against older persons in the workplace? The recent Age Discrimination in Employment Act (ADEA) legislation makes it imperative that both employers and workers clearly understand the reality of the older person as an employee.

MYTHS ABOUT OLDER WORKERS

The prevalent myths about older workers are similar to the contemporary beliefs about older people generally. For some groups, myths are overwhelmingly positive, idealizing the virtues and values of a particular status or period of life. That is not the case with old age: myths about the later years are generally negative. They assume that decline in abilities and productivity is greater than reality would indicate, and they lead to stereotyping a very diverse group of people into categories of incompetence.

Space does not allow an exhaustive listing of the myths of the older worker, so we have chosen five, which we hope will provide a reasonable sample. First, there is a general belief that increased age results in generally poor health, loss of physical energy, and increased illness. This myth leads to the assumption that older workers are physically incapable of performing their tasks, that they are often absent from work for health reasons, and that they do not have the stamina to complete demanding tasks.

Second, there is a general belief that increased age results in higher accident rates, more lost workdays, and increased insurance and medical costs. This myth leads to the assumption that older workers are more expensive to the company, that their presence increases company risks, and that they are a danger to themselves and their co-workers.

Third, there is a general belief that increased age results in lowered productivity because of slower actions, greater absence, and less commitment to the employer. This myth leads to the assumption that older people retire because they cannot compete with the productivity of younger workers and thus are an economic drain on the employer.

Fourth, there is a general belief that increased age results in rigidity of behavior, an inability to learn new skills, and a rejection of the innovative. The myth results in older workers being passed over for new positions, for retraining, and for challenging assignments that may require changes in traditional behavior.

Fifth, there is a general belief that increased age reduces the potential value of retraining, job development, and skill upgrading. This myth leads to the assumption that age makes worker development impossible, that costs would be indefensibly high, and that anticipated length of service after training would not justify the investment.

A survey of corporate managers reported in the *Harvard Business Review* indicated the depth and strength of these myths (Rosen & Jerdee, 1977). The questionnaire was in the form of a managerial decision making exercise in which the respondent was to assume the role of a "troubleshooter" and asked to make decisions regarding organizational and personnel problems. Two versions of the questionnaire which were equally used. In one, a 32-year-old was the key individual in the problem situation, while in the other, it was a 61-year-old. Otherwise the two questionnaires were identical. Thus, managerial decisions based on the age of the employee could be identified.

Although the respondents to the survey stated that they valued both younger and older workers, their recommended solutions to the problem situations did not indicate an unbiased position. For instance, the respondents: (1) saw more difficulty in changing the behavior of older employees; (2) suggested that items be routed around the older employee rather than presented to him directly; (3) did not attribute positive motives to older workers desiring retraining; (4) favored career development for younger workers, but not for older workers; and (5) saw older workers as less likely to be promoted than younger workers. In this study, age stereotypes clearly influenced management decisions, in each case to the detriment of the older worker.

INDIVIDUAL DIFFERENCES

Before providing some data on the realities of the older worker, a note of caution needs to be added. The older population is composed of tens of millions of individuals. Some are intelligent; some are healthy; some are creative; others are not. No matter what criterion is chosen, there are major variations within the older adult population. This means that we must be careful not to conclude that because the average older person is active, or creative, or cautious, that all older people are. With many variables, data clearly show that there are greater differences within the older population than between older and younger people. Thus we emphasize that we are discussing central tendencies of these myths and realities; determination of the status of any particular older person requires that some individual measurement be undertaken.

This is especially true for persons in the age group from 60 to 80. Individuals may change rapidly during this time, and age alone becomes a very poor predictor of health, vitality, or performance. Physical and intellectual change occurs very rapidly for some persons, while others show little or no decrement through this period. On the average, however, this is the period when some decline affects most people.

The work environment may greatly affect this. Persons actively continuing their work role may suffer detrimental effects if the required work is too heavy, too pressured, or too fast. On the other hand, a retirement that includes no challenges, interests, or rewards may also be detrimental. Thus there continues to be a reciprocal relationship between the physical and mental functioning of the individual and the environment. The conclusion to be stressed is that characteristics of the older population in general need not be true of any individual older worker.

REALITIES OF THE OLDER WORKER

Data clarifying the realities about the older worker are drawn from a variety of studies done both within the workplace and by gerontological researchers in universities. These studies allow us to conclude that the myths are generally inaccurate, and in some cases totally opposite of the facts. They will be dealt with on an individual basis, although the studies do not necessarily coincide with the myths that have been identified.

Illness and Old Age

The myth of illness in later life has some basis in fact. It is true that persons over the age of 65 have more sick days, more hospital stays, and more days of limited activity than younger persons (U.S. Department of Health, Education and Welfare, 1978). This is especially accurate for individuals over the age of 80. But this correlation between illness and increased age does not mean that old age is the cause of illness. An individual's stamina, resistance, and reserve capacity decline with increased age; thus, older people become more likely victims of illness.

Those who do become ill are likely to contract chronic conditions that cannot be easily cured and are likely to require medication or therapy over an extended period of time. Respiratory disorders occur more frequently in older workers; often they are caused or exacerbated by the conditions of the workplace and may result in the transfer of the worker to a different job situation. The increase in chronic conditions, however, is somewhat counterbalanced by the decline in acute conditions. Overcoming the restrictions and handicaps of chronic illness is more likely to occur through the development of adaptive mechanisms by the older person. There are many situations in which we are forced, or choose, to change our behavior in order to adapt to alterations in our environment or ourselves. Thus, in 1982, 89% of men aged 45 to 64 and 69% of men aged 65 and over reported that they were able to work in some capacity (Newquist, 1984).

Although illness is not directly caused by aging, there are some changes that do seem to occur as a part of the aging process. The senses all decline in acuity, and visual and auditory declines are probably the most pervasive and important. However, corrective measures can help many people regain normal functioning. Muscle strength is reduced with age, but experience and job redesign can generally overcome any major limitations that result. Reactions slow with increasing age—the neural system does not carry messages to and from the brain as rapidly, and psychomotor performance generally slows. Experience and preparation, however, may greatly reduce the impact of this decline in many settings. Aging also brings reduced reserve capacity; this is often evident in a need for more frequent rest periods and caution in physical activities. The effect of this decrement must be assessed primarily in relation to the requirements of the particular work role.

Although these changes do reduce the potential of the older worker, collectively they seldom interfere with activities until the individual is in his or her seventies. On the other hand, most employment does not use the maximum potential of the older worker; thus older people are able to compensate for aging changes and illness with adjustments made possible through experience, increased knowledge, foresight, and workplace accommodations (Robinson, 1986).

Most people continue to function very well until they are in their seventies and need have little fear of precipitous decline. The conditions they experience are generally of slow onset, develop somewhat gradually, and can be overcome with the normal adjustments that most people make to their physical and social situations. Thus illness and health, while posing potential problems for persons over the age of 70 (see Table 3.7 in Chapter 3, this volume), generally are not considered to be detrimental to the viability of the older worker.

Accidents and Old Age

The myth that older workers are subject to a greater number and severity of accidents would lead an employer to reject the retention or recruitment of older workers because they would be an excessive risk. The myth, however, is generally untrue and should not be used as an excuse to avoid consideration of the ways in which older workers can best contribute. In 1981, for example, workers age 55 and older made up 13.6% of the labor force, but accounted for only 9.7% of all workplace accidents (U.S. Administration on Aging, 1984).

In general, older workers have different types of accidents from younger workers, and overall their record is better. Older workers are more likely to be involved with falls or to be hit with flying objects, but they are less likely to be caught in a machine or be injured in starting a machine (Sheppard, 1978.) Once injured, however, the older worker is generally off the job longer than his younger counterpart (Coberly & Newquist, 1984).

Birren (1964) concluded that accidents that are preventable by judgment based on experience decrease with greater age, while accidents that could be avoided by quick evasive action increase with age. Thus older people are more likely to appreciate the demands of the situation and use their experience to predict situations in which an accident is likely to occur; consequently, they avoid accidents more frequently than younger workers.

Some of the avoidance of accidents is dependent upon the greater experience of the older worker. However, even when older workers have no more experience than younger workers, their accident records are better (Sheppard, 1978). Older workers are likely to be more cautious, take fewer risks, and value risk taking less; they are likely to select themselves out of areas where they feel uncomfortable or unsafe, and thus they avoid situations where accidents are likely to occur. Those tasks in which judgment and expecting the unexpected are important in accident prevention are ones in which the older worker is especially likely to be superior. However, in a work setting where both task and pace are rigidly structured, older workers will function less effectively and with a higher level of accidents, since they cannot use their experience or develop ways to compensate for aging-related changes.

Job Performance

The myth that job performance automatically declines with increased age is not supported by the facts (see Rothstein, Chapter 10, this volume). In most occupations overall work productivity does not decrease with age, at least up to the age of 65. The many studies that have been conducted in this area indicate that there is no consistent pattern of superior productivity by any age group. Doering and her colleagues reviewed 28 empirical studies of the relationship between age and performance spanning 30 years (Doering,Rhodes, & Schuster, 1983). No clear pattern of decreases in performance with age was found. Some studies reported a nonsignificant relationship; several found performance to improve with age; still others showed a decline in performance. Occupations in which performance increased with age included salespersons, paraprofessionals, clerical workers, and fabric examiners and handlers. Declining performance with age was reported for such occupations as printers, production workers, factory workers, mail sorters, sewing machine operators, and air traffic controllers (Doering, Rhodes, & Schuster, 1983). If any generalization can be made, it would be that losses in performance with age are associated with jobs requiring physical strength and a rapid work pace. Older workers may be at an advantage, however, in jobs where performance is positively associated with experience or the building of a clientele (Robinson, 1986).

Variation in worker productivity is much greater within any age group than it is between age groups (Baugher, 1978; Sheppard, 1978). That is, the difference in productivity between younger and older workers is generally less than the differences within the ranks of younger workers or any age group.

More recent research on productivity suggests that the issue of age and productivity in the workplace may need to be reframed. Paul (1984), for example, found that employers were more interested in whether older employers met productivity standards per se than in whether older workers were as productive as younger employees; age comparisons were of little concern. Employers are also beginning to realize that standard measures of productivity, such as units produced per standard interval of time, do not fully capture a worker's contribution to the organization. Defined more broadly, productivity can also encompass loyalty and the contribution the worker makes to morale and efficiency within the organization (Coberly & Newquist, 1984).

While the findings regarding productivity and age vary by occupation, it nevertheless seems fair to conclude that age is not an automatic detriment to productivity. If the industrial mix continues to shift away from manufacturing toward the service and knowledge sectors, the impact of age on job performance may be mitigated even further (Robinson, 1986).

Decline in Ability to Learn and to Change

Performance on intelligence tests is the usual measure of the individual's ability to learn. The earliest studies of adult intelligence indicated that IQ increased through adolescence and peaked at approximately 22 or 24 and then declined slowly throughout the rest of the adult years. These studies were cross-sectional in design and compared scores from persons of different ages; the differences in scores were assumed to be caused by age.

Subsequent studies used longitudinal designs, which tested the same individuals at different points in their lives. The result has been called the classic aging pattern, in which verbal abilities decline very little if at all during the years before age 65 while psychomotor and performance abilities decline earlier and more rapidly (Botwinick, 1978). This pattern holds for men and women, black and white adults, individuals from various economic strata, and persons in and out of mental hospitals (Eisdorfer, Busse, & Cohen, 1959).

A slightly different view of intellectual change has been suggested by Schaie (1975), who undertook a study using both cross-sectional and longitudinal design. He reported that verbal intelligence changes little over the lifespan, at least until age 65, but that each succeeding generation scored slightly higher than the preceding one. Thus comparisons of different age cohorts show older groups as receiving lower scores. The explanation, however, is not that IQ declines with age but that education, nutrition, and the mass media continue to form persons who score higher on the test; so IQ continues to rise.

Intelligence across the lifespan has been the subject of extensive study. Most researchers today have concluded that intellectual functioning holds up very well for healthy adults throughout the major portion of the lifespan. As Birren has pointed out, changes in intellectual performance as they relate to the work role are likely to be affected more by perception, set, attention, motivation, and physical state than they are by the capacity of the individual (Birren, 1964).

Thus the older worker is generally able to learn, to change behavior, and to develop new skills. The questions we must address are whether the worker desires to do so and whether we can be creative enough to encourage this change. This topic is dealt with in the following section.

Retraining

The final myth to be dealt with holds that retraining of older workers is an inefficient use of corporate resources, because older persons cannot be effectively retrained for work roles. Like the other myths, this one is false. Although it may take the older worker somewhat longer to learn the new skill or knowledge, experience has shown that the retrained worker is likely to be more dependable, have a better attendance record, stay on the job longer, and do as much work as the younger employee (U.S. Senate, 1977). Recurrent education of workers is needed to reduce or prevent obsolescence and structural unemployment, but this need must be met throughout the entire work history of the individual and not only during the later years (Sterns, 1986).

A variety of retraining programs have been conducted in diverse businesses and industries. The results of these programs and the accompanying research support the contention that the older person is capable of being retrained and that the results are satisfying to both the individual and the employer (Mullan & Gorman, 1972; Paul & Coberly, 1983).

In the future, more attention needs to be focused on the most effective methods to be used and the motivation of the potential learner. Many educational approaches have been shown to work, but Belbin's "discovery method" appears to have been especially successful (Belbin, 1969). Through a step-by-step approach to concrete learning, it helps the older learner discover for him or herself how and why things work as they do. The approach seeks to involve the learner actively in the process through seeking solutions to specific tasks. It has been used in several studies and gives every appearance of being unusually successful. Sterns (1986) notes, however, that the careful development of the entire training program, irrespective of specific educational technique, is the key variable in determining successful training of the older worker.

We currently have a great deal of knowledge about the way older people learn and the manner in which instruction can best be organized. For instance, laboratory research on learning has shown that building upon past experience, providing advanced learning cues, assisting the learner to use memory devices, developing a supportive environment, providing positive feedback, allowing self-pacing, and encouraging active participation will all facilitate more effective learning. However, the application of these principles in specific settings is yet to be consistently undertaken in training situations.

We may conclude, then, as did Fleisher and Kaplan (1980) after reviewing a great body of literature, that the potential of the older worker for developing and improving skills can be met through creative approaches to training and employment policy. If utilized in an appropriate and knowledgeable manner, it will result in substantial value to both the individual and the employer.

CONCLUSION

Since we have concluded that each of the myths is partially or totally false, it is not surprising to find that some employers have already realized the potential of the older worker. They have consciously chosen to retain or hire persons beyond 65 years of age and report that they are very pleased with the result (Paul, 1983). Many have provided alternative work arrangements, such as part-time work schedules and job sharing, in order to encourage older employees to stay on the job (Coberly, 1985).

The older worker, then, should be considered as a potential resource for any employer. In general, they have fewer absences, fewer accidents, and equal or higher productivity than younger workers; they can continue to learn, and they can benefit substantially from retraining. They may well be preferred to younger workers if judgment, experience, safety, reduced risk, caution, stability, and company loyalty are desired.

REFERENCES

Baugher, D. (1978). Is the older worker inherently incompetent? *Aging and Work, 1,* 243–250.

Belbin, R. M. (1969). *The discovery method: An international experiment in retraining.* Paris: Organization for Economic Cooperation and Development.

Birren, J. E. (1964). *The psychology of aging.* Englewood Cliffs, NJ: Prentice-Hall.

Botwinick, J. (1978). *Aging and behavior.* New York: Springer Publishing.

Coberly, S. (1985). Keeping older workers on the job. *Aging, 349,* 23–25, 36.

Coberly, S., & Newquist, D. (1984). Hiring older workers—Employer concerns. *Aging, 343,* 23–25.

Doering, M., Rhodes, S. R., & Schuster, M. (1983). *The aging worker.* Beverly Hills: Sage.

Eisdorfer, C., Busse, E. W., and Cohen, L. D. (1959). The WAIS performance of an aged sample: The relationship between verbal and performance IQs. *Journal of Gerontology, 14,* 197–201.

Fleisher, D., & Kaplan, B. H. (1980). Characteristics of older workers: Implications for restructuring work. In P. K. Ragan (Ed.), *Work and retirement: Policy issues.* Los Angeles: University of Southern California, Andrus Gerontology Center.

Mullan, C., & Gorman, L. (1972). Facilitating adaptation to change: A case study of retraining middle-aged and older workers at Aer Lingus. *Industrial Gerontology, 15,* 20–39.

Newquist, D. (1984). *Trends in disability and health among middle-aged and older persons.* Unpublished paper prepared for the National Policy Center on Employment and Retirement. Los Angeles: University of Southern California, Andrus Gerontology Center.

Paul, C. E. (1983). *Work alternatives: A human resource planning tool for managing older workers.* Unpublished report prepared for the National Commission for Employment Policy. Los Angeles: University of Southern California, Andrus Gerontology Center.

Paul, C. E. (1984). *Company productivity and worker age.* Unpublished paper prepared for the National Policy Center on Employment and Retirement. Los Angeles: University of Southern California, Andrus Gerontology Center.

Paul, C. E., & Coberly, S. (1983). Retraining the older worker for changing technology: Programs and practices. Unpublished report prepared for the United States Congress Office of Technology Assessment. Los Angeles: University of Southern California, Andrus Gerontology Center.

Robinson, P. K. (1986). Age, health and job performance. In J. E. Birren, P.K. Robinson & J. E. Livingston (Eds.), *Age, health and employment.* Englewood Cliffs, NJ: Prentice-Hall.

Rosen, B., & Jerdee, T. H. (1977). Too old or not too old. *Harvard Business Review, 55,* 97–106.

Schaie, K. W. (1975). Age changes in adult intelligence. In D. S. Woodruff & J. E. Birren (Eds.), *Aging: Scientific perspectives and social issues.* New York: Van Nostrand Co.

Sheppard, H. L. (1978). *Research and development strategy on employment-related problems of older workers.* Washington, DC: American Institute for Research.

Sterns, H. L. (1986). Training and retraining adult and older adult workers. In J. E. Biren, P. K. Robinson & J. E. Livingston (Eds.), *Age, health and employment*. Englewood Cliffs, NJ: Prentice-Hall.

U.S. Administration on Aging. (1984). *Promoting employment of older workers: A handbook for area agencies on aging*. Washington, DC: Author.

U.S. Department of Health, Education and Welfare, Public Health Service, National Institute on Aging. (1978). *Our future selves—A research plan toward understanding aging*. Report of the Panel on Research on Human Services and Delivery Systems, National Advisory Council on Aging. Washington DC: U.S. Government Printing Office.

U.S. Department of Labor, Bureau of Labor Statistics. (1985, January). *Employment and earnings*. Washington, DC: U.S. Government Printing Office.

U.S. General Accounting Office. (1985). *Retirement before age 65 is a growing trend in the private sector*. Washington, DC: Author.

U.S. Senate, Committee on Human Resources, Labor Subcommittee. (1977). *Findings on age, capacity, and productivity*. Washington, DC: U.S. Government Printing Office.

9

Work Continuity Versus Retirement: Reasons for Continuing Work

Harold L. Sheppard

This country, along with many others in the industrialized world, has been experiencing ambivalence (some might call it schizophrenia) about its older worker policies. The same is true when it comes to actual behavior patterns of work continuity and early retirement. The ambivalence is reflected in the simultaneous espousal of (1) the rights and needs of older persons in the world of work; (2) the need to retire such persons in order to "make room" for younger ones; and (3) the "burden" imposed by a constant mushrooming of a population of retirees. All this is accompanied by data pointing to the growing desire for, and reality of, early retirement, and by anecdotes and survey reports suggesting the longing of older Americans to find employment.

At least during most of this century, retirement—especially early retirement—has been considered a hallmark of a civilized industrial society. But at the same time, the need to feel useful is deemed by many to be fulfilled only or primarily through participation in the paid labor force. Furthermore, economic demographers are projecting within the next few decades an age profile that implies a labor shortage if current retirement patterns and trends are allowed to continue.

The actual behavior patterns include a trend toward early (before age 65) retirement, the growth rate of which may decline at times, but so far has not reversed. In contradiction to this trend, we also find a large number of persons in their late 50s or older seeking employment or reemployment, after many years of nonparticipation in the labor force, or after becoming recently unemployed as a result of recessions, company shutdowns and mergers, "skill obsolescence," or other causes. Included in this category are also many persons who had retired but who later want or need employment for financial and/or social-psychological reasons.

The casual observer, therefore, can easily be confused by anecdotal and statistical reports pointing to the increasing stream of retirees, on one hand, and on the other, to the many older job seekers and the growing number of private and public projects dedicated to assisting them. These two simultaneous but countervailing phenomena may be likened to the existence of layers of wind currents of opposite directions and with varying speeds. These dual patterns increase the difficulty in stating any simple formulation of an "older worker" policy on a national scale.

Conventional wisdom has it that workers retire earlier than otherwise because of attractive pension benefits. Little thought has been given to the possibility that there is a policy underlying this, that the very purpose of certain types of pension provisions is exactly to achieve this result—to rid the enterprise or the economy in general of an unwanted class of employees. A variety of reasons may be involved, primarily having to do with costs. Schiller and Snyder (1982) have written extensively on restrictive pension provisions, the primary impact of which is to "limit or reduce the value of continued labor by older workers."

> These "restrictive provisions" sometimes establish an absolute limit on the duration of employment, but more often simply reduce the total compensation paid for continued employment. As a consequence, older workers confront lessened incentives to remain with their employers or in the larger labor force. The net reduction in total compensation is often substantial and can be an effective barrier to continued employment. (p. 486)

This chapter, in contrast to the typical approach which delves into the reasons and conditions for retirement, attempts to focus instead on the opposite inquiry—the reasons and conditions for work continuity. An attempt will also be made to compare the financial and social-psychological conditions of work continuers with those of retirees.

Thus it concentrates, in large part, on the issue of work continuity for older person. This is done primarily through some comparisons of work continuers with retirees of the same age. Inevitably this will involve discussions of the role of expected retirement income levels and of health status, a topic that need not be belabored here. For certain purposes, comparisons of workers and retirees aged 55 to 64 will be the focus; for other purposes, the groups aged 65 and over.

The covert and overt bias of the chapter lies in its effort to discern what we might be able to say, to persons contemplating early retirement, about the advantages of remaining in the workforce and, conversely, the "penalties" of early retirement. In addressing this issue, the results may point to some policy and program directions that warrant consideration.

Most of the empirical bias for the discussion is derived from published and unpublished findings from the 1981 National Council on Aging (NCOA)/Louis Harris survey, for which the author was the NCOA project director.

ADEQUACY OF INCOME

One obviously germane way of determining the advantages of work continuity over retirement is to compare the differences in financial status between the work continuers and the retirees. It should come as no surprise that the work continuers report higher household and personal incomes than the retirees. The corresponding figures for their 1980 incomes can be discerned in Table 9.1.

The sources of income for work continuers and for retirees differ considerably, as might be expected. For the two groups of 55-to-64-year-olds, Tables 9.2 and 9.3 report, respectively, the current sources

TABLE 9.1 Median 1980 Household and Personal Incomes of Older Work Continuers and Retirees

| | 55–64 | | 65+ | |
	Work continuers	Retirees	Work continuers	Retirees
Household	$21,800	$13,500	$14,200	$ 8,700
Personal	$14,000	$ 8,400	$11,700	$ 6,100

Source: Unpublished tables from 1981 Louis Harris Associates Survey for National Council on Aging.

TABLE 9.2   Sources of 1980 Household Income for Work Continuers and Retirees, 55–64 Years Old

	Work continuers	Retirees
Earnings from own current job	91%	6%
Earnings from spouse's job	41%	25%
Social Security (and/or Railroad Retirement)	14%	61%
Company or public employer pension	6%	46%
Savings	30%	30%
Investments	19%	23%
VA, other government pension	8%	22%

Source: Unpublished tables from 1981 Louis Harris Associates Survey for National Council on Aging.

TABLE 9.3   Largest Income Source

	Work continuers	Retirees
Earnings from own current job	66%	4%
Earnings from spouse's job	20%	15%
Social Security (and/or Railroad Retirement)	6%	36%
Company or public employer pension	1%	25%
Savings	—	3%
Investments	1%	3%
VA, other government pension	2%	8%

Source: Unpublished tables from 1981 Louis Harris Associates Survey for National Council on Aging.

of household income and the one source supplying the largest part of such income.

While equal proportions (30%) of work continuers and retirees cite savings as one source, and 3% of retirees cite savings as the largest supplier of income, a critical comparison lies in the fact that 39% of the retirees, but only 29% of the work continuers, reported that they were saving or investing less than they were two or three years previously (30% and 27% respectively, were saving more). Contrary to what may have been expected, only a slightly higher proportion of retirees (49%) than of work continuers (43%) reported that they had had to take money from savings to pay bills or expenses.

We do not have available the data that take age into consideration in examining household incomes by number of years in retirement. But it may still be worth reporting—as a possible indicator of the "longitudinal price" for retirement—that for retirees as a group, median household and personal incomes vary with the number of years a worker has been in retirement. Table 9.4 shows this relationship.

To be sure, these are cross-sectional results, but they are suggestive of the erosion of retirement income during the retirement years. At least from a strictly financial point of view, they constitute an argument for continued labor force participation.

Further evidence for this viewpoint can be gleaned more directly by inquiring into the age at retirement for different household income groups among the 65-and-older retirees. As Table 9.5 shows, there is a positive relationship between household income and the proportion who waited until at least age 65 to retire. This suggests the "payoff" for work continuity.

There is some suggestion, in the disaggregated data from which Table 9.5 is derived, that the relationship between age at retirement and current household income may not be unilinear. Some of the upper-income retirees could have retired quite young because of expected retirement income and their general financial status at the

TABLE 9.4   Median 1980 Household and Personal Income by Years in Retirement

	2 years or less	3 to 4 years	5 or more years
Household	$14,200	$10,100	$ 8,500
Personal	$11,200	$ 5,900	$ 5,800

Source: Unpublished tables from 1981 Louis Harris Associates Survey for National Council on Aging.

TABLE 9.5   Percent Retiring After Age 65, by 1980 Household Income, for Retirees 65 and Older

	Under $5,000	$5,000 –9,999	$10,000 –19,999	$20,000 and –above
% Retired at age 65 or older	45%	53%	60%	60%

Source: Unpublished tables from 1981 Louis Harris Associates Survey for National Council on Aging.

time of retirement. But the more general finding is that the later one retires, the greater the odds for higher income.

But information about the comparative dollar incomes of different categories of people does not provide us with immediate insights as to the meaning of the incomes and the differences. Even if we were to go through the overly complicated process of including a dollar-value equivalent of noncash services and subsidized goods, as well as other benefits (e.g., tax deductions, tax shelters, and other forms of government assistance), we would still end up with quantitative dollar figures, with the underlying question still begging to be answered. That question has to do with standard of living and with the adequacy of income from the standpoint of the income recipient.

One (but only one) alternative to the "objective" approach to comparing the income status of work continuers to that of retirees is to develop a typology based on how adequate the total income of such persons is from their point of view, that is, perceived income adequacy.

In a special analysis of the NCOA/Harris 1981 data (funded by the Travelers Insurance Group), Sheppard and Mantovani (1982) used two key questions in the survey interview to construct such a typology:

Forced choice questions such as:
1. Please tell me which one of the statements on this card best describes your situation:
    A. I really can't make ends meet with the income I have now.
    B. I just about manage to get by with the income I have now.
    C. I have enough to get along and even a little extra.
    D. I can buy pretty much anything I want with the income I now have.
Open end questions such as:
2. Whether "not having enough money to live on" is a very, or somewhat, serious problem—or hardly a problem at all, *personally*, to the respondent.

Persons choosing statement *A* or *B, and* saying that not having enough money to live on is a very or somewhat serious problem personally, were classified as "hard-strapped." Those respondents with the directly opposite responses were designated as "well-off."

All remaining respondents, who, in effect, gave inconsistent responses to the two items used to construct the typology, were called "intermediates."

The first major finding to present here is the difference between work continuers and retirees. Among the work continuers, 51% were well-off and only 24% hard-strapped. In contrast, 41% of the retirees were well-off and 35% hard-strapped. This comparison—which is virtually unchanged if we show separate percentages for the 55-to-64 and 65-and-over groups—is at the very least an indirect measure of the income advantage of work continuity.

In our opinion, the perceived income adequacy approach is a more reliable indicator of degree of satisfaction with one's income or standard of living, compared to the use of dollar or dollar-equivalency income. Table 9.5 does not, however, constitute a clearcut answer to the question about the "costs" of early retirement ages or the advantages of later retirement. In the Sheppard and Mantovani report, the authors claim that:

> The risks involved in retiring "too early" are suggested by our analysis of the relationship between the age at which the retired respondents left the labor force and the income-adequacy typology. (p. 14)

As Table 9.6 makes clear, the later the workers retired, the higher the proportion who were well-off and the lower the proportion who were hard-strapped. Nearly one half of those retiring at 70 or later fell into the group of the well-off, in contrast to only 38% of those retiring as young as 55 to 59 years of age and 43% of those retiring between the ages of 60 and 69. Conversely, the hard-strapped proportion was negatively associated with age at retirement. Only 29% of persons retiring at 70 or older were hard-strapped, compared to as much as 38% of those who retired when 55 to 59 years old.

Of course, the age at which a person retires is not the only influence or variable involved in the making of adequate income. Retiring at a young age does typically mean more years in a nonwork status, but early retirement can occur because of the prospect of an attractive retirement income, at least at the time of retirement.

However, we cannot neglect the finding by Sheppard and Mantovani concerning perceived income adequacy and the *reason* for retirement. We know that younger retirees are more likely to have health problems. But the more critical point is that among those workers reporting they were "forced" to retire because of disabilities

TABLE 9.6   Perceived Income Adequacy by Age at Retirement

	55–59	60–64	65–69	70+
Hard-strapped	38%	35%	32%	29%
Well-off	38%	43%	43%	49%

Source: Sheppard & Mantovani (1982).

or other health problems, as shown in Table 9.7, 56% were hard-strapped, in contrast to only 26–29% among those retiring voluntarily or because of mandatory retirement rules (a very small proportion of all retirees). Of those giving health problems as the reason for retirement, only 22% were well-off —far below the 50% figure for the retirees who retired by choice or through mandatory retirement rules.

Another factor that may hinder or facilitate work continuity is the extent of home ownership, or more precisely, whether a worker rents or is still paying off a mortgage, as opposed to mortgage-free ownership. The NCOA/Harris data are informative on this matter. A much larger proportion of work continuers than of retirees are either still buying their homes or are renting. Table 9.8 certainly suggests that as long as a worker must continue to pay off a mortgage, or is renting, his or her odds for remaining in the labor force will be higher than otherwise.

It has become increasingly popular to claim that the socioeconomic status of America's retirees is quite secure—more secure than many advocates for the elderly claim, especially because such a relatively large percentage of retirees own their homes mortgage-free (compared to only 26% of all persons aged 18 and older). But there is no assurance that mortgage-free ownership in retirement versus employment is a worry-free bulwark against income inadequacy. Mortgage-free ownership while *still* employed is still to be preferred—at

TABLE 9.7   Income Adequacy Level by Reason for Retirement

	Voluntary	Mandatory	Health problems
Hard-strapped	26%	29%	56%
Well-off	50%	50%	22%

Source: Sheppard & Mantovani (1982).

TABLE 9.8   Housing Situation of Work Continuers Versus Retirees, by Age

| | 55–64 | | 65+ | |
	Work continuers	Retirees	Work continuers	Retirees
Mortgage paid off	44%	57%	56%	67%
Still paying mortgage	42	30	21	10
Renting	32	11	16	18
Other arrangements	2	2	7	5

Source: Sheppard & Mantovani (1982).

least when measured by perceived income adequacy. To be sure, the mortgage-free retirees have a higher proportion who are well-off, and a lower proportion hard-strapped, compared to all other *retirees*. But when the retired mortgage-free homeowners are compared to the *employed* mortgage-free owners, the differences are quite impressive. A lower proportion of the *employed* mortgage-free homeowners than of the *retired* mortgage-free homeowners are hard-strapped (21% versus 28%). And a much higher proportion are well-off (62% versus 46%). The costs of house maintenance and taxes, along with generally lower incomes, can keep a large proportion of retired mortgage-free homeowners out of a well-off status.

There should be little doubt, of course, that mortgage-free home ownership, as a concrete example of "retirement resources," is a primary condition for early retirement: nearly three fifths of the retirees aged 55 to 64 (57%) indicated they were in that enviable position, in contrast to only 44% of their work-continuer age peers (Table 9.8) (Sheppard & Mantovani, 1982).

Summarizing up to this point, the evidence as far as income is concerned is that (1) work continuers are better off than retirees; (2) later retirement is better than early retirement; and (3) even when mortgage-free home ownership (higher among retirees than the others) is taken into consideration, income adequacy is still higher among the work continuers.

A major exception to the first assertion is that, while work continuity among whites and blacks is associated with a better income adequacy than is retirement, the same cannot be said for the Hispanics in the NCOA/Harris sample. Regardless of labor force status, about 68% of them are hard-strapped and only 15% well-off.

The current income, as well as expected retirement income, of the still-employed older workers has a bearing on *planned* retirement age.

The hard-strapped work continuers indicated they would retire later than the Intermediates or the well-off, which suggests that they had taken into account their current low level of income adequacy as a tenuous base for retirement.

WHO RETIRES?

Which types of workers, by occupation, are most likely to be work continuers? In the 55-to-64 age group professionals and the category of skilled workers, craftsmen, and foremen were overrepresented among the work continuers, while unskilled and other operatives were underrepresented. In other words, the first two occupational groups are more likely to be work continuers than the third. By *industry*, persons in health care, education, and social services were more likely to be work continuers than to be retirees, while the opposite is true of government workers, whose retirement provisions typically are conducive to early retirement.

The *lack of job opportunities* was deemed a personal problem by a higher proportion of work continuers—28%, compared to 18% of the retirees. This higher proportion in the case of the work continuers may reflect a number of conditions, including frequent spells of unemployment or dissatisfaction with the socioeconomic status of the current job. But we should not ignore the percentage of retirees claiming not enough job opportunities as a serious personal problem. This may be an indication of another motive for retiring or remaining retired, that is, discouragement in previous job hunts.

The concern with job opportunities among the 55-to-64-year-old work continuers (28%) itself is an indication of the importance of a "decent" job among labor force participants of this age group. To be sure, younger members of the labor force complain much more about the lack of job opportunities (37% of those aged 18 to 54), but the 28% figure for the 55-to-64-year-old group is still relatively high, in our opinion.

Just as important, nearly half of these older work continuers said they would be interested in learning new skills or participating in a job-training program in order to take on a different type of job. About one-sixth had actually taken courses in the past year, and nearly three-fifths of these persons gave as a reason the acquisition of job skills. These findings should help put to rest any notion of the irrelevance of skill training for older persons. Indeed, the lack of any positive and effective national policy regarding large-scale retraining programs for middle-aged and older workers underlies many of the individual and societal problems of unemployment, low income, and slackened economic growth.

Work commitment and the need to remain in the labor force (as measured by negative responses to the question about whether they look forward to retiring completely) are just as strong among the work continuers aged 55 to 64 as among workers aged 40 to 54 (49% and 45%, respectively). But more adamantly against total retirement are the work continuers aged 65 and older: more than 80% said that they do not look forward to retiring completely.

That antiretirement sentiment is also shown in the finding that one-third of the work continuers aged 65 and over, when asked at what age they planned on retiring completely, replied instead, "Never, if I can help it." More than one half of those not covered by a pension expressed that same sentiment. Among all the subsamples categorized by age and labor force status, the work continuers aged 65 and over expressed the greatest amount of disagreement with the statement, "Older people should retire when they can to give younger people more of a chance on the job" (National Council on Aging, 1981). Nearly 7 out of every 10 (68%) of the continuers aged 65 and over disagreed with this statement (with more than half disagreeing *strongly*). These older workers are clearly thinking of their own jobs when faced with giving an agree–disagree response. But among the work continuers aged 55 to 64, disagreement on the statement about requiring older people to retire is not as keenly felt: only 49% disagreed (with less than half of these disagreeing strongly). But if a worker persists in the labor force beyond the age of 64, he or she is likely to want to hold on to the job much more than the age group typically called the "preretirement" generation. That group (the 55-to-64-year-olds) includes workers who either can or want to retire and do not hold any strong feelings about the right of older workers to continue in the world of work.

To be sure, most American workers are retired before the age of 65, but as far as the group of workers past that age is concerned, complete retirement is out of the question for most of them.

LIFE SATISFACTION

It may be instructive to discuss the relative advantage of work continuity, not from a financial standpoint, but from a social-psychological one, as well as with regard to such other issues as social roles and employment. Life satisfaction as measured by the Havighurst Scale does not seem to be much greater among the work continuers, at least in comparing the median scores of workers aged 55 to 64 and retirees. But among the 18 items in the Life Satisfaction Scale, there were 3 on which the work continuers expressed more satisfaction by 10 or more percentage points than did the retirees.

	Continuers	Retirees
This is the dreariest time of my life. (% disagree)	84%	74%
I expect some interesting and pleasant things to happen to me in the future. (% agree)	83%	71%
The things I do are as interesting to me as they ever were. (% agree)	80%	61%

By six or seven percentage points, work continuers were more satisfied or positive on two items:

	Continuers	Retirees
I am just as happy as when I was younger. (% agree)	65%	58%
Compared to other people, I get down in the dumps too often. (% disagree)	83%	77%

On only one item was the Life Satisfaction response more positive among retirees by more than six percentage points:

	Continuers	Retirees
I have gotten more of the breaks in life than most people I know. (% agree)	50%	59%

The risks of dreariness, unhappiness, and low expectations of interesting and pleasant things in the future thus seem to be lower for work continuers 55 to 64 years old. The contrast between Continuers and retirees is even greater among the men and women aged 65 and older. Indeed, the median life satisfaction score for the subsample of work continuers 65 and older is the highest score among all persons 55 and older, when comparing work continuers and retirees.

We should point out here that if there is any single variable that is unambiguously related to life satisfaction, it is health status, much more than labor force status.

In sharp contrast to the group aged 55 to 64, there were sharp differences between work continuers and retirees aged 65 and older in the life satisfaction responses, on 9 of the 18 items in the Havighurst Scale; the disparity on these questions was at least ten percentage points. On *none* of the 18 items was there a more positive response from the retirees than from work continuers.

	Continuers	Retirees
As I grow older, things seem better than I thought they would be. (% agree)	63%	53%
This is the dreariest time of my life. (% disagree)	88%	70%
I am just as happy as when I was younger. (% agree)	68%	48%
Most of the things I do are boring and monotonous. (% disagree)	89%	76%
I expect some interesting and pleasant things to happen to me in the future. (% agree)	79%	61%
The things I do are as interesting as they ever were. (% agree)	80%	70%
I feel old and somewhat tired. (% disagree)	66%	52%
I have made plans for things I'll be doing a month or a year from now. (% agree)	63%	50%
Compared to other people, I get down in the dumps too often. (% disagree)	88%	78%

In response to another question about how personally serious were several problems, poor health was considered as a very or somewhat serious problem by only 24% of the work continuers, compared to approximately one half of the retirees in that same age group (55–64). There is no intent here to claim that poor health is one of the *results* of retiring, as opposed to continued labor force participation. Indeed, if anything, the best evidence of the relationship of health status to work continuity, derived from longitudinal analysis, is that workers with no work-limiting conditions have the greatest odds for retirement after age 65.

Loneliness can be an salient element in a person's morale or life satisfaction, a dimension not tapped in the Havighurst Scale. It was listed in the NCOA/Harris survey as one of the possible problems. Loneliness was deemed as a very or somewhat serious problem by a lower proportion of the work continuers than of the retirees, especially for respondents aged 65 and older (20% of the work continuers versus 30% of the retirees). The salience of this problem for retirees is suggested by their proportions stating loneliness to be a very serious problem, by roughly a 2 to 1 ratio over work continuers.

Did the retirees miss anything about not being at work any longer, and if so, what were the aspects of the job that were missed the most? For both age groups of retirees, the two most frequently reported things missed were the income and the people at work, a point that needs attention in any future probing of loneliness among retired workers. Neither was more frequently cited than the other. "Having a fixed work schedule every day" was the least frequently cited as something missed about being retired from their jobs. But as far as the *one thing missed the most* is concerned, the money it brought in was chosen by 31% of all the retirees, with the "people at work" a close second at 26%. The "work itself" was cited by 12%, and the "feeling of being useful" by only 10%.

But these percentages varied considerably, depending on the former occupation of the retiree (Table 9.9).

As Table 9.9 makes clear, the extent to which money from the preretirement job was missed was inversely related to the level of skills, with professionals, managers, and proprietors citing it the least and the blue-collar retirees (skilled and unskilled) citing it the most—by a 2-to-1 margin over the former. Conversely, the feeling of being useful was cited more frequently by former professionals, managers, and proprietors, along with retirees from clerical and sales positions.

One might expect that retirement would mean more time to be involved in activities, but work continuers—regardless of age—were just as likely as retirees to be engaged in volunteer activities. Among those aged 55 to 64, the proportion of work continuers reporting they were currently doing volunteer work was 30%, compared to 32% of retirees. For the cohort aged 65 and over, the corresponding proportions were 25% and 24%. However, in this latter group—the men and women aged 65 and over—work continuers' median weekly

TABLE 9.9   The One Thing Missed the Most About the Job by Occupation

	Prof./Mgr./ Prop.	Clerical/ Sales	Skilled/ Foreman	Unskilled
The money	20%	23%	42%	40%
The people	30%	27%	13%	24%
Feeling useful	11%	12%	6%	8%
Work itself	15%	11%	15%	10%

Source: Sheppard & Mantovani (1982).

volunteer hours were substantially below those of the retirees, 3.9 compared to 5.1 hours. Among those who said they had not done any volunteer work, retirees were less likely to say that they would like to do so, when compared to work continuers of the same ages. Thus a substantial minority of older retirees assume some roles outside the realm of paid work and make a potential contribution to society that may also provide them with a feeling of self-worth.

Another unexpected finding pertains to the topic of caring for other members of the family (younger or older). The frequency with which work continuers and retirees spent time in this type of activity differed hardly at all.

JOBS FOR OLDER WORKERS

Much can be learned from census data, or from specific older-worker projects, on the concrete occupations in which older persons are employed. Such information is an antidote to the notion that there is only a limited range of jobs "best suited" for older persons, mostly on a part-time basis and with low wages.

Take, for example, the experience of Operation ABLE (Ability Based on Long Experience), a private nonprofit agency established in Chicago in 1977. Operation ABLE now has similar programs in other parts of the country, including Boston, San Francisco, and Little Rock. Data provided by the agency for the first half of 1986 can be used to illustrate the point about a wider range of occupations for which older workers are hired. Examples of *full-time* occupations in which such people are employed are as follows:

librarian	dining-room manager
sales clerk	driver
purchasing agent	tool-and-die maker
switchboard operator	administrative assistant
rental agent	secretary
dental assistant	

Examples of the types of *part-time* jobs are:

telemarketing salesperson	receptionist/typist
bookkeeper	information-center assistant
file clerk	full-charge bookkeeper
cashier	labhelper II
baker	maintenance worker
waitress	data-entry clerk
tutor	

In less than ten years, the Chicago Operation ABLE has been able to place more than 30,000 older men and women in these and other kinds of jobs. The experience of this and similar projects elsewhere demonstrates how "intervention" or "intermediary" mechanisms can succeed in the labor market on behalf of older workers.

Lest the important point be missed, these men and women were hired *after* reaching the age of 55. The success of the project involves a capacity and a willingness on the part of employers to disregard age per se as a factor in making hiring decisions. Much of that is a product of the "marketing" of the skills of the older applicants by Operation ABLE's staff and that of its constituent agencies. It is not just the use of the most recent computer technology matching job seekers with employers.

The agency also participates in the U.S. Department of Labor's Joint Training Partnership program (JTPA), and the information on that project again suggests that the opportunities for older workers need not be restricted to low-wage, lesser-skilled occupations. The following refers only to the hourly wages of the nearly 125 JTPA participants in the last six months of 1985: $3.35–4.50, 49%; $4.51–5.99, 25%; $6.00–8.99, 17%; $9.00 and over, 9%. The median wage for these workers was $4.55/hour.

To be sure, nearly one half were employed at jobs through the JTPA program paying relatively low hourly wages ($3.35 – 4.50), a wage range that might otherwise comprise the vast majority of jobs available to older job seekers. The more impressive point is that over one fourth of the jobs paid at least $6.00 an hour. Examples of the types of jobs in each of the four wage brackets above are shown in Table 9.10.

Operation ABLE's enrollments are heavily skewed toward participants *under* age 62. Only one fifth are 62 and older, which reflects both the importance of retired workers Social Security benefits (available only at 62) and the fact that for men and women aged 55 to 61 there remains a widespread and basic need for employment. Typically, they consist of (1) persons who carry much of the brunt of economic and technological shifts in the society (through mass layoffs or "skill obsolescence," for example) and (2) older homemakers who—because of widowhood, late-life divorce, or a need to add to household income—enter or reenter the world of work in late life.

Nevertheless, one can still cite examples of very old men and women remaining in employment or reentering the job world. As an illustration, each year in Florida, the state's Department of Labor and Employment Security sponsors an Older Worker Week Employer

TABLE 9.10 Types of Jobs in JTPA Program

| | Hourly Wage | | |
$3.50–$4.50	$4.51–$5.99	$6.00–$8.99	$9.00 and over
Security guard	CRT operator	Payroll clerk	Quality control engineer
Merchandiser	Typist	Licensed Practical nurse	Electrician
Dishwasher	Household supervisor	Receptionist	Auto mechanic
Auto-parts dealer	Caretaker	Accountant	Insurance underwriter
Cashier	Recreation supervisor	Painter	Secretary
Janitor	Companion	Cashier/ hostess	Carpenter
Kitchen aide	Court clerk	Secretary	Auto body dealer
Nurse's aide	Bookkeeper	Shipping/ receiving	Painter
Sales clerk	General maintenance worker	Copy messenger	Credit manager's assistant
Car washer		Electrical salesperson	Dockworker
Survey interview		Credit/ collection worker	Inspector
News ad interview		Traffic manager	
Bartender		Office manager	

Seminar, at which "You're Still Ticking" awards are given to senior employees and to model employers. The top 8 awardees—chosen out of more than 500 nominations—included:

1. A 72-year-old woman working as a home health aide in a private-sector long-term care facility, averaging 32 hours a week.
2. An 80-year-old physical education instructor for a community college, with a perfect attendance record.

3. An 82-year-old employment counselor for the Florida Department of Health and Rehabilitative Services, developing job openings for AFDC clients. She holds the state record for placing the most clients in jobs by a single counselor and had previously retired from two other employers before joining the state in her current capacity.

4. An 83-year-old maintenance supervisor with a private aircraft filter manufacturing firm for the past 12 years (hired at age 71); he supervises 16 maintenance helpers and is responsible for housekeeping of a 160,000 square-foot facility. He has had a perfect attendance record (with the exception of one day off for cataract surgery).

5. An 85-year-old saw operator for a lumber company for the past 40 years, with an almost perfect attendance record.

6. An 87-year-old tax preparer with more than 10 years employment with the same employer (hired at age 76).

7. An 88-year-old accounting clerk previously working on C.O.D. collections. According to her employer, "Her productivity is incredible, not for a person of her age, but for a person of any age."

Whether they were employed long before becoming "old-old" workers, or hired only after entering that age category, these employees' stories are at least anecdotal evidence of the durability of many older persons in the labor market—and of the value placed on their performance in the workplace.

The hope for any "intervention" into what might otherwise be seen as an inexorable pattern of continuing retirement before 65 or even before 60, coupled with frustration for those older workers seeking jobs, presumably lies in small-scale, typically local projects. Despite the national aggregate macrodata that may tend to discourage any thought of keeping older workers employed or finding them new jobs, these nevertheless are remarkably impressive projects that succeed in these goals. The national Title V program of Senior Community Service Employment remains a good example of this point, but it is limited to fewer than 75,000 positions per year, to part-time jobs only for low-income men and women. By conservative estimates at least 500,000 persons would apply for these types of employment opportunities.

But the overall experience of such projects demonstrates that there are many employers who do not hesitate to retain and/or to hire older persons. Furthermore, the jobs in which they are employed contradict many of the stereotypes that abound in the world of work and aging. A casual observation of detailed census data would reveal that there are few occupations in which persons in their 60s and older are *not* found to be employed. There are three main factors that influence the overall picture: (1) the *demand* for such persons among employers; (2) the efforts of older job seekers; and (3) the necessary linkages to match the older workers with the willing employers.

REFERENCES

National Council on Aging (1981). Unpublished tables from a 1981 survey conducted for the National Council on Aging by Louis Harris Associates. Washington, DC: National Council on Aging.

Schiller, B. R., & Snyder, D. C. (1982). Restrictive pension provisions and the older worker. *The Gerontologist, 22,* 482–487.

Sheppard, H. L., & Mantovani, R. E. (1982). *Hard-strapped and well-off retirees: A study in perceived income adequacy.* A report for the Travelers Insurance Companies by the National Council on the Aging. Washington, DC: National Council on the Aging.

10

Older Worker Employment Opportunities in the Private Sector

Frances R. Rothstein

The first step toward increased older worker participation in the private sector must be a recognition by employers that older workers represent solutions to specific business problems. It is the recognition of need, rather a sense of corporate social responsibility, that offers the most promise for continued growth in older worker employment opportunities. However, at the same time that some business leaders are promoting age-neutral personnel policies and special programs to encourage older people to remain in or reenter the labor pool, other forces continue to limit older workers' employment opportunities. This chapter discusses some of the conditions that promote and inhibit older worker employment and offers a look at a few private sector responses that have resulted in improved older worker opportunities and productivity.

Increasingly, forward-looking corporate managers are acknowledging that older workers can help companies meet some of their human resource requirements in an era in which both demographic and economic conditions are changing quickly. However, the vast majority of American businesses have a long way to go in revising policies and practices to allow older people to make their maximum contribution to the economy. Businesses need to attract or retain older workers for numerous reasons.

BUSINESS NEEDS

Need for a Flexible Workforce

Companies have long hired older workers during peak workload seasons; perhaps the most common example of this is found in the retail industry during the weeks before Christmas. However, the increased availability of older people willing and able to work, combined with the cyclical nature of many service industries, has caused an upturn in the use of various types of flexible workers to fill in as needed. To avoid getting caught in a hire-and-fire, or a hire-and-layoff, pattern, many companies with the need for fluctuating staff sizes are maintaining a smaller core workforce and using temporaries, part-time workers, job-sharing arrangements, and other alternative staffing patterns. Because these options often dovetail with older people's interest in reduced work schedules, workers approaching traditional retirement age and retirees interested in returning to the workforce present a valuable supplement to full-time staffs.

Costs of Losing Experienced Employees

Special arrangements that allow businesses to retain top executives—perhaps through part-time consulting contracts, perhaps through special assignments—are not new. Most companies acknowledge the unique value of executive judgments based on long experience, and many find a way to tap into that expertise. What is new, however, is the degree to which companies are making similar overtures toward managerial and technical personnel. This has been particularly true in some of the high-tech industries, both because of staff raiding within geographically concentrated clusters of related companies (e.g., California's Silicon Valley and Boston's Route 128) and because of the relatively large percentage of entrepreneurs who leave established high-tech companies to start new ones. For example, Aerospace Corporation of Los Angeles hires its retirees aged 55 and over for a variety of technical and nontechnical jobs of less than 1,000 hours per year or 20 hours a week; employees hired under this "retiree casual program" retain all health and pension benefits. Likewise, Oregon's Tektronix encourages its retired workers to return, with more flexible working conditions as an attraction.

Inadequate Numbers of Younger Workers

In 1976, management authority Peter Drucker predicted, based on documented demographic changes, that the retirement age in the United States would have to be raised to 70 or eliminated entirely within a decade (Drucker, 1985). Despite the skepticism expressed by experts at first, Drucker's prediction came true in record time, with the elimination of mandatory retirement in California in 1977 and the increase to age 70 for mandatory retirement in the rest of the country by 1978. In recent years, California was followed by Florida, Iowa, Maine, New Hampshire, and Tennessee (Gollub, in press); most states have also eliminated mandatory retirement for public employees, creating a climate conducive to future elimination of mandatory retirement in the private sector as well. These legislative changes, while spurred by strong state lobbies on aging issues, are a clear instance in which public policy directly reflected the changing labor supply available to businesses, as well as more equitable treatment of older people who wished to continue to work. Perhaps the most visible example of the use of older workers to fill in the gaps left by a shrinking pool of younger employees is the McMasters program recently initiated in selected pilot sites by McDonald's Corporation; that program is discussed later in this chapter.

Unstable or Unprepared Young Workers

Both the popular and the business press document a growing concern about the poor work habits and work behavior of entry-level young people. Many approaches are being considered and tried; one promising strategy is the introduction of work maturity and preemployment skills into the remedial education available to high-school-age youngsters during the summer. Unfortunately, despite some hopeful signs, all too many youngsters enter the workforce without the habits and attitudes employers prefer. Some youth-dominated industries, such as food services, have found that older workers can serve as role models for younger workers, demonstrating a strong work ethic, loyalty to the firm, and stability that can be contagious.

ADVANTAGES OF OLDER WORKERS

In addition to their value to businesses with the staffing needs noted above, older workers offer special advantages as a direct result of their visibility in a company's workforce.

Positive Public Image

Because of the growing media focus on issues related to aging and the recognized political and economic implications of the swelling ranks of older Americans, the general public tends to look kindly on firms that treat this segment of the population well. As long as the presence of older workers does not close off promotion opportunities for younger and middle-aged workers, opportunities for older people to continue working tend to have a beneficial effect on the morale of a company's own workforce.

Increased Market Share Among Older Consumers

A positive public image, while valuable, is difficult to relate to bottom-line concerns. However, there is no question but that the presence of older people in a company's workforce exerts a peer-to-peer attraction on older customers. With people over 55 responsible for over one quarter of the consumer purchases in this country (Bloom, Korenman, & Sanders), savvy companies seeking a segment of that lucrative market may utilize older workers in visible positions in the hope of enlarging their percentage of older customers.

Compliance with Government Policies

As noted earlier in this chapter, a good portion of those companies that have increased the proportion of older people among their employees have done so primarily to comply with federal and state policies and programs, especially the Age Discrimination in Employment Act and some states' prohibition of a mandatory retirement age. Age discrimination cases filed by the Equal Employment Opportunity Commission increased from 11.6% of total cases filed in 1981 to 23.3% of the 1985 total (U.S. Equal Employment Opportunity Commission, 1982, 1986); that sends a strong message to businesses about the need to exercise considerable sensitivity in dealing with older employees and applicants.

However, at the same time that the federal government is applying the "stick" of potential lawsuits, there is also the "carrot" of some limited public funding support for companies that do make the effort to increase the numbers of older people they employ. These government programs are targeted toward economically disadvantaged people aged 55 and older and have their roots in the principle expressed by the National Commission for Employment Policy in its ninth annual report: "Although employer actions are critical to the improvement of the employment situation of older workers, many older workers have a need for training and other services that cannot be adequately addressed by employers alone" (National Commission for Employment Policy, 1985, p. 41). The Job Training Partnership Act of 1982 earmarks 3% of each state's grant for training older workers and is the first federal job training program to specify funding for people 55 and over. That act also allows for special funds to retrain experienced workers who get laid off or who are the victims of plant closings; many of those who qualify are middle-aged and older. Both the act's older worker set-aside and its displaced worker provisions are incentives for employers to hire older people, because the federal funding enables businesses to offset substantially the costs of training those workers.

BARRIERS TO OLDER WORKERS

Despite the changing economic and demographic realities and the positive qualities of older workers themselves that promote their wider acceptance among private sector employers, there remain a number of critical barriers that continue to limit older worker employment opportunities.

Employer Attitudes

The most serious challenge facing older workers is overcoming negative attitudes held by individual managers and peers—attitudes often caused by unconscious adherence to common but usually inaccurate stereotypes. The American Association of Retired Persons (1983) has identified some of these stereotypes —poor attendance, declining productivity, diminished learning capacity and intellectual functioning, decreased motivation, and increased rate of on-the-job accidents—and found that research fails to link those qualities conclusively to advanced age. (See also Peterson & Coberly, Chapter 8, this volume.)

Employer attitudes toward older workers have improved considerably in recent years. For example, 90% of the chief executive officers of 552 large industrial and service firms surveyed by the W. M. Mercer Corporation in 1981 agreed that older workers perform as well as younger workers (Mercer, 1982). A 1984 Conference Board survey of 363 companies found few managers or co-workers who held negative beliefs about older workers, with the one exception that a slight majority characterized older workers as less flexible and more resistant to change than their younger counterparts (Rhine, 1984). That latter perception—whether or not it is an accurate one—is enough to limit older people's success severely in businesses and economic segments being radically and rapidly transformed by computer technology.

Business Practices

Beyond problems arising from employers' perceptions about older workers, there are also barriers caused by employer practices. Many firms still have mandatory retirement policies on the books; true, the age at which an employee must retire has risen, but *any* limit that prevents able and willing workers from continuing to work needs rethinking. The provisions of some pension programs also encourage early retirement; others penalize workers who continue drawing salary past customary retirement age. Some firms have been slow to adopt the alternative work arrangements that enable older workers to maintain a flexible or reduced work schedule. Perhaps most discouraging to the dedicated older worker is the common practice of limiting training and promotional opportunities to younger workers at the expense of older ones.

Older People's Personal Limitations

Some older people elect to retire when faced with health problems or age-related decreases in physical abilities. Others, however, would choose to continue working in a different capacity or on a reduced schedule, both for the sense of purpose derived from employment and for the income that may be necessary in order for the "golden years" to retain their shine. Still others—such as displaced homemakers who have no recent history of paid employment or minorities who may have been limited by past discrimination to low-wage, low-skilled positions—may need special training and placement services to move into appropriate employment. Public programs such as the Job Training Partnership Act and the Senior Community Service Employment Program represent a small step toward addressing these very serious problems. The Job Accommodation Network, an information network for employers operated by the President's Committee on Employment of the Handicapped, helps businesses access information about how their peers have successfully accommodated disabled workers (Bowe, 1985). Despite these few programs, though, older workers who are unskilled, disabled, or suffering from multiple employment barriers generally have very few options.

BUSINESS INITIATIVES

Examples do exist, in growing numbers, of companies that have begun to eliminate discouraging or unfair policies and practices and that are moving in new directions to accommodate and take advantage of the aging American workforce. In most cases, these changes have occurred as a result of direct business needs. In a series of issues forums conducted in July 1985 by the National Alliance of Business and SRI International, businesses in a variety of industries expressed interest in using older workers to alleviate temporary labor needs caused by seasonal fluctuations in business and to fill part-time permanent staffing needs. Interestingly, a number of the companies represented at the forums expressed their frustration in attracting older workers and welcomed a stronger relationship with the many national and local groups whose mission includes job placement for older people.

Although critical issues such as the need to fill staffing gaps are understandably the catalyst for most older worker initiatives in the private sector, a few companies have moved beyond strict bottom-line concerns, devising comprehensive strategies that illustrate their basic commitment to older people as well as their accurate reading of demographic change. The Travelers Insurance Companies set the standard. Their age-neutral pension policy allows workers to accrue benefits for 40 years regardless of age; its internal job bank, established to meet the fluctuating staff needs of the insurance industry, draws primarily upon Travelers retirees for part-time and temporary work. In a perfect example of a mutually beneficial arrangement, the Travelers customer hot-line is staffed by 16 older workers who share four job slots. These job-sharers have the years of company experience that help them answer a wide range of questions, and they have the patience required to handle callers who may be confused or irate; the job-sharing situation helps the workers remain pleasant and helpful in what would be a high-stress, potentially explosive situation for a 40-hour-a-week person. Travelers continually expands its Older Americans program, demonstrating that maximizing the use of older workers boosts everything from public image to bottom line. "This is one of the few human resource policy areas that is really a win–win situation," claims Travelers' director of personnel administration, Don DeWard (DeWard, 1986). "After having our Older Americans Program in place since 1980 and evaluating its results, we are more committed than ever to expanding it. "

Perhaps the most common older worker employment practice among private sector companies is the establishment of temporary agencies that funnel retirees back into temporary part-time or short-term full-time jobs. Ted K. Cobb, founder of TOPS* Temporary Office Personnel Service in Denver, formed the Prime-Staff Division of his company, with a mandate to recruit older people who could satisfy his clients' repeated requests for mature, experienced workers. The Equitable Life Assurance Society followed Travelers' lead, establishing a Retiree Talent Bank in 1982 to serve as an in-house temporary agency drawing upon The Equitable's own retirees.

Flexibility is the watchword for other pioneering companies, with flexible hours, part-time work, and jobsharing becoming less unusual. Northern Natural Gas Company of Nebraska has developed job-sharing options that offer reduced work schedules for older workers; the older workers share their jobs with younger ones and provide then with on-the-job training. Woodward & Lothrop, a Washington, D.C.–based department store chain, attracts older salespeople through flexible full-time and part-time schedules; people over 50 make up 40% of the Woodward & Lothrop workforce, and store managers expect that percentage to grow (Berlow, 1986).

McDonald's Corporation has begun field-testing its new McMasters initiative in some of its Maryland restaurants. Tying into the federally funded Job Training Partnership program, McDonald's offers a special four-week training program to people over 40, who learn their trade through a combination of classroom training and supervised work experience. In preparation for a higher percentage of older workers among its restaurant staff, McDonald's is reviewing specific tasks required for various positions to determine which ones can be redesigned with older people's particular "people skills" or physical needs in mind. Pat Brophy, head of special employment at McDonald's, told a 1985 National Alliance of Business forum that assembling the company's new line of prepared salads requires the care and attention to detail that often characterizes older workers; she also cited older women's success as hostesses for birthday parties, a role in which they draw upon their years as homemakers and mothers.

Naugle's, Inc., a California-based restaurant chain, developed a special recruitment program called "Oldies But Goodies," designed to attract older workers. Naugle's leadership sees that program as a key part of a strategy aimed at reducing turnover costs, stabilizing an otherwise very young workforce, and creating a positive public image (National Alliance of Business, 1985).

Service industries are not alone in tailoring recruitment and job design efforts toward older people. Texas Refinery Corporation, a Fort Worth manufacturing company with an international market base, regularly conducts national advertising campaigns to encourage retirees from unrelated industries to join its sales force (U.S. Senate, 1985). Company spokesmen explain that their justification for that action is based strictly on analysis of sales figures: some of the company's top sales representatives are well over 60. In a 1985 statewide conference on senior employment and retirement issues, Texas Refinery's vice president for personnel, Jim Rosenthal, attributed the success of the older sales people to their excellent "people skills," developed over years of living rather than as a result of previous job-related experience. One aspect of the job that appeals to retirees is the flexibility they have to decide their own schedules. People who want to sell "round the clock" do so; others take extended vacations interspersed with months of full-time or part-time work.

Also in Texas, Automatic Data Processing's San Antonio region hired two older workers through a 90-day on-the-job training agreement with the Senior Texans Employment Program. When those initial hires worked out well, ADP recruited and trained additional older people with the program's assistance (National Alliance of Business, 1985).

Stouffer's Food Corporation has taken a different approach, one aimed at retaining and maximizing the productivity of its experienced workers. Supervisors watch to see whether age-related changes are causing older workers to perform less efficiently in the fast-paced retail products assembly line; if so workers may then transfer to the institutional products line, where speed is less a factor for success than meticulousness (U.S. Senate, 1985).

When small and medium-sized companies need older workers, they often rely on the brokering services that are available through national or community organizations with programs set up for that purpose. When Geomet Technologies, Inc., a Germantown, Maryland, scientific consulting firm, began planning a statewide indoor air quality survey of Florida homeowners, nine new hires were required. Seeking responsible people with good driving records and communication skills for the five-month assignment, Geomet sought help from the American Association of Retired Persons' Florida office; AARP had 30 individuals for Geomet officials to consider. "What we liked was that AARP could provide us with a ready pool of qualified people who are available on short notice," attested Geomet treasurer Stephen S. Wolk (Wolk, 1986).

Two common elements link the business initiatives described here, as well as most of those around the nation that succeed in utilizing older workers productively. First, they build upon the natural strengths that older people bring to the workplace: good judgment born of years of experience, patience in dealing with customers, and a strong belief in the traditional American work ethic. Second, they are innovative, offering older people productive employment opportunities that are flexible enough to appeal to people who want to mix work with family life, hobbies, or simply relaxation. Companies that are able to attract and retain older employees tend to have personnel policies that are people-oriented—policies that keep those companies competitive in attracting workers of all ages.

However, it is important to realize that, despite some of the encouraging business practices noted in this chapter, and despite a growing understanding of the value of older-workers, economic expansion will be the key determinant of future older worker employment opportunities. While demographics show that additions to the workforce will be smaller through the end of the century than they were in the last two decades, a continuing decline in early retirement incentives and an increase in employers' willingness to hire older workers will not necessarily result from those demographic changes. After surveying its member businesses, the Conference Board drew a conclusion that is an apt one for this chapter:

> Vigorous growth in demand for goods and services, translated into strong demand for workers, would certainly create a climate more conducive to the encouragement of extending years of labor force participation. A slack economy with high employment rates could hardly be expected to engender strong interest in discouraging older workers from leaving the labor force. (Rhine, 1984, p. 34).

This chapter draws in part upon work done under award number 90 AM 0088, from the Administration on Aging, Office of Human Development Services, Department of Health and Human Services. Points of view or opinions do not necessarily represent official Administration on Aging policy.

REFERENCES

American Association of Retired Persons. (1983). *Training older workers for employment.* Washington, DC: AARP.

Berlow, E. (1986, June 12). Going for the gold-collar worker. *Washington Post*, p. 5.

Bloom, D. E., Korenman, P., & Sanders, D. (1986, March). Habits of American consumers. *American Demographics*, p. 24.

Bowe, F. (1985). Intercompany action to adapt jobs for the handicapped. *Harvard Business Review*, Jan-Feb, p. 166.

DeWard, D. D. N. (1986). Personal communication to author.

Drucker, P. F. (1985). *Innovation and entrepreneurship: Practice and principles.* New York: Harper & Row.

Gollub, J. O. (1987). Increasing employment opportunities for older workers: State and local initiatives (pp. 143–164. In S. H. Sandell (Ed.), *The problem isn't age: Work and older Americans.* New York: Praeger.

Mercer, W. M. (1982). *Employer attitudes: Implications of an aging work force.* Chicago, IL: William M. Mercer, Inc.

National Alliance of Business & SRI International. (1985). *Invest in experience: New directions for an aging workforce.* Washington, DC: Author.

National Commission for Employment Policy. (1985). *Older workers: Prospects, problems and policies.* Washington, DC: Author

Rhine, S. H. (1984). *Managing older workers: Company policies and attitudes* (Conference Board Report No. 860). New York: The Conference Board.

U.S. Equal Employment Opportunity Commission. (1982). *Annual Report.* Washington, DC: U.S. Government Printing Office.

U.S. Equal Employment Opportunity Commission. (1986). Unpublished figures from a report on operations of the EEOC Office of the General Counsel and of the Office of Program Operations.

U.S. Senate, Special Committee on Aging. (1985). *Personnel practices for an aging workforce: Private sector examples.* Washington, DC: U.S. Government Printing Office.

Wolk, S. (1986). Personal communication to author.

11

Employment Opportunities for Older Workers (and Others): A Labor View of Short- and Long-Term Prospects

E. Douglas Kuhns

At the present time, and under all circumstances, it is very difficult to discern any concerted trade-union or "labor" view regarding employment opportunities for older union members. Part of this disorganization is related to the general disorganization of the trade-union movement in the current economy. A contributing factor is its own preoccupation with short-term problems and a related disinclination to focus on long-term issues.

There are exceptions to this generalization. For example, the International Association of Machinists and the United Auto Workers have a long history of comment and even of action on such long-term labor force issues. But in general, unions have concentrated on job security for those in the main work years (20–60) and on winning and protecting adequate retirement benefits.

The long-run demographic projections appear to be quite clear. The proportion of the population in excess of age 65 is rapidly increasing. At the same time, the proportion projected as new entrants to the workforce is rapidly decreasing. Quite clearly, there will be serious social, political, and economic consequences as a result, including serious financial considerations for Social Security and similar programs, not to mention the general tax base. Demographic trends do suggest the development of a massive labor shortage within the next two decades, but that lies in the future. Critical shorter-term developments demand full attention now: unemployment in heavy industry, youth and minority unemployment, and the uncertainties deriving from technological change and international competition.

National productive capacity has undergone extensive change as well. During the course of recovery from two successive recessions, long-term expectations of profitability reached a low and competitive pressures resulting from distorted exchange rates forced manufacturers overseas, all of which have had a negative effect on domestic employment.

LIMITING CONDITIONS IMPOSED BY CURRENT ECONOMIC CONDITIONS

The following comments do not directly address the prospects for work among the retired; rather, the conditions that make for a decrease in elderly employment *in the short run* are outlined. Only then can we consider policies that so energize the economy that increased employment *in the long run* can be considered.

While it is not true that we are on the road to becoming a nonmanufacturing economy, we have allowed considerable erosion of the industrial base on which employment for older workers depends. This has proceeded to the point that many of our secondary industries, including many military-related industries, are beginning to be alarmed. While the total volume and value of our manufacturing output continues, on balance, to climb year by year, there is no disputing the declining role of manufacturing as a proportion of the total economy. Manufacturing employment has had an even sharper proportionate decline, and usage of plant capacity has declined to 80%.

A contributing factor to the decline in employment levels has been technological change at accelerated rates induced by adaptation of computer technology and the proliferation of robotics. While some of this developing technology has enhanced the productivity of the remaining labor involved, much of it has reduced the use of labor, particularly skilled labor, drastically. The point of this is that, historically, technological change has taken the form of heavy equipment that enhanced the productivity, and therefore the value, of the labor retained. It sufficiently reduced the cost of the product for everyone else, including even the displaced workers, that the stimulation of overall purchasing power provided continued growth in the economy. Much of the current technology, however, is addressed as much to capital saving as to labor saving. The ultimate nightmare in this scenario is that we may finally reach a point at which increases in purchasing power are insufficient to absorb the products of that improved productivity. Meanwhile, over the course of the last decades, investment expenditure has languished. While it appears that total government expenditure—for all of the efforts to the contrary— remains as a fairly stable portion of total expenditure, consumer expenditures overall have been widely recognized as "carrying the load" of growth.

During the same period, the expanding segments of the economy, which appear to be absorbing much of the displaced labor of the last decades and most of those coming into the labor force, are the service industries. Many of these pay such low wages that there is little incentive for the development of labor-saving devices, and heavy investment expenditure generally is not required. In most instances, highly technical skills are not required, either, and employment patterns have reflected a disproportionate increase in part-time labor in the last decade.

Although the development of low-paid, part-time occupations in the service trades would appear to favor employment opportunities for older workers, there has been no marked development in this direction. Recruitment practices in these industries are clearly directed toward the younger age groups.

UNION PROTECTION OF OLDER (NONRETIRED) WORKERS

For the trade union movement, the preceding described pattern of economic and occupational development has been a major disaster. The decline in heavy industry, where the strongest trade unions have historically been concentrated, has brought precipitate declines in their membership and a diminished capacity to present their members' interests. While there has been some accompanying increase in union membership among the service industries, it has been far from proportionate to the growth of these industries. Increase in union membership among government employees has been impressive, but these organizations often have limited powers of collective bargaining. On the whole, the proportion of the labor force that is an active trade union membership is lower then it has been in many decades.

In the course of this transition, the trade union movement—inadvertently—has become a major factor in the employment of older workers, up to age 65. Seniority provisions governing layoffs have substantially raised the average ages of the retained workforces in the traditionally unionized sectors of the economy. This development itself has put increased strain on those already damaged industries in the form of accelerated costs of pensions and other benefits.

In response to the Age Discrimination in Employment Act (ADEA) amendments of 1978, unions generally have paid attention to implementation of the regulations concerning continued extension of welfare benefits to their working members over age 65. This includes previously existing efforts to extend pension credit to years of service after age 64, still not required under the law.

But none of this is to say that unions have any concerted policy in effect, or even on the drawing boards, with respect to employment of workers over 65. Generally speaking, unions at this time, particularly given the unfriendly legal as well as economic environment, are more concerned about discrimination against active *union* workers of *any* age.

Indeed, it is almost impossible to focus on employment of members over 65 when unions are almost constantly in the process of negotiating earlier retirement ages in response to employers' initiations of special early retirement arrangements to facilitate their workforce reductions in force.

INADEQUACY OF CURRENT NATIONAL FULL EMPLOYMENT POLICIES

It is no longer sufficient to say that employment of people over 65 depends upon the fashioning of a national full-employment policy for all workers; it goes much further than this. As we approach a social and economic cataclysm down the road, as we most assuredly will if the current course of events continues unabated, we will ultimately have some form of national industrial policy to provide some framework for economic and job stability. The current penchant for less government involvement in the economy clearly is an aberration, which even now is honored more in the breach than in the observance.

The relative decline in investment in heavy industry, the relative decline in manufacturing, the shifting of jobs and investment overseas, the incapacity of enterprises to compete—these are not symptomatic of the resurgence of private enterprise. They are symptoms of an economy approaching crisis. The entrepreneurs insist that this is a result of failures in productivity, and, in a sense, this is true, because increased productivity in the past bailed them out. It would be much more to the point, however, to simply admit that, increasingly, private enterprise is in crisis, that private enterprise is merely responding, albeit efficiently, to the problems it encounters. And it is producing results we may not wish to live with.

THE DRAG OF SOCIAL COSTS

Whether we like it or not, many desirable acts of legislation impose costly burdens on our productive system. Economic or social "impact" assessments place an additional strain on industry; environmental requirements impose social costs, as do antidiscrimination requirements; overlaying this entire structure and helping to maintain it, there is a burden of legal costs.

The response of private enterprise to the imposition of all of the new social costs has been to attempt to push them back upon the people in increased prices in times of inflation, when they can pass the burden through; back upon workers and employees when they cannot. And, in a very real sense, again, they are right. Social costs are people costs. They are the costs of maintaining reasonable life, socially and politically determined. Their ad hoc imposition on first one industry and then another in varying forms knows no equality and comes to be distributed disproportionately. Consequently, it distorts the entire pattern of production from what the pattern might otherwise be. (See Chen, Chapter 5, and Crown, Chapter 6, this volume, for discussions of dependency ratios as examples of social cost).

There is no point at this juncture in begging the question of what the pattern should otherwise be. No one knows with certainty at this point. What *is* required is some mechanism by which all of the social costs can be distributed throughout the society in an equitable, even manner in such a fashion that private productive activity can be left to its conventional role of dealing with the basic economic conditions related to the conversion of materials, labor, and capital into finished goods and services. It is under these conditions that private enterprise can best fulfill its functions.

Other industrial democracies, including some non-Western ones, provide health care, education and training, retirement income, and environmental protection, as well as many insurance coverages, through their public economies. In addition, there is considerable regulation through the channels of existing national industrial policies in many of these nations, lending elements of subsidization or security to the operations of private companies once they have approval under such policy. It is no wonder that many U.S. companies move overseas.

John Maynard Keynes, contemplating the antecedents to some of these long-term economic problems, saw the problem as identifying the conditions and policies of statecraft under which capitalism could best and most efficiently fulfill its role as the main vehicle of productive activity. That capacity now increasingly is beset by conflicts— over who, industry or government, shall cover social requirements.

The longer-run problem obstructing full employment results from inadequate income distribution. This inadequacy is identified by many as based on the unbalanced relation of income to work.

Wassily Leontief, trying to evaluate the economic implications of the advent of the electronic chip and related developments, has offered a disturbing hypothesis. He believes that the explosive rise in overall output and economic well-being provided through the Industrial Revolution depended not only on the functioning of the market system, propelled by the profit motive, but also on the intrinsic nature of nineteenth-century technology. He notes that the replacement of muscle power by mechanical power actually expanded the role of labor as the most important factor of production. In other words, labor productivity was enhanced. "The demand for skilled workers needed to operate complex (but dumb) machines replaced the demand for unskilled physical labor" (Leontief, 1983, p. 16). Labor's increased productivity increased its share of the national income, and all levels of society benefited.

By contrast, in the age of the electronic chip, "not only the physical but also the controlling 'mental' functions involved in the production of goods and services can be performed without the participation of human labor" (Leontief, 1983, p. 16). And "the displacement of labor by increasingly efficient machines seems to have no limits," leaving labor's function as an indispensable factor of production progressively diminished, leading to increasing unemployment and socially undesirable effects upon income distribution.

If he is correct, increasingly higher unemployment in the world economy cannot be corrected simply by accelerating investment or by increasing fringe benefits, since such investment will only aggravate the problem by speeding up the introduction of technology. While it is true that these developments in technology are not as apparent in the service industries, the service sector cannot indefinitely continue to offset job losses in agriculture and industry, and the displacement capacity of the new technology seems to have no limits.

Given a course of events in which a great deal of this comes to pass, people's roles as producers will cease to be as important as their roles as consumers. Income receiving will have to be detached from work (although not necessarily from production) if the total output is going to be sustained. It may be of some interest to note that some of this structure is already in place.

RETIREMENT BENEFITS: ECONOMIC STABILIZER OR DESTABILIZER?

Total federal social welfare expenditures for 1983 approached $400 billion. State and local outlays for similar purposes (though not pro-portionate across the board) were $243 billion during the same year, providing a total of $643 billion, or 23% of total personal income. So much for the effort to dismantle the Rooseveltian revolution! Of the total federal portion, $220.2 billion was allocated to those aged 65 and older, or 55% of the total. If (somewhat arbitrarily) we allow a similar proportion of state and local allocations to this group—about $134 billion—a total of around $354 billion is paid to the population over age 65. This would mean that very close to 13% of the total personal incomes of that year were transferred to an over-65 population from which virtually no productive services were returned.

Since most of this income is expended in one form or another, it should not take any great stretch of the imagination to envisage the economic impact upon total production and income if this ex-penditure were nonexistent.

At this point in time, according to the census figures (U.S. Bureau of the Census, 1984), approximately 11.8% of the population is over age 65. Only 4% of them are classified as in the labor force. Given the number of people retired at ages under 65, the number of retired people has to be one eighth of the population. If their number approaches 30 million, their size is one fourth the size of the total labor force (population age 16 and over). Their incomes (private pensions, public pensions, Railroad Retirement, and Social Security) are more or less related to work—past work—if we accept the legal dictum that these payments constitute deferred wages. In economic theory, wages are the share of production allocated to labor as a factor

of production. Wage payments are related to work and are said to be
related to the value of labor in its various uses. A sizable amount of
economic theory is devoted to the circular reasoning (i.e., the marginal productivity theory of wages) as to how this comes about. But the
payments are related to production, and they could otherwise be
designated as shares.

RETIREMENT WORK OR RETIREMENT BENEFITS: TOWARD A SHORTER WORK WEEK

If Leontief is right, and the amount of robotization and computerization that now appears within reach is realized, the achievement of
potential full production (full employment will no longer be a standard) will depend on reorientation of income distribution.

The first logical step in this process, and one that would provide
the least dislocation in the private economy, would be a revived
movement toward a shorter standard work period. It would coincide
with some already current trends, embodied in the growth of part-
time employment and flex-time arrangements, as use of labor (even
skilled labor) is reduced.

The 8-hour day and the 40-hour week have been cast in stone since
after World War II. The rationale for the "normal" work period was
fairly well established by that time and rather solidly grounded in a
number of economic studies of the period. Particularly in manufacturing, there were a number of experiments suggesting that the optimum working period from the point of view of economic efficiency
(output per worker-hour, if you will) was, depending somewhat on
the nature of the enterprise, in the range of seven and one-half to
eight and one-half hours a day. But the emphasis then was on
manufacturing. The service industries are different, and certainly,
with the development of the new technologies, there is room for new
study of the optimum workday. In some cases, it is not even clear
that the old principles of increasing and diminishing returns even
apply.

Paradoxically, however, whatever the conditions may be in a number of cases, they are confounded by the effects of fringe benefits and
social costs that are not directly related to the operation.

Reducing the length of the normal workday increases the pressures
for scheduling overtime. Assuming that longer hours are compensated with overtime premiums, the practice can be costly. An
alternative, if the normal workday is reduced, may be addition of

another shift. This only compounds the cost problem and replaces overtime costs with the greater cost of fringe benefits or social costs for another shift. But the more difficult problem for any employer to surmount is the fact that, if the workday is shortened, workers want no commensurate reduction in a day's pay. So the "shorter hours" movement is not growing.

There has, however, been some experimentation, for a time relatively successful, with a four-shift schedule in some industries with continuous operations (e.g., some container manufacturers' operations in the Midwest in the 1960s, when times were relatively good and fringe-benefit costs were low). At this point, the main factor militating against additional shifts is the cost of fringe benefits, primarily medical insurance.

Fringe-benefit costs in relation to incomes vary widely, but amount to anywhere between 25% and 45% of compensation; The costs of medical coverage alone range up to $1.25 an hour. There are many industries in which the statutory minimum wage would be exceeded by the hourly cost of fringe benefits. And the most recent legislation, including changes in the tax code, indicate that the end is nowhere in sight.

Nowhere in current developments is there any sign that these costs are ever going to be substantially reduced. What *is* happening, however, is that the uneven distribution of these costs, and of social costs in general, is distorting production and employment and impeding growth. While one can, up to this time, be impressed with the resilience of the system in making adjustments and adapting to changes, the noose is tightening. The current, increasing concentration of income does not augur well for the future of the system; it threatens an increasingly polarized society.

ELEMENTS OF NATIONAL POLICY PREREQUISITE TO WORK FOR ALL

The broad outlines of policy generated by these conditions are fairly clear, even if the specifics are not.

1. We must have some form of federally sponsored medical and health maintenance system that is accessible to all. (This would go beyond national health insurance; participation by the insurance industry is not necessary, and it not even clear they want this business, anyway.)

2. We need a centralized, no-fault type liability insurance system covering all forms of liability, industrial and otherwise.
3. We need a centralized system for the financing and handling of social costs problems related to all environmental and safety issues in order to get the weight of these costs off the back of the private sector.
4. In response to the question, "How is all of this to be paid for?" the answer is, "Taxes, of course, what else!" But the consolidation of all of these costs and the spreading of them more proportionately across the economy would eliminate the distortive effects on production and employment even if no savings were achieved—and we would expect the savings to be considerable.
5. We need a centralized, integrated retirement system that divorces retirement income from work and abandons the notion of that income as deferred wages.
6. We need a national industrial policy that is designed to, at least, monitor the economy in terms of making determinations of what industries should be maintained at what minimal levels, including government operation when the private sector cannot maintain it.
7. Along with this, we need an international trade policy that will permit the operation of comparative advantage in production (the true "fair trade" everyone talks about), freed from the distortions to competition afforded by a free-wheeling (floating exchange rates) international money market.
8. Finally, to provide the catalyst to assure that the savings from fringe benefit and social costs are channeled back into the system, there should be a legislatively mandated reduced working day. (While the six-hour day is the most logical for continuous operations, some flexibility could be allowed for.)

When, and if, these changes can be made in the economic climate, there will be economic "room" for business enterprises to manage multiple shifts and shorter hours. Had these conditions been possible over the last decade, reduced work schedules could have taken the place of "concession bargaining"; sharing of work could have taken the place of job displacement. The end result is not likely to be worse than the displacement of many from high-paying jobs to low-paying jobs in the service industries and increased hidden unemployment.

If these policy changes can be managed over the course of the next decades, with the continuing development of the new technologies and the resulting reduction of the labor content in all productive activity, the stage may be better prepared for the final adjustment. This would consist of the set of economic decisions to be made about the distribution of income in order to insure a market for full production. It is not at all clear how the system can handle those decisions in its present form. How the shares of production are determined may ultimately be a political decision. The "bargaining" process is likely to be one in which all groups will have to participate, unless the decisions are going to be autocratically managed.

The major policy innovations that have been suggested would give the capitalist system a renewed lease on life, and perhaps prolong it indefinitely. If income is not too concentrated, the ongoing development of technology, as it permits shorter working hours, will encourage the development of industries catering to leisure time, recreation, the retired, and, particularly, education. For if labor's physical input no longer is to be required in many cases, its mental input will be and may ultimately provide some answers as to how the "shares" of work and income may be divided.

In the course of this process, workers over age 65 will be placed much more on a par with those under 65. Shorter hours and less physical labor will make them more competitive with younger workers, pressures to retire will be reduced, and their medical needs may be reduced. Recent studies have suggested that their mental capacities generally are as good as those of younger workers (at least until illness, or very old age), and the computer age may be made to order for their capacities.

If it appears from much of the foregoing that the entire economic system must be reformed before there can be employment opportunities for older people, this is partially true. The fact of the matter is that the system as currently constituted is in no position to do what is necessary to provide those opportunities. It is beginning to experience difficulty in providing wider opportunities to others. The policies suggested would rearrange some of the elements in the system. Some service components would be removed to the public economy, to reduce the crushing burden of cost and regulation imposed on some private industries.

There are nice stories of what private enterprise has done in some special cases of disabilities or older employees. Once a manager has been able to determine that such a case may involve no financial loss or extensive liability, these cases make very good public relations material. But, at bottom, it should be clearly understood that private enterprise is strictly in the business of making money. Compassion, social conscience, humanity, and morality are not the primary motives of business. And it is not at all clear that, in the interests of economic efficiency, it should be any other way. To improve the results of the market the broader society needs to provide suitable political and economic parameters within which the system is to function. Removing some of the heaviest millstones from the market system as it advances toward the new technologies would facilitate greater participation from all of the needy inhabitants.

REFERENCES

Leontief, W. (1983, November 7). *Business Week*, p. 16.
U.S. Bureau of the Census. (1984). *Statistical abstract of the United States.* Washington, DC: U.S. Government Printing Office.

12

Able Elderly in the Family Context: Changes, Chances, and Challenges

Gunhilde O. Hagestad

We live in a watershed period, characterized by revolutionary demographic changes (see, e.g., Rappaport & Plumley, Chapter 3, Chen, Chapter 5, and Crown, Chapter 6, this volume.). It is an era that challenges us to reexamine old assumptions, perceptions, and expectations. As Laslett (1977) put it in a discussion of aging in recent history: "Our situation remains irreducibly novel; it calls for invention rather than imitation." Comparing the life experiences of age-cohort groups currently in our population can help illustrate the magnitude of demographic and social changes that have reshaped the social context of lives and relationships. Two groups are chosen here: individuals currently over the age of 85 and early baby boomers, the first of whom are now turning 40. These two groups represent yesterday's and tomorrow's young-old. Contrasts between them reflect dramatic changes in mortality and life expectancy, fertility patterns, educational attainment, and work careers. These contrasts point to sharply different adult experiences among those who entered old age in the mid-twentieth century and those who will be the young-old in the first decades of the twenty-first century.

Although sweeping changes associated with the aging of our society have opened up new vistas for individual life experiences and the maintenance of family ties, recent literature has focused on the problematic aspects of recent demographic change. It is high time that we look at the opportunities presented in an aging population, which comprises millions of able, independent elders. In the family realm, recent changes offer increased complexity of family networks, relationships of unprecedented duration, decades of shared experience, and the opportunity to forge new roles. Modern grandparenthood illustrates all of these possibilities.

In mortality patterns, life paths, and family role constellations, recent changes have affected men and women differently. Some emerging contrasts between men and women provide ground for reflection and present challenges to policy makers as well as researchers.

THE CHANGING CONTEXT OF LIVES: CONTRASTING TWO COHORTS

Our society currently has cohorts of people whose experiences of given life phases have been worlds apart. To illustrate how dramatically lives have changed, let us contrast two age groups: our present "oldest old" (Suzman & Riley, 1985), those 85 and older, and the first waves of the postwar baby boom—individuals who are now approaching midlife and will constitute the young-old in the early part of the twenty-first century.

Many of the current oldest-old probably never expected to reach their present age. At the time they were born, general life expectancy was 49. For people who had survived to the age of 20, the average length of remaining life was about 42 years (Torrey, 1982). These elderly remember a past when death was a part of life for all age groups. A majority of them had lost a parent or a sibling by the age of 15 (Uhlenberg, 1980). In their youth, they survived an influenza pandemic that killed millions, young and old. Later, among those who became parents, there was a constant fear of childhood diseases, many of which were potential killers.

Less than a third of these men and women finished high school, and fewer than 10% attained a college degree (Rosenwaike, 1985). Many of them had worked for nearly two decades when Social Security was introduced in 1935. Almost half of the men in this group were still employed in their late sixties (Siegel & Davidson, 1984). While we lack strong data on how many of the oldest have children, it is reasonable to assume that close to 70% of them have at least one living child (Shanas, 1979; U.S. Bureau of the Census, 1984). The average age of these children is about 59 (Torrey, 1985). Among oldest-old parents, three-fourths are also grandparents and great-grandparents.

This society currently has approximately 2 million members who are counted among our oldest-old. It is estimated that by the time the first cohorts of baby boomers reach this age bracket about 10 million Americans will be over 85 (Suzman & Riley, 1985; Siegel & Davidson, 1984). The twenty-first century's 85-year-olds with roots in the post-war baby boom will look back at lives that were strikingly different than those remembered by today's oldest-old.

As the first baby boomers are approaching their 40th birthdays, most of them have both parents living. It is estimated that by the time they reach their late sixties, nearly one third of the women in this group will still have at least one surviving parent (Winsborough, 1980; Wolf, 1983). Some of them have living grandparents. In the world of their childhood, deaths in the nuclear family were rare and unexpected crises, and they have come to think of serious illness and death as events that typically occur in life's later decades. During their early years, recent advances in medicine had produced inoculations for most serious childhood diseases, and antibiotics kept common infections from becoming life threatening. At the time of their birth in the early postwar years, general life expectancy was about 67. By the time they reached 20, they could expect an average of 53 more life years. More than 80% of these baby boomers graduated from high school; 20% have a college degree. Because of their educational level, members of this group were relatively late in entering the labor force, but they are expected to leave it at an earlier age than was the case for people born early in this century. It is estimated that less than 10% of the men in these cohorts will be in paid employment when they reach their late sixties (Siegel & Davidson, 1984).

Between the baby boomers and the oldest old are today's young-old. These are transitional cohorts—individuals who have some knowledge of a demographic world we left behind and who have been characterized as "demographic pioneers" (Shanas, 1980). Having survived to the age of 65, they can expect nearly two more decades of life (Siegel & Davidson, 1984). Constituting about 60% of those classified as "old," individuals aged 65 to 74 overwhelmingly function without limitations on activities due to health problems. Less than 10% of them require institutional care or assistance with daily living (U.S. Senate, 1983).

NEW PATTERNS OF AGING: PROBLEM OR PROMISE?

Recent changes in mortality, work patterns, and educational levels represent whole new potentials for family life and individual life careers. Yet the mass media, as well as gerontological literature, have taken a surprisingly dim view of the new demographic realities. All too often, the word *aging* is associated with the word *problem*. The old *are* and *have* problems. The dominant popular image of old age is one of inevitable decline, senility, and dependency. At the World Congress of Gerontology in New York in 1985, a participant could have spent the entire time listening to papers on Alzheimer's disease and senile dementia. On the other hand, an attendee looking for sessions on the old as a resource would have had a lot of free time.

In discussions of the family, the recurrent theme in recent gerontological literature has been the burden of parent care. There is growing concern over the strain experienced by families who provide care for impaired elderly members (e.g., Brody, 1984; Cantor, 1983; Ory, 1985). Many of these discussions focus on women in middle generations, who tend to be the main providers of care. It is frequently argued that today's families face more of a care load than was the case before societal aging. Unfortunately, we do not have the historical data to judge the accuracy of such claims, but it is important to keep in mind that before our society had a rectangular survival curve, illness and death were experiences that were encountered in all phases of family life. Families have always been caregiving units. The most significant difference between today's families and families of the past is not likely to be in the number of hours spent on the provision of care, but in the *focus* of care.

In no way would we want to forget the problems and heartaches that confront many families in our aging society. But when are we going to look at the positive outcomes of demographic change? When are we going to realize that more financial support goes from old to middle-aged and young family members than flows in the opposite direction along generational lines (Hill, Foote, Aldous, Carlson, & MacDonald, 1970; Morgan, 1983)? When are we going to understand than an aging society offers expanding, not constricting, opportunities for family life? When are we going to acknowledge that even in advanced old age, millions of people function independently? When are we going to recognize that most old people do not represent dependency and a drain on familial and societal resources—but rather that they indeed constitute a vastly underutilized social resource? When are we going to grasp and realize the rich new possibilities presented by recent demographic and social changes?

In a recent discussion of emergent patterns of longevity, Riley and Riley (1986) list four types of new potentials presented by recent demographic change: increased complexity of social networks, increased duration of relationships, prolonged opportunities to accumulate experience, and new chances to complete or change role assignments.

The Rileys point out that such potentials are not fully realized in our society, because we currently have an imbalance between a rapidly growing, vital older population and opportunities available in the social structure. Similar points have been presented by Rosow (1974, 1976) in his discussions of aging in modern society. He argues that our society currently offers "tenuous roles" to its older members. These authors are focusing on a macrosocial level, an aging society that may be experiencing what M. Riley earlier has referred to as "a gap between people and roles." On a microlevel of social reality, however, such as in family groups, the four types of potential outlined by the Rileys may be considerably closer to being realized than in society at large.

NEW POTENTIALS FOR FAMILY LIFE

Complex Family Networks

A growing number of families now have four or more generations (Shanas, 1980; Townsend, 1968). Members of multi-generational families interact in a complex set of family roles and relationships. For example, in a four-generation family, there are three "tiers" of parent–child connections; two sets of grandparent–grandchild relationships, and two generations of people who are both parents and children. Older members of such families typically have steady contact with siblings, children, grandchildren, and great-grandchildren. Most of these ties endure for decades.

Durable Relationships

As was briefly outlined above, family relationships now have an unprecedented duration (Hagestad, 1986). Siblings may share eight decades of life, and for most of those years, they will regard each other as age peers. The majority of parents and children will have about half a century of shared lives; many will have 60 to 70 years together. Grandparents and grandchildren will have relationships that last two or more decades. These figures represent not only rich, varied personal experiences, but also an enormous wealth of shared living and interdependent biographies.

The Accumulation of Experience

In enduring family relationships, individuals build their own unique webs of experiences, memories, stories. The longer the relationship, the more complex the web. "As two or more persons have a succession of shared experiences, they develop a wider and more firmly rooted common conception of reality—setting them apart from others, who have not been part of the same experience circle" (Turner, 1970, p. 82). Recent research on marriages that have survived into the retirement years has demonstrated the effects of accumulated shared experiences. The longer a couple has been married, the higher their rates of agreement on personal goals (Atchley & Miller, 1983). In the case of parents and children, the passage of time often leads to the softening of earlier contrasts, to the development of common ground, and to greater tolerance of differences. At a recent social gathering, a woman in her late sixties—the mother of four—commented on her current phase of life: "I love being my age! It's the first time in my life that all my children liked me!"

Through long-lasting ties in the family, individuals not only build bonds through the accumulation of shared experience, they also help one another deal with a changing historical context. In a society that often erects structural barriers against contact and communication between members of different age-cohort groups, the family provides critical generational bridges. Interwoven lives, longstanding personal knowledge, and long-term reciprocities can help soften and modify the age-related contrasts and chasms that exist in society at large. Older family members help the young build bridges to the past, and the young can help make a rapidly changing culture and technology more understandable. Today's elderly often rely on younger generations to help them deal with complex bureaucracies (Shanas & Sussman, 1977), and in many modern families, children are tutors for parents and grandparents who find it trying to adjust to the computerization of everyday life. Some years ago, we interviewed a middle-aged woman who gave a vivid illustration of how intergenerational family ties bridge generational contrasts in society at large. She was worried about how long the interview would take, because she had a full program that evening: her mother and grandmother were going to teach her how to can fruit the old way, and her grandson was taking her disco-skating.

Changing Roles

At this time in history, the number of life years has increased, but the proportion of adulthood spent actively involved in two key roles has decreased. As we mentioned above, the work role is entered later and left earlier than was earlier the case. It has been estimated that it may now be common to spend one fourth of adulthood in retirement (Riley & Riley, 1986; Torrey, 1982). In the family, the trend toward fewer, closely spaced children means that a decreasing number of years are spent involved in the day-to-day tasks of childrearing, and the empty nest phase is a normal, predictable part of modern family life (Glick, 1977). These role changes in our long-lived society may have shaped a new kind of grandparent.

There are several trends worth noting with regard to modern grandparenthood. While the entry into the grandparent role most likely has always been a transition that typically took place in middle age (Sprey & Matthews, 1982), it is now more clearly sequenced in relation to parenthood than it was earlier (Hagestad & Burton, 1986). Because women finish childbearing fairly early in adulthood, the days of active parenting are likely to be over by the time they become grandmothers. After the emptying of the nest, they may function as what Gutmann (1985) calls "emeritus parents," monitoring and supporting members of the younger generations:

> Precisely because she is now detached from active, hands-on parenting, the older woman can graduate to the next vital parenting level: The management of the extended rather than the nuclear family; and, by extension, of the individual parental couples within the extended family. (p. 57)

Grandparents have been found to be important supports for their children's parenting (Tinsley & Parke, 1984). With nearly half of all grandparents becoming great-grandparents (Shanas, 1980), we may also find that they become important stabilizing forces for adult grandchildren. While many young children have grandparents who are actively involved in work roles, the grandparents of young adults are likely to be retirees, and many of them will have experienced widowhood. The few investigations that have explored relationships between young adults and their grandparents (Hagestad & Speicher, 1981; Hoffman, 1979–1980; Robertson, 1976) have found that these grandchildren see grandparents as highly important people in their lives. The emerging picture of today's grandparent, especially in the later phases of grandparent–grandchild relations, is one of a family member who operates without some of the role constraints characteristic of earlier adulthood; who has lived and learned to put things in perspective; whose most important function may just be *being there* for younger generations (Hagestad, 1985). The comforting presence of grandparents may often be felt despite geographic distance between them and the younger generations.

For members of several younger generations, grandparents serve critical "safety-valve" functions: they are people who can be counted on in case things go wrong (Troll, 1983). There is growing evidence that in times of crises, grandparents do indeed step in with help and support. A case in point is divorce. Recent research has found that grandparents serve as significant "stress-buffers" following family disruption (Cherlin & Furstenberg, 1986; Hetherington, Cox, & Cox, 1978). While we do not know how often divorce leads to three-generational living, or how often grandparents provide substantial financial support to grandchildren following divorce, recent studies show that grandparents on the "custodial side" are significant factors in postdivorce adjustment. Marital breakup often intensifies relationships with maternal kin but presents a threat to relationships in the paternal line (Furstenberg, Peterson, Nord, & Zill, 1983; Hagestad, Smyer, & Stierman, 1984). Research on divorce has confirmed previous findings regarding the role of men and women in the maintenance of family ties.

THE WORLDS OF MEN AND WOMEN

It has repeatedly been found that women are the linchpin of family contact and cohesion. They are the kin-keepers, the ministers of the interior, who orchestrate family get-togethers, monitor family relationships, and facilitate intergenerational contact (Rosenthal, 1985). Women in middle generations are most centrally involved in kin-keeping, and the mother–daughter link is pivotal, both in the maintenance of family contact and the flow of support across generations (Daatland, 1983; Kendig & Rowland, 1983). As was mentioned above, daughters are more involved in parent care than men are. A recent study of family caregivers (Horowitz, 1985) found that two-thirds of them were adult children and that, among offspring providing care, daughters outnumbered sons three-to-one. This research also show-ed that when sons were caregivers they relied heavily on assistance from their wives. In other words, "caregiving as a primary female role clearly extended to daughters-in-law as well as daughters" (Horo-witz, 1985, p. 615). It has been common, especially in the popular press, to suggest that when women are in the labor force, they will spend less time and effort on kin-tending. There is little empirical evidence to support this claim (Cantor, 1983; Horowitz, 1985; Noelker & Poulshock, 1982; Soldo & Myllyluoma, 1983). Indeed, a recent study by Stoller (1983) found that employment significantly reduced caregiving to aging parents among sons, but this was not a statistical-ly significant trend for daughters. (See Gibeau, Chapter 13, this volume for more on the role of women as family caregivers.)

Because of gender differences in life expectancy and age at mar-riage, the oldest member of a family lineage is likely to be a woman. In society at large, as well as in families, the world of the very old is a world of women. Among today's oldest old, there are only 41 men for every 100 women (Siegel & Tauber, 1986). Even among the young old, those aged 65 to 74, there are only 75 men per 100 women (Siegel & Davidson, 1984). The steady increase in the number of old people living alone that has been observed over the last two decades (Kobrin, 1976) is mostly accounted for by women, who constitute 80% of elderly "primary individuals." There has been public concern over the well-being of the old who live alone, but a current national study found that they are far from isolated (Kovar, 1986). The vast majority live close to family, have frequent contact with them, and live within a matter of minutes from them. Only 5% of people living alone reported no contact with family or friends during the two weeks prior to the interview. Most of these isolated individuals were men. The first reports from this study conclude that it may indeed be steady contact with family and friends that makes it possible for older women to live alone and function in everyday living. Although they are somewhat older than people who are living with others, they rate their health more positively and two-thirds perceive themselves as a lot more active than other people their own age. It appears that although most women in the later phases of old age do not have a "horizontal" linkage to a spouse, they have strong intergenerational, "vertical" ties that help them sustain independent living. There are few indications that this will change in the near future. Some things are likely to change, however.

As we enter the twenty-first century, a generation of women with high levels of education and high rates of labor-force participation will be in the early phases of old age. About half of them will have experienced marital disruption earlier in adulthood and will have spent a number of years on their own. The needs of these older women are going to confront social service agencies and informal networks with a different challenge from that represented by past cohorts, who after decades of traditional marriage and motherhood faced decades of widowhood.

Young-old mothers in the twenty-first century may have more shared experiences with their daughters than has been the case for older women at the end of this century. In the future, mothers and daughters will typically look back at involvements in education, work, and family. Many of them will also share some of the life changes associated with aging. A greater fund of shared life experiences may make the "female axis" even more central as the dominant force in the maintenance of intergenerational cohesion and continuity. In addition, there are recent social trends that may weaken men's intergenerational ties. Divorce has already been mentioned. Often marital disruption leads to what Preston (1984) calls "the disappearance act of the American father." The increase in nonmarital fertility is another trend that entails young generations who grow up with little or no contact with a father and paternal kin. While women's intergenerational ties are more durable, rich, and varied than ever before in history, a growing number of men may now have highly precarious vertical family ties (Eggebeen & Uhlenberg, 1985; Hagestad, 1986). In contrast with recent discussions of how demographic and cultural changes may have created new gaps between the worlds of men and women, we also find suggestions that male and female life patterns may show increasing convergence in our aging society. Three trends have been identified as contributing to such convergence: the decreasing life-course involvement in work and parenting, "the androgyny of later life," and the "feminization" of our population.

As was discussed in the comparison of yesterday's and tomorrow's young-old, two key role activities now occupy a smaller proportion of the adult years than was the case for previous cohorts: work and day-to-day parenting. Many observers have noted that men's and women's differential investments in these roles create sharp gender differences in early adult experiences, but wane in importance after midlife (Gutmann, 1985; Livson, 1983; Rossi, 1986).

From psychodynamic and biological perspectives, it is also argued that, as men and women age, they become more alike (Turner, 1982).

Giele (1980) discusses this as part of what she calls "the cross-over pattern." Gutmann (1985), who sees the parent role as the critical factor in early adult gender differentiation, argues that older men gravitate toward the domestic sphere and an emphasis on affiliation. Aging women, on the other hand, become more aggressive and agentive, assuming a role as administrators of extended family networks.

Rossi (1986) reminds us that the larger the proportion of elderly in the population, the greater the tendency to a female majority in that population. Thus, an aging population is one in which androgynous qualities may be more in evidence, but also one in which we may see greater salience of "female values," such as an emphasis on connectedness and reciprocal caring. Increasingly, for men and women, the strongest thread of continuity across eight or more decades of life will be found in the fabric of family life.

CONCLUSIONS

While much recent attention has focused on issues of dependency in an aging society, we need to recognize the enormous potentials for family life under the new demographic conditions. Current patterns of longevity create new opportunities for long-lasting, complex relationships and emerging roles for the able elderly. They represent a major family and societal resource.

Gutmann (1985) discusses the challenge facing social scientists in today's society. His words would apply to policy makers as well:

Instead of thinking of the aged as helpless recipients of services over which they can have little control, they can begin to study the ways in which postparental potentials can be transformed—into resources and capacities—not only for the elders, but for us all. (p. 59)

This is a revised version of a paper presented at the Ollie Randall Symposium, Annual Meetings of the Gerontological Society, New Orleans, November 1985. It is reprinted here by permission of *The Gerontologist*.

REFERENCES

Atchley, R. C., & Miller, S. J. (1983). Types of elderly couples. In T. H. Brubaker (Ed.), *Family relationships in later life* (pp. 77–90). Beverly Hills, CA: Sage.

Brody, E. M. (1984). Parent care as normative family stress. *The Gerontologist*, 25, 19–29.

Cantor, M. H. (1983). Strain among caregivers: A study of experience in the United States. *The Gerontologist, 23*, 597–604.

Cherlin, A., & Furstenberg, F. F., Jr. (1986). *The new American grandparent: A place in the family, a life apart.* New York: Basic Books.

Cherlin, A., Furstenberg, F. F., Jr., Lee, S., & Miller, C. A. (1983, October). *Grandparents and divorce.* Paper presented at the Grandparenting Conference, Racine, WI.

Daatland, S. O. (1983). Use of public services for the aged and the role of the family. *The Gerontologist, 23*, 650–656.

Eggebeen, D., & Uhlenberg, P. (1985). Changes in the organization of men's lives: 1960-1980. *Family Relations, 34*, 251–257.

Furstenberg, F. F., Jr., Peterson, J. L., Nord, C. W., & Zill, N. (1983). The life course of children of divorce: Marital disruption and parental contact. *American Sociological Review, 48*, 656–668.

Giele, J. Z. (1980). Adulthood as transcendence of age and sex. In N. J. Smelser & E. Erikson (Eds.), *Themes of work and love in adulthood* (pp. 151–173). Cambridge, MA: Harvard University Press.

Glick, P. C. (1977). Updating the family life cycle. *Journal of Marriage and the Family, 39*, 5–13.

Gutmann, D. L. (1985). The parental imperative revisited: Towards a developmental psychology of adulthood and later life. In J. A. Meacham (Ed.), *Contributions to human development* (Vol. 14) (pp. 31–60). Basel, Switzerland: Karger.

Hagestad, G. O. (1985). Continuity and connectedness. In V. L. Bentson & J. Robertson (Eds.), *Grandparenthood* (pp. 31–48). Beverly Hills, CA: Sage.

Hagestad, G. O. (1986). The aging society as a context for family life. *Daedalus, 115*, 119–139.

Hagestad, G. O., & Burton, L. (1986). Grandparenting: Life Context and Family Development. *American Behavioral Scientist, 29*, 471–484.

Hagestad, G. O., Smyer, M. A., & Stierman, K. L. (1984). Parent-child relations in adulthood: The impact of divorce in middle age. In R. Cohen, S. Weissman, & B. Cohler (Eds.), *Parenthood: Psychodynamic perspectives* (p. 375). New York: Guilford Press.

Hagestad, G. O., & Speicher, J. L. (1981, April). *Grandparents and family influence: Views of three generations.* Paper presented at the biennial meeting of the Society for Research in Child Development, Boston.

Hetherington, E. M., Cox, M., & Cox, R. (1978). The aftermath of divorce. In J. H. Stevens, Jr., & M. Matthew (Eds.), *Mother–child, father–child relations* (pp. 149–170). Washington, DC: National Association for the Education of Young Children.

Hill, R., Foote, N., Aldous, J., Carlson, R., & MacDonald, R. (1970). *Family development in three generations.* Cambridge, MA: Schenkman.

Hoffman, E. (1979–1980). Young adults' relations with their grandparents: An exploratory study. *International Journal of Aging and Human Development, 10*, 299–310.

Horowitz, A. (1985). Sons and daughters as caregivers to older parents: Differences in role performance and consequences. *The Gerontologist, 25,* 612–617.

Kendig, H. L., & Rowland, D. T. (1983). Family support of the Australian aged: A comparison with the United States. *The Gerontologist, 23,* 643–649.

Kobrin, F. E. (1976). The fall in household size and the rise of the primary individual in the United States. *Demography, 13,* 127–138.

Kovar, M.G., (1986, May 9). Aging in the eighties, age 65 years and over and living alone, contacts with family, friends, and neighbors. In *Advance data from vital and health statistics* (No. 116, DHHS Publication No. PHS 86-2350). Hyattsville, MD: Public Health Service, National Center for Health Statistics.

Laslett, P. (1977). *Family life and illicit love in earlier generations.* New York: Cambridge University Press.

Livson, F.B. (1983). Gender identify: A life-span view of sex role development. In R.B. Weg (Ed.), *Sexuality in later years* (pp. 105–127). New York: Academic Press.

Morgan, J.N. (1983). Intra-family transfers revisited: The support of dependents inside the family. In G.J. Duncan & J.N. Morgan (Eds.)., *Five thousand American families—patterns of economic progress* (Vol. 6) (pp. 347-365). Ann Arbor: The University of Michigan, Institute for Social Research.

Noelker, L.S., & Poulshock, S.W. (1982). *The effects on families of caring for impaired elderly in residence* (Final report submitted to the Administration on Aging). Cleveland, OH: The Margaret Blenkner Research Center for Family Studies, The Benjamin Rose Institute.

Ory, M.G. (1985, Fall). The burden of care: A familial perspective. *Generations,* pp. 14–18.

Preston, S.H. (1984). Children and the elderly: Divergent paths for America's dependents. *Demography, 21*(4), 435–457.

Riley, M.W., & Riley, J.W., Jr. (1986). Longevity and social structure: The potential of the added years. In A. Pifer & L. Bronte (Eds.), *Our aging society: Paradox and promise* (pp. 553–577). New York: Norton.

Robertson, J.F. (1976). Significance of grandparents: Perceptions of young adult grandchildren. *The Gerontologist, 16,* 137–140.

Rosenthal, C.J. (1985). Kinkeeping in the familial division of labor. *Journal of Marriage and the Family, 47,* 965–974.

Rosenwaike, I. (1985). A demographic portrait of the oldest old. *Milbank Memorial Fund Quarterly, 63*(2), 187–205.

Rosow, I. (1974). *Socialization to old age.* Berkeley: University of California Press.

Rosow, I. (1976). Status and role change through the life span. In R.E. Binstock & E. Shanas (Eds.), *Handbook of aging and the social sciences* (pp. 457–482). New York: Van Nostrand Reinhold.

Rossi, A. (1986). Sex and gender in the aging society. In A. Pifer & L. Bronte (Eds.), *Our aging society* (pp. 111–139). New York: Norton.

184 *Choices About New Policies*

Shanas, E. (1979). Social myth as hypothesis: The case of the family relations of old people. *The Gerontologist, 19,* 3–9.

Shanas, E. (1980). Older people and their families: The new pioneers. *Journal of Marriage and the Family, 42*(9), 9–15.

Shanas, E., & Sussman, M.B. (Eds.). (1977). *Family, bureaucracy, and the elderly.* Durham, NC: Duke University Press.

Siegel, T., & Davidson, M., (1984). Demographic and socioeconomic aspects of aging in the Untied States. In *Current population reports* (Series P-23, No. 138). Washington, DC: U.S. Bureau of the Census.

Siegel, J.S., & Tauber, C.M. (1986). Demographic perspectives on the long-lived society. *Daedalus, 115,* 77–118.

Soldo, B.J., & Myllyluoma, J. (1983). Caregivers who live with dependent elderly. *The Gerontologist, 23*(6), 605–611.

Sprey, J., & Matthews, S.H. (1982). Contemporary grandparenthood: A systematic transition. *Annals of the American Academy of Political Science, 464,* 91–103.

Stoller, E.P. (1983). Parental caregiving by adult children. *Journal of Marriage and the Family, 45*(4), 851–858.

Suzman, R., & Riley, M.W. (1985). Introducing the "oldest old." *Milbank Memorial Fund Quarterly/Health and Society, 63*(2), 177–186.

Tinsley, B.R., & Parke, R.D. (1984). Grandparents as support and socialization agents. In M. Lewis (Ed.), *Beyond the dyad.* New York: Plenum.

Torrey, B.B. (1982). The lengthening of retirement. In M.W. Riley, R.P. Abeles, & M. Teitelbaum (Eds.), *Aging from birth to death: Vol II Sociotemporal perspectives* (181–196). Boulder, CO: Westview Press.

Torrey, B.B. (1985). Sharing increasing costs on declining income: The visible dilemma of the invisible aged. *Milbank Memorial Fund Quarterly/Health and Society, 63*(2), 377–394.

Townsend, P. (1968). Emergence of the four-generation family in industrial society. In B.L. Neugarten (Ed.), *Middle age and aging* (pp. 255–257). Chicago: University of Chicago Press.

Troll, L.E. (1983). Grandparents: The family watchdogs. In T. Brubaker (Ed.), *Family relationships in later life* (pp.63–74). Beverly Hills, CA: Sage.

Turner, B.F. (1982). Sex-related differences in aging. In B.B. Wolman (Ed.), *Handbook of developmental psychology.* Englewood Cliffs, NJ: Prentice-Hall.

Turner, R.H. (1970). *Family interaction.* New York: Wiley.

Uhlenberg, P. (1980). Death and the family. *Journal of Family History, 5,* 313–320.

U.S. Senate, Select Committee on Aging. (1983). *Aging America: Trends and projections.* Washington, DC: U.S. Government Printing Office.

Winsborough, H.H. (1980). A demographic approach to the life cycle. In K.W. Back (Ed.), *Life course: Integrative theories and exemplary populations* (pp. 65–76). Boulder, CO: Westview.

Wolf, D.A. (1983). *Kinship and the living arrangements of older Americans: Final report submitted to the National Institute of Child Health and Human Development* (Contract No. N01-HD-12183). Washington, DC: Urban Institute.

13

Working Caregivers: Family Conflicts and Adaptations of Older Workers

Janice Gibeau

As the numbers of elderly mount, and the longevity of the elderly increases, their needs for assistance also mount. Oriol (1985) notes the results of a national health survey indicating that there were 2.8 million people aged 65 and older who needed the help of another person in carrying out the activities of daily living. While the incidence was 1 in 10 for those aged 65 to 74, it jumped to 4 in 10 for those aged 85 years or older. He further notes that those people 85 and older residing in the community are six times more likely than people aged 65 to 75 to be dependent in activities of daily living.

With the changes in the age structure of our maturing society comes the growing likelihood that midlife and older workers will be expected to serve as caregivers for elderly family members at a time of their lives when they are also deciding whether to remain on their jobs. Employers, facing a projected shortage of young workers, will be needing more midlife and older workers. The cost of retirement programs, including health care for retirees, may generate even more pressure on employers to retain their older workers. The costs of early retirement, encouraged when there was less need for older workers, now represent a potential threat to the stability of the employment sector. Older workers, much in demand by their employers and their dependent family members, may be caught in the middle as breadwinners and caregivers. If they stop working to care for their elders, both they and their employers may be negatively affected. Employers may experience a crucial reduction in their supply of labor. Workers may unwittingly mortgage their own accrual of resources and benefits needed for retirement. If workers reduce their level of caregiving while remaining in the labor force, both the elderly and the service sector relying on the work of caregivers may be severely threatened. Consequently, a matter that seems to be personal and intimate, the care of a loved one, once again demonstrates that work and family lives are closely related in a amalgam of concern for families, employers, and the government.

OLDER WOMEN AT WORK: SOME UNEXPECTED PROBLEMS

This Chapter examines the convergence of work and family life from the perspective of the stresses noted and adaptations made by families with older working caregivers who are trying to manage multiple family responsibilities. The focal point in any discussion of family stresses is most commonly the perspective of the woman in the family. Although it is estimated that about 28.5% of the 2.2 million caregivers in a national survey of informal caregivers were men, the majority were women (Stone, Cafferata, & Sangl, 1986). Other studies also indicate that caregiving is primarily associated with women (Brody, 1981; Brody & Lang, 1982; Hendricks & Hendricks, 1977; Horowitz, 1985; Lee, 1980; Tennstedt, 1984). Therefore, understanding family patterns for older working caregivers requires an examination of changing family structures related to older women, differences in the labor force attachments of older men and women, the economic risks faced when work is terminated, and the balance of labor in older families.

Many of the problems facing older workers are relatively recent. At the turn of the century, when life expectancy was age 49 (Blau, 1981) and the median age was 22.9 (Soldo, 1980), a working man could anticipate that his parents would die before he reached the age of 30 and that he would probably die before he stopped working. If he was married, his wife could expect to outlive him, although she would probably not live beyond her menopause. After her husband's death, she and any children she had would have to rely on any resources accumulated prior to his death, unless she was one of the small minority of women in the labor force at that time. The main source of the family assets would be property.

Today, with a life expectancy of 79 years for men and 83 years for women, one's chances at birth of living until the age of 65 are currently better than 75% (Maddox, 1981). A working man now faces a different set of expectations. Unlike his ancestors of the early 1900s, this man may leave the workforce at the age of 60 and live in retirement for another 18 years or more. His parents may well be alive for all or part of that time. His wife will probably be caring for his parents, although he may help by paying their bills and doing some of their shopping. His wife will still outlive him, but she may rely more on resources linked to his work than those tied to ownership of property. Glendon (1981), in describing changes in family structures, points to changes in the labor laws, property laws, and social welfare programs that have been shifting the location of one's economic security away from the family toward the workplace. The job has become the new property.

For the women in today's society, several other circumstances stand in contrast to life at the turn of the century. A working woman today who reaches the age of 49 can easily have an elderly family member, aged 67, who will live another 16 years or more, and a grandparent 85 years of age or older. If one or both are ill or functionally impaired, she may be caring for them as well as for relatives of her husband. If she continues to work until she is 73, as about 41% of women 70 years or older are expected to be doing by 1990, she may be carrying multiple responsibilities for as many as 25 years. She will probably be caring for a woman, not a man, in the family. For every man over 85, there are three women (Oriol, 1985). It is also not that uncommon for women in their sixties to be caring for family members 90 years old or older. In an exploratory study of 40 working caregivers (Gibeau, 1986), 5 of the women interviewed were caring for a parent 90 years of age or older. Another study by McKinley and Tennstedt (1986) indicated that the frequency of caregivers having responsibilities for someone over the age of 90 was about 1 in 11. For those reporting on the care of people 85 years of age and older, the frequency is 1 out of 4 (Horowitz & Dobrof, 1982; Stephens & Christianson, 1986; Stone, Cafferata, & Sangl, 1986).

In addition to the probability that a woman in her sixties will be working while caring for an old-old parent, it is highly likely that she will be doing so alone. As married women age, they are more likely to be alone. Widowhood is a status for 51% of all elderly women, and women make up 80% of the 7 million elderly people who live alone. Projections for the year 2000 indicate that there will be an increase of 10% in the number of women being divorced (Glick, 1979). Many women function as the sole support for dependent children and caregivers for their frail elderly. If the average family size continues to drop to 3.1 by 1990 (Callahan, Diamond, Giele, & Morris, 1980), the number of female children available to care for the elderly will also be limited.

Regardless of age, women caring for their families and their elders are now in the workplace in unprecedented numbers. Statistics on the general participation of women in the labor force illustrate several themes. More women are working; women constitute a growing proportion of the workforce; women earn less than men; and women often work more during their older years. Compared to men, women begin old age poorer and become more so as age advances (Oriol, 1985). In 1900 women represented abut 18% of the labor force. Of women 14 years of age and older, 20% were working. In 1980, 42% of the labor force was composed of women and nearly 52% of all women were working (U.S. Department of Labor, 1982). Although single women and women who are widowed, separated, or divorced have always been in the labor force, married women have been participating in greater numbers. In 1981, more than 60% of married women aged 20 to 44 were in the labor force. This is nearly double the rate for 1960 (O'Neill & Braun, 1981).

MIDDLE-AGED WORKING WOMEN ON THE INCREASE

Middle-aged and older women have been noted as the most common age groups providing care to the elderly. How many are available for these tasks and how many are working? It has been noted that the work participation of middle-aged and older women doubled between 1954 and 1974 (Block, Davidson, Grambs, & Serock, 1978), and Brody (1981) reports that women aged 45 to 64 accounted for the largest increase in labor force participation of women between 1950 and 1970. Projections indicate that approximately 75% of women between the ages of 45 and 60 may be in the labor force after the turn of the century (Cooperman & Keast, 1983). Remaining in the workforce after the age of 55 is becoming more common. In 1960, women's participation was 33% for those 55 to 59 years old and 26% for those aged 70 and older. By 1970, 38% of those aged 55 to 59 were working and 32% over the age of 70 were working. It has been projected that by 1990 the proportion of women from these groups who will be in the labor force will be 41% for both groups, while the participation of men aged 65 to 69 in the workforce has steadily declined (Coser, 1984).

Because caring for a dependent elderly family member is often a long-term, not a short-term, responsibility, women making the decision to discontinue work in order to become caregivers must face several facts that have serious implications for their status as tomorrow's elderly.

COSTS TO WOMEN WHO COMBINE PAID WORK AND CAREGIVING

Some of the benefits they may need in the future will no longer be available. Eligibility for disability benefits requires that someone has worked 5 of the 10 years prior to their disability. If a women has been out of work caring for a husband or parent, she will not be eligible for disability benefits until she begins work again and remains in the workforce for the time required. If she becomes disabled while she is a caregiver, she is not eligible for Social Security benefits.

Early departure from the workforce often means sacrificing accrued pension benefits if the required vestment period is not achieved prior to leaving. Group health benefits, life insurance, and wage benefits tied to longevity are also sacrificed. As women and their families rely more heavily on women's work as major sources of economic security, the risks of caregiving weigh more heavily on the working caregiver's mind.

Although it has been commonly acknowledged that midlife and older women have been caring for their elders, what is known about the working experiences of these women?

Several studies have indicated that many caregivers are working either full time or part time in the labor force. Horowitz and Dobrof (1982), in a study of 203 caregivers, found that 58% of the children were working full time and 9.2% were working part time. The average age for the caregiving children was 50.8 years. Brody (1981), in a study of 172 middle-generation women with a mean age of 49.1, found that 60% were working. Rimmer (1983) reports that women caring for the elderly were less likely to be working and, if they were working, they were doing so part time. In referring to a study by Hunt, she indicates that 1 out of 10 working women and 1 out of 8 unemployed women were responsible for the care of at least one elderly or disabled person. In a study of 78 never-married women caregivers, Burnley (1985) reports that all of the women, most of whom were in their forties and fifties, were employed full time.

Given the evidence that caregiving can, for some, become a full-time job, what are the consequences of caregiving? One early study of families providing care found that 80% described disruptive problems and 40% reported severe problems (Sainsbury & Grad de Alarcon, 1970). Of the families studied, 50% said that their social time was restricted; 60% reported a decline in the physical well-being of the primary caregivers. Other studies note emotional exhaustion, depression, family stresses, physical fatigue, and stress-related illnesses (Cantor, 1983; Cicirelli, 1983; Frankfather, Smith, & Caro, 1981; Gibeau, 1986; Horowitz, 1985; Mace & Rabins, 1981).

Horowitz and Dobrof (1982) report that 52% of the children who were caregivers said that their emotional state had changed for the worse and 33% said that their physical health had declined. Davis (1978), in a study of 51 caregivers, reported that caregivers had difficulty getting out of the home and having free time. When women in another study of 40 caregivers (Gibeau, 1986) were asked to describe what their lives had been like, they frequently mentioned time conflicts as a problem:

> It's rough, very rough. It seems like I just don't have enough hours in a day to get everything done. I have no time to myself. . . . I have a grandchild coming I want to spend time with.
>
> There are not enough hours. . . . I've had a family, work and I have her. Once in a while, I feel a little resentful. I don't have any time for myself.
>
> It's very difficult emotionally, mostly because I have a family other than my mother, and I haven't been able to lead that part of my life the way I'd like to. It's very frustrating. I can't give her the time I would like to, and she requires it. I feel I can't do enough. Sometimes I rush in and out, but I feel guilty. I have a husband and housework that doesn't get done. It was great when I wasn't working.

When these women were asked to describe what things they had given up in order to help their mothers and mothers-in-law, slightly over half of those who described things they had given up identified the loss of free time. Others said they had lost sleep, privacy, travel, or vacation opportunities. The quality of the responses as well as the categorization of responses suggests some of the emotional stress these women often feel. One caregiver, in assessing what she had given up since her mother had been living with her, said, "My life and my home." She went on to add that she cannot leave the home without great difficulty. She described giving up friends and travel and added, "My home is not my home."

The stresses of caregiving are not always related to the level of frailty or specific physical needs of the elderly, but relate more to emotional strains. Poulshock and Demling (1984), in a study of 614 families caring for an impaired elderly family member in the home, found that a severe level of burden in caregiving was associated with negative relationships, not the elders' level of functioning.

The tasks that the majority of respondents in a study by Gibeau (1986) selected as their most important contribution was the provision of emotional support. This task was also cited as the most difficult. In describing the problems these women faced, the caregivers expressed varying degrees of frustration, stress, and feelings of helplessness in trying to cope with the emotional needs of their mothers and mothers-in-law. The following represent some of the feelings expressed:

> It's very difficult because of her personality. I deal with the elderly all day. . . . It's wonderful. Then I go to my mother! I think she is the most difficult person in town to deal with.
>
> It's her attitude. She was . . . always negative. She doesn't stop to think. She only has two friends.
>
> It's very difficult, lots of times. She gets upset, I get upset. Then my husband and the kids get it. It's a big responsibility. . . . We feel that the roles are reversed. She's a difficult person to help. The more I do, the more she wants. It leaves me feeling that I'm not enough.

It should also be noted that while caregiving can be very time-consuming, it is not always associated with marked stress. Some of the women in Gibeau's study described a positive feeling, such as the following:

> There's a great change in our relationship. . . . She needs me . . . a good feeling. The only thing is once in a while it takes away from my children and grandchildren.
>
> It hasn't been bad. I don't know what I'll do when she doesn't need me. I'll feel very empty.

Other studies suggest that some caregivers do not experience undue stress or high levels of burden (Morris, Sherwood, & Gutkin, 1981; Noelker & Poulshock, 1982; Zarit, Reeves, & Bach-Peterson, 1980).

COPING WITH TWO JOBS

Whether stressful or not, many caregivers who are working must find a way to balance their responsibilities at work and at home with the care of their elders. How have they and their families managed thus far? Many studies have found that caregiving responsibilities have not been relinquished easily by women (Brody, 1981; Cantor, 1983; Horowitz & Dobrof, 1982; Noelker & Wallace, 1985; York & Calsyn, 1977). Most data suggest that the women in the family have made the major adjustments, either by maintaining their caregiving while reducing or eliminating their paid work, by reducing their caregiving hours, or by trying to maintain both roles simultaneously.

While Doty (1984) notes some contradictory evidence from published studies on the impact of work on women's caregiving activities, Stueve and O'Donnell (1984) report that daughters working full time tend to be less involved in parent care. They also present some evidence suggesting that women are equally reluctant to relinquish their paid work lives. It has also been suggested that the increased employment of women has precipitated increased admissions to long-term care facilities (Schorr, 1980). One study involving an analysis of data from the 1982 National Long-Term Care Survey indicates about 9% of the caregivers reported leaving the labor force to care for disabled family members or friends. Reports of spouses and daughters leaving the labor force clustered around 12%, but only 5% of the sons had made this decision. Of the 1 million caregivers who had been employed, 20% had cut back on their hours, 29.4% had rearranged their schedules, and 18.6% had taken time off without pay (Stone, Cafferata, & Sangl, 1986).

Wright (1983), in a survey of single caregivers, found that about half of the women in the sample had given up work to care for a disabled parent, but none of the men had done so. The women also adjusted their normal work hours more than men. In general, women appear to provide twice as much care as men. But the personal cost of adjustment is great. Brody (1981) found that the hours spent in caregiving were no different for working and nonworking daughters. A review of several other surveys indicates that between 20% and 25% of caregivers in studies who have quit work list their caregiving responsibilities as the reason they are not looking for work (Horowitz & Dobrof, 1982; Rimmer, 1983; Stueve & O'Donnell, 1984). Over half of the caregivers or other relatives in the study by Horowitz and Dobrof (1982) had had to miss work.

Reports of time missed vary. Some caregivers report missing one week or less, while others report taking extended leaves of absence.

Twenty-three of the 40 women in one study missed work for an average of 50 hours annually. Nine of the women in this study also had to turn down opportunities for overtime, and 10 said that they had considered quitting work (Gibeau, 1986).

What are the consequences of their taking time off from work? Whether women take brief periods of time off in order to take a family member to a medical appointment, turn down overtime because of the need to provide care to an elderly person after work, or take extended leaves, the consequences can be expensive and wages are often lost. Some women describe being penalized in their performance evaluations, which determine merit increases in pay (Gibeau, 1986).

For those women who maintain dual lives as breadwinners and caregivers, what supports are available? What adaptations do they and their families make to reduce the stresses associated with competing demands? These questions explored in the Gibeau study suggest that working women rely on a triad of supports: family assistance, available community services, and supports within the workplace. Selected findings from that study are presented to illustrate how these supports affect the daily lives of these women and their families.

QUANTIFYING THE PRESSURES OF TWO JOBS

In order to get some idea of how much various family members helped, women in this study were asked to identify how much help they received and who provided that help. Findings indicated that while caregivers reported having help in all areas of their care of an elderly family member, some types of tasks involve more family members than others. The most common activity other family members participated in was shopping, with about a third of the caregivers reporting help in this area. The tasks associated with the least amount of help were ones of personal care. The only people assisting with these activities, which involved bathing, dressing, and grooming, were sisters or sisters-in-law. This was very consistent with other studies reporting gender differences and family differences in care of elderly family members (Brody, 1981; Horowitz, 1985; Horowitz & Dobrof, 1982; Wright, 1983). Other findings, also similar to those in other studies, include the common involvement of siblings and husbands in transportation, assistance from sisters in cleaning or laundry, and assistance from husbands and siblings in helping the elderly person to manage his or her finances (Horowitz & Dobrof, 1982; Stephens & Christianson, 1986).

The range of hours of family assistance was from 0 to 45 hours, compared to the range of 1 to 105 hours for the caregiver. While the mean number of hours of care to the elderly was 12.1 for the primary caregiver, the mean hours of family help was 1.8. Compared to family members, caregivers spend nearly seven times the hours in caring for their elderly family member. For some caregivers, the differences are more striking. One married 58-year-old secretary living with her husband, a computer programmer, provided 26 hours a week of care, while her husband helped with the shopping for about an hour.

Others had a better balance in time spent on caregiving. Another 52 year old secretary lived with her husband, who is an engineer, and her 22 year old son. She had three daughters living in nearby communities, as well as two brothers and a sister. She identified receiving help from her husband, her son, and her sister. Although she did not say that her brothers helped with specific tasks, she turned to them for support when she was upset with her mother. Her husband and her sister helped with the cooking and shopping, and her sister also helped with transportation. This caregiver said that her mother appointed her "the boss" because she was the oldest, but that everyone helped out. She spent about 14 hours a week in caregiving while her family provided 8 hours.

Because caring for the family home also constitutes a cumulative burden for the working caregiver, added to her usual homemaking responsibilities, each woman was asked to review specific homemaking tasks with reference to the help she received from other family members. Findings indicated that family members provided an average of 9.6 hours of weekly help, compared to the 26 hours of the caregiver.

There was no consistent pattern followed when women described the help they received from family members, except to say that husbands were mentioned more frequently than others as sources of support. Husbands were also more active in caring for the home than they were in caring for the elderly. Of the tasks included in care of the family and home, 15 husbands helped with shopping and 14 helped with cooking, while nearly a third helped with cleaning and a majority of husbands helped with repairs. The assistance of children occurred less often. Usually it was a matter of a son helping with repairs or a daughter helping to clean; this breakdown is consistent with traditional gender divisions in household tasks.

While it is clear that husbands do help the working caregiver, how much do they help? Of those helping with specific tasks, husbands spent an average of nearly 5 hours on cooking, 3 hours shopping, 7 hours cleaning, 5 hours on repairs, 5 hours on childcare, and 1 hour providing transportation services. Despite the contributions made, women spent almost twice as much time cooking and over twice as much time on childcare. The most balanced sharing of responsibilities occurred around cleaning, with about 7 hours each: shopping, with 3 hours each; and transportation. The caregiver spent nearly 3 times as many hours in the combined tasks of homemaker as the family members provided. Data analysis also suggests that as the age of the husband increased, the hours spent by the caregiver on homemaking decreased, indicating that older husbands were helping more at home. While these are interesting averages to consider, it should also be noted that some women reported that their husbands, particularly the retired husbands, spent as much as 20 hours in cooking, cleaning, and shopping. Unlike the limited hours frequently noted in studies exploring the sharing of household responsibilities in younger households, this sample includes husbands working as many as 36 hours at home. On the other hand, the caregiver's hours of homemaking increased with the size of her household. Many of the households had adult children, which suggests that the help one might expect them to provide was either not occurring or not significantly reducing the burden on the caregiver. In fact, it may have increased.

How did women feel about their homemaking responsibilities and the help they received? Nearly half of the women said they were satisfied with things the way they were or described the balance of responsibilities as fine. The remaining half said that they had mixed feelings, were dissatisfied, or were just resigned to things the way they were.

No clear patterns emerged in terms of variations according to specific family or work characteristics. Some women would smile and speak of men's inability to cook, children not being helpful, or ways in which people relied on the caregiver to look after them. When asked how they would change things, a third said that they would not change them, while nearly a half said that they would have the family provide more help.

DILEMMA AND LIMITED POLICY OPTIONS

Whether women speak of conditions at home, at work, or of caring for the elderly, strikingly few complained, spoke of demands, or identified changes that they wanted. The women in this study seemed to be compliant and resigned to their situations. When asked to identify the changes they would like to see in their work, they often said things were okay or that they could not think of any. The responses of the women in this study did little to support the view that jobs are seen as the "new property" (Glendon, 1981) or that women are making claims on the workplace (Peattie & Rein, 1983). On the other hand, the reluctance to make demands or express dissatisfaction may simply support the suggestion that working-class women are not likely to complain (Rubin, 1976). For many women, work may serve as a helpful boundary separating them from even greater family demands that would be made if they were not in the labor force. It may be that women still feel caught in the middle and are not yet prepared to make additional demands on their employers or their families. Some may not want to increase their claims, preferring instead to keep limits on their jobs as an adjunct to their family responsibility.

As we face the marked demographic changes associated with the aging of the baby boomers, women may find it increasingly difficult to balance or limit work and family responsibilities. What can be done within the family in the future to reduce the stresses placed on the working caregiver? Because women report that they currently rely heavily on employee benefits in the workforce and would be willing to pay for additional benefits, family members could be helpful by supporting the development of cost-shared work benefits linked to elder care. Without the support of husbands, these benefits are unlikely to gain acceptance. Conceptually, this means that men must be seen as having something to lose as well as women. Men also need to become more directly involved in the care of the elderly family member. Findings in the Gibeau (1986) study are similar to others in showing that men often help with transportation and shopping but seldom with personal care.

As women find themselves caught in the vortex of conflicting demands, what changes might be made to best reduce stresses placed on working caregivers, support the economic security of women and their families, and maintain the level of care the elderly require if they are to remain in the community?

Policies for the future should be linked to reflect the interdependence of work and family life. It would also be reasonable to address the importance of the service sector in the efforts made to balance and stabilize family life.

Because women report that they currently rely heavily on community-based services for their elders, these services must be preserved. Women speak more of needing homemakers and home health aides than of financial issues as major sources of support. Were these supports to diminish or be eliminated in the service of cost containment in long-term care, the delicate balance between working and caregiving might collapse. It is important to note the policy implications of caregivers' not knowing about the source and funding of services for their elders. This places both the elders and their caregivers at risk of being unable to act quickly enough as advocates for the preservation of critical services.

The service sector must also advocate strongly to include the needs of the caregivers as an integral and legitimate factor in assessing the vulnerability of the elder. Providing services to support the caregiver's involvement is critical to the balance of working and caring.

Because it is clear that women often must leave work in order to take an elder to a medical appointment, we must reexamine and expand the definition of family medicine. How medical professionals, clinics, or other group practices structure their hours must be made more responsive to the needs of the family. In some instances, this would mean having more evening hours, while in others it could involve locating more routine health care at senior centers or adult day health centers.

Because women report that they currently rely heavily on employee benefits, both employers and employees must become more informed about the role of these benefits in reducing caregivers' stress. Benefits targeted for elder care should be developed. The feasibility of offering elder care benefits is enhanced by the finding that women are willing to share the costs of these benefits.

By placing a value on the unpaid labor of caregiving as equal to wages lost, the benefit can be made to cover the contributions of men as well as women. It avoids the struggle to attach a market value to caregiving as a paid service. This would not help the caregivers who are outside the labor force, but is a step toward attaching value to the labors of caring.

In addition to expanding employee benefits packages to include elder care, employers could provide other employee assistance programs that would make education, counseling, and case management services available to working caregivers.

Even if employers support the development of benefits for working caregivers, such benefits are also going to require the strong support and participation of husbands. Without the support of both men and women, these benefits are unlikely to gain acceptance. Conceptually, this means that men must be seen as having something to lose as well as women. Men also need to become more directly involved in the care of the elderly family member. Findings in the Gibeau study are similar to others in showing that men often help with transportation and shopping but seldom with personal care. That is not to say that men are simply unwilling to assist with more of the care. Sometimes women do not include men in their caregiving domains.

Critical to the restructuring of responsibilities along the parameters of gender is the acceptance, if not endorsement, of women. Women have joined the workforce and must be willing to relinquish some of their homemaking and caregiving responsibilities. Moreover, it is interesting to hear more women describing their husbands' increasing interests in cooking, shopping, and cleaning as the age of the husbands increases or as they adjust to retirement. Previous boundaries may blur as they age and work together. More study is needed of the role retirement or work reduction plays in the caregiving activities of men. It is clear that men cannot cross over into the world of caregiving without the encouragement and support of the women who now occupy those roles. The asymmetry of gender in caring for elders needs to be reduced if families, or particularly the women, are to endure the future increase in the need for personal as well as supportive services and to maintain and enhance their capacity to contribute to society in the workplace as well.

This study was supported in part by funding from the Administration on Aging (#90 - AM - 0158 awarded to the National Association of Area Agencies on Aging) and from the Gerontology Institute of the University of Massachusetts, Boston.

REFERENCES

Blau, Z. S. (1981). *Aging in a changing society* (2nd ed.). New York: New Viewpoints.

Block, M., Davidson, J., Grambs, J., & Serock, K. (1978). *Uncharted territory: Issues and concerns of women over 40.* College Park, MD: Center on Aging, University of Maryland.

Brody, E. M. (1981). Women in the middle and family help to older people. *The Gerontologist, 21,* 471–480.

Brody, E. M. & Lang. (1982). They can't do it all: aging daughters with aged mothers. *Generations,* Winter.

Burnley, C. S. (1985, August). *Never married women caregivers.* Paper presented at the 35th annual meeting of the Society for the Study of Social Problems, Washington, DC.

Callahan, J., Diamond, L., Giele, J. Z., & Morris, R. (1980). Responsibility of families for their severely disabled elders. *Health Care Financing Review, 1,* 29–48.

Cantor, M. H. (1983). Strain among caregivers: A study of experience in the United States. *The Gerontologist, 23,* 597–604.

Cicirelli, V. G. (1983). Adult children and their elderly parents. In T. H. Brubaker (Ed.), *Family relationships in later life* (pp. 31–47). Beverly Hills, CA: Sage.

Cooperman, L. F., & Keast, F. D. (1983). *Adjusting to an older work force.* New York: Van Nostrand Reinhold.

Coser, R. L. (1984). Old age, employment and social network. In S. F. Yolles, L. W. Krinsky, S. N. Kieffer, & P. A. Carone (Eds.), *The aging employee.* New York: Human Service Press.

Davis, B. G. (1978, Nov.). *Stress in individuals caring for ill elderly relatives.* Paper presented at the annual meeting of the Gerontological Society, Dallas, TX.

Doty, P. (1984). *Family care of the elderly: Is it declining? Can public policy promote it?* Working paper. Washington, DC: Office of Policy Analysis, Health Care Financing Administration.

Frankfather, D., Smith, M. J., & Caro, F. G. (1981). *Family care of the elderly: Public initiatives and private obligations.* Lexington, MA: Lexington Books.

Gibeau, J. L. (1986). *Breadwinners and caregivers: Working patterns of women working full-time and caring for dependent elderly family members.* Unpublished doctoral dissertation, Brandeis University, Waltham, MA.

Glendon, M. A. (1981). *The new family and the new property.* Toronto: Butterworth's.

Glick, P. D. (1979). The future marital status and living arrangements of the elderly. *The Gerontologist, 19,* 301–309.

Hendricks, J., & Hendricks, D. C. (1977). *Aging in mass society: Myths and realities.* Cambridge, MA: Winthrop.

Horowitz, A. (1985). Sons and daughters as caregivers to older parents: Differences in role performance and consequences. *The Gerontologist, 25,* 612–617.

Horowitz, A., & Dobrof, R. (1982). *The role of families in providing long-term care to the frail and chronically ill elderly living in the community.* Final report submitted to the Health Care Financing Administration (DHHS Grant # 18-P-97541/2-02), Washington, DC.

Lee, G. R. (1980). Kinship in the '70s: A decade review of marriage and the family. *Journal of Marriage and the Family, 42,* 923–936.

Mace, N. L., & Rabins, P. V. (1981). *The 36-hour day.* Baltimore: Johns Hopkins University Press.

Maddox, G. (1981). *Perspectives on aging: Exploding the myths.* Cambridge, MA: Ballinger.

McKinley, J. B., & Tennstedt, S. L. (1986). *Social networks and the care of frail elders.* NIH/National Institute of Aging Grant #AG 03869, Boston University, Boston.

Morris, J. N., Sherwood, S., & Gutkin, C. E. (1981). *Meeting the needs of the impaired elderly: The power and resiliency of the informal support system.* AoA Grant #90-A-1294, Hebrew Rehabilitation Center for the Aged, Boston.

Noelker, L.S., & Poulshock (1982). *Effects on families of caring for an impaired elder in residence*. Final Report to the Administration on Aging. Cleveland, OH: Benjamin Rose Institute.

Noelker, L. S., & Wallace, R. W. (1985). The organization of family care for impaired elderly. *Journal of Family Issues 6*, 23–44.

O'Neill, J., & Braun, R. (1981). Women in the labor market: A survey of issues and policies in the United States. In Committee on Post Office and Civil Service, *Pay equity: Equal pay for work of comparable value* (Part II) (Serial No. 97-53). Washington, DC: U.S. Government Printing Office.

Oriol, W. (1985). *The complex cube of long-term care: The case for next step solutions-now*. Washington, DC: American Health Planning Association.

Peattie, L., & Rein, M. (1983). *Women's claims: A study in political economy*. New York: Oxford University Press.

Poulshock, S. W., & Demling, G. T. (1984). Families caring for elders in residence: Issues in measurement of burden. *Journal of Gerontology, 39*(2) 230–239.

Rimmer, L. (1983). The economics of work and caring. In J. Finch & D. Groves, *A labour of love: Women, work and caring* (pp. 131–147). London: Routledge & Kegan Paul.

Rubin, L. B. (1976). *Worlds of pain: Life in the working class family*. New York: Basic Books.

Sainsbury, P., & Grad de Alarcon, J. (1970). The psychiatrist and the geriatric patient: The effects of community care on the family of the geriatric patient. *Journal of Geriatric Psychiatry, 1*, 23–51.

Schorr, A. (1980). *Thy father and thy mother: A second look at filial responsibility and family policy* (ORS/OP/SSA/HHA Publication #13-11953). Washington, DC: U.S. Government Printing Office.

Soldo, B. (1980). *America's elderly in the 1980s (Population Bulletin, 35)*. Washington, DC: Population Reference Bureau.

Stephens, S. A., & Christianson, J. B. (1986). *Informal care of the elderly*. Lexington, MA: Lexington Books.

Stone, R., Cafferata, G. L., & Sangl, J. (1986). *Caregivers of the frail elderly: A national profile*. Unpublished manuscript. (Available from Robyn Stone, Division of Intramural Research, National Center for Health Services Research, 5600 Fishers Lane, Park Building MS3-40, Rockville, MD 02857.)

Stueve, A., & O'Donnell, L. (1984). *Interactions between daughters and aging parents: Conditions and consequences of daughters' employment* (Working Paper No. 146), Wellesley, MA: Wellesley College, Center for Research on Women.

Tennstedt, S. (1984). *Informal care of frail elders in the community*. Unpublished doctoral dissertation, Boston University, Boston, MA.

U.S. Department of Labor. (1982). *Labor force statistics derived from the current population survey: A databook, Volume 1*. Washington, DC: U.S. Government Printing Office.

Wright, F. (1983). Single careers: Employment, housework and caring. In J. Finch & D. Groves (Eds.), *A labour of love: Women, work and caring* (pp. 89–106). London: Routledge & Kegan Paul.

York, J. D., & Calsyn, R. J. (1977). Family involvement in nursing homes. *The Gerontologist, 17,* 500–505.

Zarit, S., Reeves, K., & Bach-Peterson, J. (1980). Relatives of the impaired aged: Correlates of feelings of burden. *The Gerontologist, 20,* 649–655.

Part III

Policy Options: Small and Large Steps to the Future

14

Economic Incentives and Disincentives for Developing Purposeful Roles for the Elderly

George Rohrlich

It has been over half a century since John Maynard Keynes published his essay on "Economic Possibilities for Our Grandchildren" (1932). Writing amid the shock of the Great Depression, Keynes registered a forceful dissent from those economists who saw only a future of long-term stagnation. He foresaw a vigorous return of economic progress and prosperity giving rise to dramatic gains in the general well-being. The engine of progress in the future, as in the past, would be human inventiveness: as it yielded ever more efficient (i.e. cheaper) ways of producing, there would be manifold opportunities for profit and capital accumulation. These would, in turn, open up successive waves of massive economic expansion.

As a result, the "economic problem" as it had had to be faced over all our past in the way of a "struggle for subsistence, always . . . the primary, most pressing problem of the human race" would come to be solved; and people would be freed for other pursuits. Man's "real, his permanent problem . . . due to his freedom from pressing economic cares will be how to occupy the leisure, which science and compound interest will have won for him to live wisely and agreeably and well" (Keynes, 1932, pp. 366–367).

True, there were conditions and qualifications, chiefly the assumption of "no important wars and no important increase in population." Also, the force of habit would be bound to assert itself: "The old Adam will be so strong in us that everybody will need to do *some* work if he is to be contented" (pp. 368–369). But people will make "what work there is still to be done to be as widely shared as possible. Three-hour shifts or a fifteen-hour week may put off the problem of how to use our newly-found leisure for a great while. For three hours a day is quite enough to satisfy the old Adam in most of us!" Finally, even though the economic necessity to work will be spared to ever-larger proportions of the population, "it will remain reasonable for oneself" (p. 372).

Certainly, Keynes's expectations of a post-Depression resumption of technological advance and better living conditions have come true in the past 50 years, at least for the developed and for part of the developing world. But, alas, we have not stopped having major wars, and in large parts of the world, notably in the poorest countries, population growth has been rampant. Concomitantly, there has not appeared among the "haves" either a surfeit with ever-growing material possessions or a discernibly growing disposition to consider further work efforts to be more meaningful if turned toward our poorer fellow citizens' advancement rather than our own.

But, then, we are but little over halfway toward the targeted date, and Keynes thought of 100 years as the minimum span of time necessary to attain the changed state of affairs. Meanwhile, new concerns have arisen far and wide that make many of us wonder about hasty and unlimited economic growth as the royal road to solving the economic problem. These latter-day doubts comprise concerns about the "carrying capacity" of our planet and the possibly adverse impact of unlimited economic growth on our environment. These doubts and apprehensions have led to serious questions being raised about the possibility that the much vaunted solution— economic growth—itself could turn into a problem (Barkley & Miller, 1972). As the economist Herman E. Daly has put it succinctly, "The world economy grows, but the ecosystem does not" (Daly, 1986).

What, then, are our (tentative) conclusions in terms of economic policy directions for the future?

First and foremost, we have yet a long way to go in bringing production to a level sufficient to feed all—notably in a worldwide perspective. On the other hand, we can no longer in good conscience concentrate *only* on growth-oriented economic policies to the exclusion of all other considerations. Rather, we must aim at keeping economic growth within ecologically sustainable limits. By the same token, we must complement our growth-oriented strivings with efforts aimed at a more even distribution of the economic product, so that we can meet first needs first for all.

Even so, and perhaps even as a premise for the foregoing postulates, we will have to cultivate a shift in our motivations toward a greater willingness to work "for others," that is, for the community (however defined), to a greater extent than individual actors on the economic scene have evinced to date.

If these propositions be accepted as our general premises, how do they translate into creating greater opportunities for economic and social participation of the elderly?

Without purporting to adduce ready-made answers to this complex question, it would seem possible to identify some components of an economic policy model that would appear to be of the essence:

- A greater emphasis than heretofore on producing more of the essentials of life
- A greater share of total production being devoted to public goods, including services and merit goods, that is, goods that deserve priority on common interest grounds
- Curtailment of wasteful production and expenditures, that is, meaningful reductions in (1) the massive use of irreplaceable scarce resources and (2) any and all processes and products that jeopardize the self-renewing capacity of our environment.

There is a wide range of choice among the methods used in the pursuit of these aims. But in the broadest sense, they indicate the overall economic incentives and disincentives, respectively, within which those more specific incentives and disincentives aimed at greater involvement of the elderly will have to be found.

CHANGING PERSPECTIVES ON AGING

Not so long ago people whom we would regard today as being in their prime, if not actually their younger years, were considered in both Western and in other societies as having attained advanced age. Canon law, for example, traditionally relaxed certain strict injunctions concerning marriageable partners for women in their twenties on grounds of their presumed lessened eligibility due to age. In Japan, a woman past the age of 30 would refrain from wearing garments of a lively color or design. In many African societies, age 50, even in men, would definitely be regarded as old age. And what is more, even within the last several decades, the physiognomies and other bodily features of such persons, notably within tribal settings, tended to bear out such evaluation.

Then as now, of course, certain long-lived individuals attained much higher ages. But without a doubt, life expectancies on the whole were considerably lower in past generations than at present, all the more so the more primitive the stage of a society's development.

Moreover, judged in functional rather than chronological terms, "age" was essentially a compound of good health and bodily prowess. Working capacity was generally defined in terms of arduous work, since brawn was the single most prominent requisite of most jobs.

The current century has witnessed the culmination of long-term trends that have been mutually reinforcing in adding—as the saying goes—years to life and life to years. The relevant demographic indicator is not the *general* increase in longevity (i.e., measured from birth)—because of the dramatic progress in overcoming infant and childhood diseases—but the improvement of life expectancy in the upper age brackets.

The Notion of a Retirement Age

Elsewhere, for example, in Bismarck's Germany, the idea of a fixed retirement age took on concrete form at the end of the nineteenth century in connection with the institution of social insurance providing for old age retirement benefits. In this country the largest initial impulse to delimit people's working lives by an upper age limit came from the strong late-nineteenth-century drive to entrench a "merit," or civil-service, system in public employment. In part this movement derived plausible support from blatant abuses under the spoils systems in effect at all levels of government. Selected horror stories of disabled, blind, and lame job holders furnished the necessary emotional support. During the Great Depression of the 1930s, federal legislation put strong pressure on the states to adopt the same kind of merit system, including maximum age provisions.

With the renewed growth of pension programs in private industry following their collapse in the Great Depression, particularly during and after World War II, compulsory retirement age came to obtain virtually general acceptance. The much-cited argument in its favor was the invidious alternative, that is, the *ad personam* determination of an individual worker's capacity for continued work, or lack of such capacity. Age 65 came to obtain the widest acceptance as the normal retirement age—albeit with variations. Typically, hazardous or especially onerous occupations or those critical to public safety or security could command an earlier retirement age, for example, for miners, firemen, policemen, and airline pilots. Sometimes an earlier age would also be applied to women than to men. Higher ages, too, up to age 70, were not unusual, especially in terms of eligibility for certain noncontributory benefits. (See Chen, Chapter 5, and Crown, Chapter 6, this volume, for the effects of various possible retirement ages.)

Much more generally than these instances, there has been in evidence a clear preference among persons approaching retirement age under our Social Security program to take advantage of optional retirement at an earlier than the normal age (65), usually the earliest allowable age (62), even at a loss of nearly a fourth of the pension amount otherwise payable.

The reasons for this far-flung preference for earlier retirement are not clearcut. Is it a preference in the first place? Or is it a result of compelling circumstances beyond the volition of individual workers? (See Sheppard, Chapter 9, this volume, for reasons why many older workers prefer to continue working.) Retirement often comes about as a result of prolonged unemployment or occupational disability. Often companies make early retirement more attractive as a "come on" to rid the payroll of redundant workers.

The statistical evidence of an ever-earlier retirement from work defies any ready or reliable inference that it is a matter of pure choice on the part of older persons.

If anything, the rhetoric of many older persons, organized expressions on the part of their organizations, and, most of all, the logic of the long-term demographics pertaining to older persons point in the opposite direction. For example, perhaps the most unpopular feature of our Social Security benefit rules has been the "tax" on postretirement earning from work. Pressure from older persons has led to successive liberalizations of this feature.

The Age Range Expands

In fact, the dramatic progress in longevity and good health in the upper age brackets has made necessary, or at least plausible, a disaggregation in the grouping of the older population. This has shown itself of real merit in clarifying the operational concepts and points of reference bearing on the subject matter. A report of the U.S. Senate Special Committee on Aging (1984) offers one breakdown:

> This publication will use the chronological concept to look at the population 55 years and older. When possible, statistics will be distinguished for the "older population" (age 55 and over), the "elderly" (age 65 and over), the "aged" (75 years and older), and the "very old" (85 years and over). (p.2)

A simplified subdivision that has obtained some currency, notably in discussing work and employment dimensions of older persons, is to group together persons in the potentially working ages of 50 to 75 as the "third-quarter-of-life" cohort. Those over age 75, sometimes grouped together as the "old-old," are viewed as falling outside presumptive working-age classification.

This latter model or figure of speaking conveys in a nutshell a new and as yet tentative dividing line that could come to replace the outdated symbolism of age 65 as the "normal" boundary of people's working life and contributory role in society. The gradual increase of the statutory normal retirement age of 65 under our Social Security program to higher ages beginning at the end of the current century would then merely acknowledge a transition in our thinking that is already well under way. Of course, some qualifications are necessary. There will always be some people incapable of working to age 75, just as some of those aged 76 and older will be in possession of their full capacities. Besides, paid employment is by no means the only valuable contributory role that older persons can play in society. More on this will be said in the following section.

At this point, suffice it to reiterate the empirical fact that in the United States and elsewhere age cohorts formerly considered "old" are now commonly considered, and in fact prove themselves to be, well within their active years both in their own estimation and in the judgment of the community.

What are the corollaries to this social phenomenon, and what other demographic, social, and economic developments call for recognition? Essentially these:

1. The concomitant growth in both numbers and percentages of those who live to be "old-old," that is, into their eighties and nineties .
2. Dramatic increases in both incidence and prevalence of maladies of old age, notably degenerative diseases with attendant increases in health care costs.

Not connected by any inner logic, but simply simultaneous in occurrence, there has been a significant falling off both in the rate of new births and in the size of subsequently younger age cohorts, both below working age and in the early years of labor force participation.

In terms of social costs, this means that the maintenance of those members of society who are not self-supporting has to be borne by relatively fewer workers (of all ages) than was true in years past— until such time in the future as current demographic trends will yield a different age composition (probably by the second quarter of the next century) or until such time as persons in older age cohorts not now effectively contributing to production can be enticed and will be permitted to do so. Ways and means of achieving this are examined in the subsequent sections. But it is important not to succumb to a kind of panic that exaggerates the extent to which the older population constitutes an unfair "burden" on the active workforce. Professor Henry J. Aaron of the University of Maryland points out:

> In what sense does this cohort of retired persons burden active workers? The correct answer is that it imposes no burden whatsoever. During their working years, the current elderly added to the productive capacity of the economy by their saving. They reap the benefits of this saving during their retirement. Without this saving, output would have been lower than it is. The increase in output attributable to this saving just suffices to pay for the current consumption of the elderly. (Aaron, 1984, p. 19)

Human beings need a realm within which they can bring to bear their particular contribution to the business of life, and an outlet to do so. In most instances what they feel they can contribute is some kind of useful work, paid or otherwise.

But there is a nearly infinite variety of work or, at any rate, participation in a common work effort, and the gradations defy classification. The task consists in fitting such personal outputs to the needs of others or of society at large.

Gauges of Productivity

Commonly we regard as a valid measure of productivity the remuneration that a person's work can command on the market. This market valuation, however, is subject to several qualifying factors. Some are institutional, for example, collective bargaining concerning wages and fringe benefits. Others defy a common denominator, for example, personal circumstances of a worker or work seeker that are known to, or presumed by, the (potential) employer (e.g., the fact that he or she is enjoying an assured income from some other source, say, some kind of pension income).

In my own experience as a retired person, I have repeatedly been offered salaries that seemed to be based on just that assumption, that is, that they would serve as supplementary income.

Is this a true valuation of productivity? I would submit that this question is wrongly put. Realistically phrased so as to elicit a meaningful answer, the question ought to be asked this way: Taking into account the nature of the work, the working conditions, compensation, duration, and so forth, is the particular job worthwhile and acceptable for the one to whom it is offered?

But would not such a frame of reference constitute a violation of established labor standards? Certainly—or most likely—it might be out of compliance with prevailing labor standards. How is one to judge this in the context of providing (additional) opportunities for gainful employment to elderly person, that is, people past "retirement age"? That depends on whether one focuses on society (i.e., the community as a whole) or on just that sector of the population traditionally deemed to comprise all those of working age.

Seen from the latter point of view, the infraction or abandonment of *some* labor standards for the "oldsters" might seem no different from the analogous proposition relating to "youngsters," for example, the introduction of (lower) youth wages. Might this not put us on the road to waiving restrictions on child labor? That is the fear.

Viewed, however, from a societal vantage point, such deviation or, better, differentiation of statutory or regulatory provisions would appear to be quite compatible with the rationale underlying most labor-protective legislation or regulations in the first place. The basic goals, that constitute their justification, such as assuring workers a living wage and full-time employment, may no longer be the issue or may be relevant only in part, for example, with regard to the older worker's health and safety at work. In view of pensions and the continuing accumulation of entitlement to Social Security benefits, there would be no rationale for a guarantee that a particular postretirement job pay a living wage that will produce sufficient aggregate income by itself. Retired workers are in such a unique position that there would be no basis for apprehension that the particular arrangement would necessarily jeopardize the prohibition of child labor or lead to a whittling down of the special rights of women workers who are of childbearing or childrearing age.

A Society Where All Are Needed

An exclamation one frequently hears uttered in jest or in a mood of resignation, "It takes all kinds to make a world," has a very meaningful application in the present context: it suggests that the Good Society will welcome and accommodate, that is, endeavor to use to good advantage, the contributions of all its members, including particularly the work efforts and work products of all those willing and able to engage in work.

The question of payment or other modes of reward, if any, is a separable consideration. It is in the payment or other reward system adopted that incentives and disincentives come to the fore and gain particular importance. The greatest of disincentives, no doubt, lie in barring such contributions or in restricting them by rules that lack justification and plausibility.

Productive Work Effort Outside of Gainful Employment

Past experience in the economically developed nations has tended to focus discussions of productive work and employment almost entirely on paid work in the employ of others, especially in large enterprises—what with mass employment in large-scale industrial economies having been for so long the single most prevalent mode of gainful employment.

In recent decades, however, our growing familiarity with scenarios in newly independent developing nations has caused many economists, especially those engaged in technical assistance work in such nations, to take note of the prevalence and frequency of small-scale private efforts at newly created *self*-employment.

The sum total of these independent initiatives, variously referred to as "underground" or "shadow" economies, often constitutes an important, though elusive, component of economic development.[1]

Activities of this type know no age limits. Perhaps, by loose analogy, unused outlets could be and, no doubt, are being opened up in our type of society and economy by elderly persons retired from gainful employment.

However, monetary gain, normally associated both with employment and self-employment, need not be the only measure of pro-

[1]See, for example, Morgan (1985). Increasingly these activities have called forth positive responses by the governments of these countries in the form of incentive policies toward independent small-scale initiatives being adopted and helped along through low-interest loan programs.

ductiveness, at least in a broader sense than the usual technical economic parlance. By definition useful volunteer work is devoid of any monetary compensation feature; and so, in many instances, is family employment.

Remuneration and Other Rewards

In many cases of gainful employment and self-employment, there are present nonmonetary returns. Economists identify these as such and consider them part of the total *quid pro quo*. Sometimes persons who derive an unusual degree of gratification from their work bespeak their own good fortune over this fact—at least half seriously saying they would do the work even without pay.

Increasingly, we have come to recognize that a person's "work," in the sense of his or her exertion of creative activity, constitutes an act of self-actualization and self-fulfillment essential to human contentment. Along this line, it is maintained that this is an important contributory factor in the recent rapid growth of labor-force participation by married women, notably following their childbearing and childrearing preoccupations. In this sense, then, but not only in this sense, there is a "productivity" aspect for the worker himself or herself and, presumably, for the family and for the community.

This element of "work" seems particularly relevant in respect to elderly persons past "normal working age," and it is enhanced by their concern for full status as citizens in our work-minded society. (This is why the well-meant "alternative" of offering play-type entertainment to such persons has an offensive connotation for many.) What has recently been called the "busy ethic" (Ekerdt, 1986) bespeaks this phenomenon.

Conversely, the beneficial effect for society is widely acknowledged and has been emphasized in certain situations where the advisory role of older persons has become institutionalized. Typical of these instances is the dollar-a-year expert attached to a newly constituted business made up of persons lacking entrepreneurial, managerial, or technical savvy due to limited training or inexperience.

A wide range of such useful elder roles exists based on a variety of qualifying characteristics, from technical know-how to creativeness of an inspirational character. The latter is often ascribed to the proverbial "wisdom" of age. Yet the mere fact of long years of life's experience can be of significance even in the absence of such "wisdom."

It should be made clear that the quality referred to here is *not* primarily one of knowing how to do things. In fact, superior know-how is increasingly being questioned in our age of quick and deep-reaching changes in methods and technologies. Rather, it is the familiarity with much more general aspects of life, such as the sequence of causes and consequences in human happenings that those who have lived through them possess and those who have not, lack. There is an irreducible element of *deja vu* and "nothing new under the sun" that flows only from long years of experience with the business of living in an undulating world. They can serve as a possible knowledge base, but more likely as a source of soothing calm in the face of bewilderment, excitement, and fear entertained by the unweary.

But is it at all realistic and not merely wishful thinking, at least for the foreseeable future, to contemplate a time when all are needed? The prognostications of prominent futurists have given us widely differing scenarios bearing on this question. Robert Theobald (1965), for example, foresees an utter scarcity of jobs and employment opportunities due to the rapid progress of technological change leading to ever more labor-saving production techniques and the spread of robotics. So do others. Peter Drucker (1983), by contrast, predicts a growing scarcity of labor, what with the falling supply of new workers due to fertility declines below replacement ratios. Many economists agree, at least for the decades ahead.

Whatever happens, I would pose this question: Can anyone who takes seriously the notion of "one world," while contemplating the vastness of suffering from unmet needs around the globe, really fathom that we will run out of work at any time in the foreseeable future?

BEYOND THE RETREAT FROM THE WELFARE STATE

In his book *Beyond the Welfare State*, Gunnar Myrdal pointed to the necessary transition from mere government intervention—as and when deemed necessary—to planning, even beyond national frontiers (Myrdal, 1967).

The United States, though a welfare state in many ways, has undergone in the Reagan years an almost unbelievable retrogression in social philosophy and action. Witness the recourse to soup kitchens and charity in coping with massive hunger and to emergency shelters as the answer to homelessness. Obviously, to reverse this backsliding must be the starting point of any positive social policy, especially one aimed at fuller participation of older persons in the U.S. economy and society and built on more dignified incentives than despair born of being down and out.

This need not necessarily imply a turn to more regulation or more detailed regulation. What it would have to mean is some public concern with a place for elders (and other vulnerable groups) in the economy as part of—in Myrdal's terminology—the pursuit of a "planned coordination" of the intervention by public, semi-public, and private organizations toward the "created harmony" of the welfare state (Myrdal, 1960, p. 69). In this connection it is to be noted that to Myrdal "the industrial firm [that] is a participant in a national community" moving "in the direction of equity and solidarity," and thus, whether "a family affair or a more impersonal concern . . . is already, in essential respects, 'socialized.'"[2]

Public Policy Incentive #1: The Intergenerational Compact

The conception that all are needed seems very close to, if not implicit in, such a scenario. Its affirmation as a tenet of public policy would by itself constitute the greatest single incentive toward any and all citizen involvement. The premise for that to happen is to retrieve the path toward "the created harmony" of the welfare state.

What does that path consist of? First and foremost, the understanding that society rests on an intergenerational compact. Elders care for the well-being of the young, and the young are concerned for their elders. (This is in contrast to the intergenerational tension described by Moody in Chapter 2 of this volume.) The intergenerational commitment underlies all civilized society and sets a pattern of "creating for others," the archetype of socioeconomic redistribution.

Second, it includes acceptance of a joint responsibility in the realm of social action between government and the citizenry. This is, in essence, what makes a community. Walter Lippmann used to refer to it as a "public philosophy."

What, then, are concrete incentives to that effect, that is, the conditions for calling into being the spirit that all are needed? What are the respective responsibilities that fall to government and to the citizenry in its various private formations, notably business organizations? What are the limitations that must be faced up to, realistically, in making it happen? What are the principal disincentives?

[2]See Morgan, 1985, p. 65. Myrdal (1960) specifically rules out nationalization as not needed.

To bequeath to future generations a livable world implies, first of all, a concern for our common heritage: respect for the self-renewing productive capacity of Mother Earth, the integrity of the environment.

War is the greatest destroyer of all capital, human as well as physical. It annihilates the accumulated wealth that holds the seeds of further development. Nowadays, war is also the greatest threat to our compliance with the ecological imperative. Clearly, war is the most complete denial of the notion that all are needed. Preparation for *nuclear war* compounds the peril, since it jeopardizes the future of not only a particular society but of all humanity. Thus it can readily be seen as the prime disincentive for intergenerational harmony.

By contrast, the promotion of life- and energy-preserving pursuits that open up opportunities for the application of constructive human aptitudes could be considered the master matrix for the development of scenarios that make a place for all. The productive "payoff" of the allocation of human efforts within such a scheme must be measured not only in the direct returns but in the savings achieved by the prevention of waste and destruction.

Public Policy Incentive #2: Investment in Human Beings over the Life Cycle

Human needs change over an individual's lifetime, and so must the nature of societal support. In keeping with this transition, the process and the relative shares of the intergenerational "creating for others" change in direction and intensity. Given the ever-present overall resource limitations, unavoidable choices are bound to arise between competing needs or claims.

Investments with doubtful or unpromising returns will fall short of the urgency of those promising unquestioned success. Gains of very different types must sometimes be weighed one against the other. Some among these quandaries have come to be known as "tragic choices" (Calabresi & Bobbitt, 1978) or "painful prescriptions" (Aaron & Schwartz, 1984). Popular perceptions of these issues sometimes appear ill-informed or unclear. For example, the frequently alleged reluctance of younger cohorts to accept willingly the rising costs of adequate retirement pensions for their elders would appear puzzling—unless it is drummed up and bogus. After all, it is easy to see that in the absence of public provisions of this type, comparable burdens would fall on the shoulders of individual families.

But what about the ever-costlier life-preserving measures needed by older, and especially very old persons, as against pressing but unmet health needs of the young? No less a humanitarian than Kenneth Boulding has raised the specter of a tantalizing dilemma thus: "When it gets . . . to organ transplants, kidney dialysis, and keeping people alive in the state of fundamentally ill health by elaborate and very expensive devices, it is very hard not to feel that a certain revision of the value system is in order" (Boulding, 1985, p. 156).

Such a "revision of the value system" is no small matter, since it would presuppose "the acceptability of death after a reasonable length of life" (Callahan, 1986, p. 265). To put in concretely in terms of a current proposal: Should a right to heart transplants be added to the entitlements under Medicare while we are not providing even the most elementary health protection for the young?

Fortunately, incentives and disincentives with regard to specific public policies of investing in human beings rarely clash with such force. By and large, the wide range of need-specific support systems developed over time have proved themselves, from prepartum child-support schemes to various educational, training, and placement programs throughout the course of a person's life. The task is to make them responsive to some of the newly perceived ways in which older persons can make themselves useful to society and adding to the social product. This has to be broadly understood to comprise any progress toward meeting unmet needs, at the one end of the range, and, at its other end, advancing toward the solution of what Keynes called "man's *real*, his *permanent* problem . . . how . . . to live wisely and agreeably and well."[3]

Public Policy Incentive #3: Social Utilities

A more limited role by government that is in the nature of an incentive is that of enabler or facilitator. For example, the provision of a means of public transport, especially if free of charge or at very low cost, would clearly remove an important obstacle to the mobility of action-oriented, nonworking older persons. The notion of "social utilities," a term coined by Professor Alfred Kahn of Columbia University (Kahn, 1979, pp. 75 ff.), covers various service systems by analogy to the established concept of "public utilities."

[3]For an updated summary of the support systems for older persons, see National Council on the Aging (1986).

Beginnings have been made in several directions, to varying degrees. Free transportation is available to the elderly on the public transport systems of several municipalities, and public transportation at reduced cost or under lessened restrictions now exists on some city, intercity, statewide, and nationwide transport systems.

"Free" medical care has been brought about for the elderly, albeit with severe limitations, in the Medicare program.[4] Wider, broadgauged, in fact generalized implementation of this principle is called for. Safe housing, of course, with ready access to both work locations and recreational areas, is high on the list. Properly maintained public comfort stations of easy access are in critically short supply.

Public Policy Incentive #4: Selective Support of Private Initiatives

Corporate and other business and individual actors on the economic scene (usually epitomized by "the market") are normally profit-oriented and motivated by self-interest. The infusion of a normative content, notably a societal purpose, into their agenda and mode of action is bound to be more limited and roundabout. The most likely vehicle of this infusion will usually be subsidization. For example, retraining efforts during periods of labor scarcity are clearly in the interest of private employers and may draw on their initiative, particularly if public subsidies are available.

The same applies to individual or group-sponsored self-employment initiatives, especially when loan capital and advisory services are proffered. Whenever this is the case, such overall objectives as meeting basic needs and the production of first-rate goods and services may attract new interest. We might at long last face up to tackling the vast reservoir of undone work that cries out to be done. Suitable projects are readily spotted all around us. They bespeak our common neglect of the environment, from sheer ugliness to the existence of a wide array of health hazards. The unquestionable worthwhileness of such tasks and the great variety of work that needs to be done could open up a wide-ranging demand for talent and capacity of virtually any kind.

Moreover, the flexibility of this approach could open up a variety of innovative job content, working schedules, and payment modes or other reward systems. This range of options might open the way for

[4]Extension and ultimately generalization of the health care system and of other social utilities would be conducive not only to greater involvement of the elderly but to citizen involvement generally. For health care scenarios, see Davis (1986).

pilot efforts along unconventional lines, tailored to encouraging work sharing and newly discovered motivations for being, in Keynes's words, "economically purposive for others." Depending on the nature of the projects, there may develop an awareness of the preciousness of nonrenewable resources and the importance of respecting environmental constraints.

Because of the exploratory nature of the activities here envisioned and the variable work arrangements, there may be opportunities for the elderly to bring to bear their particular strengths, while minimizing the disincentive qualities of their particular limitations. (See, e.g., Cahn, Chapter 16, this volume, on "service credits.")

Public Policy Incentive #5: Nonmonetary Recognition of Service

A new, potentially fruitful area of incentives could be the public recognition and acknowledgment of services rendered, especially where these were rendered merely for nominal pay or without remuneration. This would tend to emphasize, in addition to any personal merit, the communal or social significance of the performance. Honorary designations or titles might go a long way in making up for lesser or no pay, especially if structured according to the length and importance of the service rendered.[5] An activity that carries recognition is much more likely to be a source of contentment for the doer. Such community recognition might bring about, for example, a conscientious environmental monitoring and public hazard detection service—no small achievement.

If incentives such as the above are introduced, a new level of public well-being can be reached. Concepts of the welfare state will no longer be limited to benefits bestowed on individuals by an all-caring government. The caring function would then be matched by the full opportunity to use the talents of all citizens in order to enrich the entire society. No people need then be shunted aside from the life of their communities.

[5]I guess, with the many years and miles that separate me from my native Austria, its splendiferous titularities continue to hold me in awe.

REFERENCES

Aaron, H. J., & Schwartz, W. B. (1984). *The painful prescription*. Washington, DC: Brookings Institution.

Barkley, P. W., & Miller, R. L. (1972). *Economic growth and environmental decay: The solution becomes a problem.* New York: Harcourt, Brace, Jovanovich.

Boulding, K. E. (1985). *Human betterment.* Beverly Hills, CA: Sage.

Calabresi, G., & Bobbitt, P. (1978). *Tragic choices.* New York: Norton.

Callahan, D. (1986). Adequate health care and an aging society: Are they morally compatible? *Daedalus,* 115, 263.

Daly, H. E. (1986, April). Toward a new economic model. *Bulletin of the Atomic Scientists,* pp. 4–44.

Davis, K. (1986). Aging and the health care system. *Daedalus,* 115, 227–246.

Drucker, P. (1983, June 7). Twilight of the first line supervisor. *Wall Street Journal,* p. 34.

Ekerdt, D. J. (1986). The busy ethic: Moral continuity between work and retirement. *The Gerontologist,* 26(3), 239–244.

Kahn, A. J. (1979). *Social policy and social services* (2nd ed.). New York: Random House.

Keynes, J. M. (1932). Economic possibilities for our grandchildren. In J. M. Keynes, *Essays in persuasion* (pp. 366–372). New York: Harcourt, Brace.

Morgan, T. (1985). The shadow economies: Steps toward estimating their size in Asian countries. *Asian Development Review,* 3(2).

Myrdal, G. (1960). *Beyond the welfare state.* New Haven, CT., Yale University Press.

National Council on the Aging. (1986). *Perspective on aging: NCOA public policy agenda 1986–1987.* Washington, DC: Author.

Theobald, R. (1965). *Free men and free markets.* Garden City, NY: Anchor Books.

Theobald, R. (1976). *Beyond despair.* Washington, DC: New Republic Books.

U.S. Senate, Special Committee on Aging. (1984). *Aging America: Trends and projections.* Washington, DC: U.S. Government Printing Office.

15

The Role of Higher Education in Creating Economic Roles

Scott A. Bass

This chapter will explore the role higher education can play in developing new opportunities for older people to contribute in significant ways to the economic and social needs of our society.

Two simultaneous changes have occurred in the United States in the last 20 years that have created new problems and, as will be discussed, new opportunities for society. The first change is an increase in the number and percentage of able, relatively healthy individuals over age 65 in the population, and the second is a dramatic reduction in the labor force participation of this age group. The following sections of this chapter will discuss the capacity of the current older population to engage in work, their relatively low representation in the workforce, and, finally, how higher education can help to train and involve older people for significant roles in society.

ACTIVE OLDER PEOPLE

The vast majority of the growing population between the ages of 65 and 80 are able and active individuals. According to the American Association of Retired Persons analysis of U.S. Department of Health and Human Services statistics, only 14% of individuals aged 65 to 74, and only 26% of those aged 75 to 84, need functional assistance (American Association of Retired Persons, 1986). Despite the attention frail elderly have received in the literature, only 5% of the elderly population are in nursing homes, and most of these elders are over 80 years old. This is not to say that older people do not have health problems or special health needs; in fact, most older persons have at least one chronic health condition, and many have multiple conditions. The most prevalent of these conditions are arthritis, hypertension, hearing impairment, heart conditions, sinusitis, visual impairments, and orthopedic impairments. Nevertheless, these conditions, although troublesome, are for the most part not debilitating problems and can be managed during routine daily activities.

LABOR FORCE PARTICIPATION

Despite the relatively good health of older people, statistics indicate that their labor force participation has dropped by nearly 45% since 1960. (See Rappaport & Plumley, Chapter 3, and Sandell, Chapter 7, this volume.) Approximately 1 older man out of every 6 and 1 older woman out of every 14 are currently in the labor force. This means that more than 82% of the male population over age 65 and more than 92% of the female population over age 65 are no longer in the labor force (U.S. Bureau of Labor Statistics, 1987).

The consequences of improved health but reduced involvement in employment raises several questions. First, do most people want to stop work? According to a 1981 Louis Harris survey (Harris & Associates, 1981) conducted for the National Council on the Aging, 48% of employees aged 50 to 64 wanted to continue working after age 65. Of those working individuals over 65 who were sampled, 81% said they were not looking forward to retirement. Second, do those who have retired not want to work? According to the same survey, regardless of the position that the older person held prior to retirement, 75% preferred to continue in some kind of paid, part-time, flexible work after formal retirement. If large numbers of older people are physically able to work, and many (though not all) would like some involvement with work, then why are there so few older people in the labor force? The answer to this question requires some further discussion of the different reasons older people are out of work and the obstacles they face in entering or reentering the workforce.

There are many different reasons why an able older worker is currently out of work. Some of these reasons include:

1. *Retirement or early retirement from a previous job.* Such retirement can be totally voluntary, with the individual seeking to end many

years of work in favor of total leisure time. However, retirement can be made so financially attractive that an older person may be seduced into it. Or, on the other hand, the job can be made so unpleasant through threats of relocation, pay increase passovers, job reassignment, and so forth that retirement seems the lesser of two evils. Finally, retirement can be compulsory in certain positions. Although mandatory retirement has been eliminated in at least 13 states, some businesses, universities, and police and fire departments have mandatory provisions that force older workers into retirement.

2. *Layoff and discouragement.* Older workers can be dismissed due to financial cutbacks and join the ranks of unemployed job seekers. Due to age or racial discrimination in employment, the older worker may find it hard to find work and can be easily discouraged, forcing the onset of involuntary retirement.

3. *An infirmity or disability.* An older worker may, for example, develop visual or dexterity problems that make it difficult to perform certain functions required in the job, although able to do other tasks. The employer may prefer to encourage the worker to retire rather than incurring additional costs by retraining the worker.

4. *A change in technology.* In jobs affected by changing technology, older workers may lack the specialized knowledge of younger, newly trained graduates. One avenue for these workers is retirement.

5. *Problems of reentry.* These affect individuals, particularly older women, who have been out of the workforce for many years but, due to a change in circumstances, seek to enter or reenter the workforce. This decision may result from the illness or death of a spouse and a need for additional income, or it may be a result of a desire for the increased social interaction found in the workplace, a desire to begin or continue a career later in life, or a combination of factors. In any case, the lack of a recent job history poses obstacles to finding desirable employment.

6. *Career switches.* Individuals who are unhappy in one career may officially retire from it so they can make the transition to another.

7. *Poor qualifications.* These affect older individuals who have chronic work problems, have a history of unemployment, or lack necessary work skills.

In summary, older people who are currently outside the labor force may be there as a result of a variety of very different circumstances. And their desire for work may vary enormously. Again, according to the Louis Harris survey, we know that if older people had the ability to choose their work situation, most would choose part-time work.

Therefore, the reason that so few older people are in the workforce is a combination of factors that include discrimination, free-market forces, personal choice, health, family obligations, confidence, and skill level. In addition, barriers to work for older people may be found in the rigidity of employment options in the primary labor market.

In seeking to develop a national older-worker policy, it should be kept in mind that, while older workers should have equal opportunity to all employment, many potential older workers may be seeking new flexibility from a job. As well as opening up current primary labor market positions to older people, new and more flexible positions may need to be established that can involve large numbers of able older people in significant productive roles. These positions could operate outside the primary labor market, in the form of a *secondary labor market*. The secondary labor market would provide services which society may find desirable but may not be willing to pay for at current market rates. The secondary labor market would provide these services at less than market rates and afford the worker an expanded level of job flexibility not currently available in the primary labor market (Morris & Bass, 1986). These new positions would allow older people the opportunity for the substantive exchanges found in the workplace, but without the heavy responsibilities traditionally associated with professional work. The capacity of a university setting to serve as a training ground and facilitator for the creation of these new positions for able older people is currently being tested on a pilot basis at the Gerontology Institute at the University of Massachusetts at Boston and will be discussed in greater detail later in the Chapter.

EDUCATION FOR OLDER PEOPLE

In 1981 the Special Committee on Aging of the U.S. Senate developed an information paper on national older-worker policy that was highly critical of the limited role that university settings have played in the area of employment and work for older people. In fact, the paper specifically criticized institutes and schools of gerontology for being "negligent regarding employment issues" (U.S. Senate, 1981).

Universities in general are not known for their responsiveness to changing societal needs. University administrations can encourage, provide incentives, and develop agendas, but the final decision on most academic matters rests with the faculty. Changes in population served, departmental structure, and curriculum are very difficult to bring about.

Robert Paul Wolff, in his book *The Ideal of the University* (1969), indicates that attitudes toward the purpose and mission of higher education within the academy are often divided. There are those academics who believe that the ideal of a university is an ivory tower of intellectual thought, a setting where science, philosophy, literature, and the arts can be studied with a select few, unencumbered by external political or social considerations.

Others view the ideal of the university as a training camp for the professions, where talented, generally young, individuals come to acquire the foundations and skills to become tomorrow's professionals. There are those who believe the university, as a microcosm of society, should strive to reflect the diversity of our society by providing access for those who historically have been excluded from the benefits of higher education. They believe the college community should seek to become the pluralistic, participatory community that has yet to exist in the larger society. Finally, there are those who believe the ideal of the university is as a social architect, providing timely and relevant technical assistance to society. As a consequence of all these conflicting purposes, the university's ability to respond to emerging social problems is limited. Change comes slowly within higher education.

It remains true, however, that over 91% of people over age 65 in the United States do not have a college degree, that many older people desire new, flexible careers, and that the university has the capacity and resources to fulfill this training need. This is perhaps a point that distinguishes public from private academic institutions, where public universities, dependent on taxpayers' support, may be more responsive to serving older learners than the private colleges and universities. Despite the disagreements among faculty as to the purpose of higher education and the appropriateness of career training, disagreement about serving nontraditional students, and disagreement about being responsive to societal needs, university institutes have given some attention in recent years to the role of the older worker. At the same time numerous programs have begun within colleges and universities to serve older people. Few of these programs, however, are concerned with career training for older people.

Essentially there are three categories of education programs being offered by higher education institutions to older people in the United States. The first category of educational programs available to the older person is the *tuition-waiver program within the regular college or university setting.* More than two-thirds of all colleges and universities sponsor tuition-waiver or reduced-rate programs for older citizens (Timmerman, 1985). Most of these programs allow the older person to enroll on a space-available basis after full-fee students have registered, but they offer few supportive services to the older learner. These older students are often highly motivated individuals who are willing to learn in a setting composed of students who, for the most part, are much younger than themselves. Although these older students are quite visible, their numbers across the United States are very small (Kingston, 1982).

The second category of educational programs that serve the older person is the *continuing-education program.* These programs account for the largest enrollments of older persons. Most of these programs are offered on a noncredit basis and are targeted at leisure time or personal-enrichment learning (DeCrow, 1975). The public or private programs that have proven most popular, such as Harvard University's Institute for Learning in Retirement, Elderhostel, or Boston University's Evergreen College, typically involve retired, professional, middle- or upper-middle-class individuals (Covey, 1980; Hiemstra, 1976; Hooper & March, 1978). They receive continuing education credits (or no credits) and carry restricted course loads in a predominantly age-segregated program. These well attended programs, nonetheless, do not reach ordinary, able, working-class seniors who may not have had the opportunity for higher education or who are seeking job skills for employment (Hameister, 1976).

The third category of education programs is the development of *institutes for retired professionals.* These institutes are often designed with university resources that allow older people to plan, administer, and teach their own educational program. Examples of such developments include the Emeritus College at the University of Illinois at Carbondale, and an emeritus center at the Brookdale Institute at Columbia University. These institutes are generally for the benefit of retired professionals and serve both social and intellectual functions.

CAREER TRAINING IN GERONTOLOGY FOR OLDER PEOPLE

Since 1980, with the assistance of a training grant from the U.S. Administration on Aging, the University of Massachusetts at Boston has sought to develop a model program for professional career training in gerontology targeted at the older person. It consists of a certificate program and a separate Gerontology Institute. The certificate program, which fits under the category of a tuition-waived educational program, is now fully operational as a regular university undergraduate training program in gerontology at UMass/Boston. It is currently funded with regular tenure-track, full-time faculty, offers the equivalent of 30 credit hours of instruction in gerontology, and conforms with all state and university requirements for accreditation. The program, however, differs from other tuition-waived programs or other university certificate programs in several important ways. Most importantly, the program was conceived from the outset to serve older learners, and this continues to be its primary objective. As a consequence, new supportive services have been created within the credentialing college unit, the College of Public and Community Service, to assist the older learner in adjusting to college responsibilities. The equivalent of two full-time staff are made available to the older learners who have been away from high school or college on an average of 50 years. The staff provide assistance with registration and other forms (college computerized op-scan forms are most difficult for individuals who have visual difficulties or have never used such forms previously), counseling, and tutoring. In addition, a faculty member has been allocated on a one-course-equivalent basis to assist students with standards for research papers, use of library, discussion of technical reading assignments, and general confidence building around routine academic assignments.

Gerontology classes for students within the program have been consolidated into one day per week, scheduled during the daytime, over two terms, so as to limit travel to and from the college for older people and eliminate rush hour or evening travel. During the second term of study, students are required to complete a supervised direct service placement with a frail elder on a different day of the week. Classes, which average about 28 students in size, are age-integrated, but no class has more than 40% younger students. Teaching in gerontology classes, as in the entire College of Public and Community Service, is designed for adults who have had previous experience and therefore uses the competency-based system of standard setting and evaluation.

As a result of very high student demand, the program doubled in size in 1983. Currently there are 60 full-time students enrolled in gerontology, and there are 124 graduates. The program also provides assistance with job or work placement for graduates and has been very successful with placement of its graduates. The reputation of the program as training highly professional older workers has grown to such an extent that the program now has more employment requests for its graduates than it has candidates.

The only difficulty is that, in keeping with the results of the Louis Harris survey described earlier, most older graduates of the gerontology program prefer part-time employment. Many are seeking professional roles, but with reduced responsibilities. The gerontology program has negotiated with numerous human-service employers about job sharing for older workers, but there are a limited number of professional positions that afford the flexibility the older graduates seek.

The gerontology program sparked a great deal of public attention, particularly around the capacity of older people to embark on significant policy or service roles in society. In 1983 the archdiocese of Boston asked the gerontology program to train in gerontology a number of older men and women affiliated with the archdiocese. For its part the church would commit itself to finding jobs for the graduates in work with the elderly, which would be professional in nature but would not be paid at market rates. As a result of filling a need for able older people affiliated with the church, and of providing rigorous training for productive but flexible roles, the archdiocese found itself oversubscribed with interested applicants.

As the gerontology program continued to grow in reputation and professionalism it became increasingly obvious that the program would have to branch out in new directions and explore possibilities for creating more flexible work options for its graduates. In 1984, the state legislature awarded an annual line item of $175,000 to the college to establish a separate but linked Gerontology Institute which would expand on the earlier work of involving older people in responding to the needs of the elderly. One of the first major programs that the Institute launched was a pilot testing of an internship program in gerontology that created new productive roles for graduates of the certificate program. This educational program fits into the second category of educational training for older people, that of a continuing education program. Graduates of the gerontology program enroll in the internship program on a noncredit basis. Interns in the program study and work together in a group of 6 to 9 people on a technical issue in gerontology. Interns commit two days a week for a one-year period; currently, 21 individuals have volunteered for the pilot program. A small honorarium is provided to the interns.

Three different categories of internships are available, in the areas of elderly housing, insurance, and legal training. Elderly-housing interns are working with the city of Cambridge and the Massachusetts Institute of Technology on the development of a 41-acre parcel in Cambridge. They are supervised as a group by a prominent retired housing expert and are involved as skilled older professionals in all phases of the development. Already, the city has begun requesting other services and analyses from the institute, involving skilled older people on a fee-for-service basis. The second internship involves the state's Medigap insurance regulations. Interns under supervision of one of the state's interveners are conducting research on the feasibility of including hospice care under the insurance regulations. The third internship involves legal training in benefits to the elderly. Training is provided by the college's undergraduate law program, with trained interns being outstationed to legal service offices. In each of these three pilot internships, the institute has sought to develop new flexible roles for able older people where none have existed previously. In this context, the older worker benefits, the community benefits, and the university benefits.

At this time, the Gerontology Institute is working on the development of the third area of education for older people: institutes for retired professionals. This is being done in two respects, the first being an alumni fellowship program that makes competitive financial awards available for ideas of merit that have been developed by gerontology graduates. A second and much larger effort is the establishment of a collaborative of retired professors in the Boston area, who, although not seeking employed roles, can be of service to the community and university.

The future research agenda of the Gerontology Institute is significant, and includes the following items: (1) an examination of the replicability in other settings of the institute's experience; (2) an assessment and review of the UMass/Boston internship program in terms of offering productive work roles responsive to the desires of older people; (3) a review and testing of potential secondary labor market roles in sectors other than gerontology; and finally, (4) an analysis of the feasibility of a state or national Elderly Technical Assistance Corps, which would provide training and stipends for professional policy, planning, or service roles involving older people.

CONCLUSION

In conclusion, the university can play a pivotal role in the training and development of new productive career options for able older people. Older people can be a viable resource, in either the primary or the secondary labor market, in responding to the current and future needs of society. They can take on roles that enhance the quality of life of the worker and those served.

REFERENCES

American Association of Retired Persons. (1986). *A profile of older Americans,* Washington, DC: Author.

Covey, H. C. (1980). An exploratory study of the acquisition of a college student role by older people. *The Gerontologist, 2,* 173–181.

DeCrow, R. (1975). *New learning for older Americans: An overview of national effort.* Washington, DC: Adult Education Association.

Hameister, D. R. (1976). Conceptual model for the library's service to the elderly. *Educational Gerontology, 1,* 279–284.

Harris, L. & Associates, Inc. (1981). *Aging in the eighties: America in transition.* Washington, DC: The National Council on the Aging.

Hiemstra, D. R. (1976). Older adult learning: Instrumental and expressive categories. *Educational Gerontology, 1,* 227–236.

Hooper, J. O., & March, G. B. (1978). A study of older students attending university classes. *Educational Gerontology, 3,* 321–330.

Kingston, A. J. (1982). The senior citizen as college student. *Educational Gerontology, 8,* 43–52.

Morris, R., & Bass, S. A. (1986). The elderly as surplus people: Is there a role for higher education? *The Gerontologist, 1,* 12–18.

Timmerman, S. (1985). Options in aging education for developing institutions. *AGHE Exchange, 8,* 4.

U.S. Bureau of Labor Statistics (1987). *Civilian Labor Force, 1959–1980.* Washington, DC: U.S. Government Printing Office.

U.S. Senate, Special Committee on Aging. (1981). *Toward a national older worker policy.* Washington, DC: U.S. Government Printing Office.

Wolff, R. P. (1969). *The ideal of the university.* Boston: Beacon Press.

16

Service Credits: A Market Strategy for Redefining Elders as Producers

Edgar S. Cahn

When a society has vast unmet needs at the same time that there are large numbers of healthy, energetic productive human beings for whom the society can find no use—even though they would like to be useful—then something is wrong. There was a time when we addressed this paradox by expanding the expenditure of public funds. At present, it appears that unmet needs will increase and human resources will remain untapped, but that there will be no increase in public spending commensurate with need. In theory, private-market mechanisms are supposed to supply what people want. Money functions as the medium of exchange, enabling the market (or the public sector) to match supply and demand and to harness productive capacity in order to meet consumer demand. So far as the people this society has designated "redundant" are concerned, the medium of exchange, money, is not doing the job.

The approach this chapter develops is simply this: *create a new currency*. I call this new currency "service credits." It has been created by law in three jurisdictions in the United States, is being tested (so far successfully) in five, and is under consideration by the legislatures of seven more states.

How does it work? The basic concept is simple: purchasing power earned by producing service is expended to consume services produced by others earning service credits.

The initial experiment took place in Missouri: persons over age 60 earn service credits by providing respite care (to relieve or "provide respite to" the primary caregiver) for older persons; they can then spend those service credits to purchase respite care or homemaker care for themselves of for someone in their family. One might call that the blood bank model—give now, draw later if needed. There are other, more far-reaching models, in various stages of planning and implementation:

- Older persons earn service credits staffing a preschool daycare program. The parents pay with service credits earned in a drivers' pool serving the elderly at night and weekends.
- A congregation, union, or other membership organization pledges to earn a total of several hundred hours per month in service credits, to be held by the organization for use by its members if they need homemaker services, daycare, or other agreed-upon benefits.

The first model, daycare, looks like an intergenerational barter program. The second resembles a rudimentary insurance plan. In short, even though initial experiments have concentrated on the elderly, all the parameters can be expanded:

1. *Services produced.* These might include tutoring for students with special problems or special talents, services to the handicapped, home repair, food preparation, cooperative food purchasing, adult daycare, removal of architectural barriers for the mobility-impaired, posthospital convalescent care, shopping, and escort service.

2. *Who earns.* Present experiments focus on the elderly; but high school students might prefer shopping and chore service; single heads of households might be trained to operate a daycare center with intensive child development components; young men and women could learn basic home repair and home renovation skills.

3. *Who can "spend."* Different degrees of transferability can be provided. For example, a grandson or granddaughter across town could earn service credits as a gift for grandparents so that they could get help when needed. Groups can combine to pool credits earned for members and their families.

4. *Mixed prices.* A two-component price can be charged for the services. Where money must be spent to pay for supplies, materials, capital equipment, or professional services, the price can include a

pass-through charge to cover the money expenditures and a service credit charge to cover the service credit component.

The basic approach is this: *we can begin to address our social problems by creating a new medium of exchange that can convert presently unutilized personal time into a marketable asset that can generate real purchasing power.* This is a local currency that can be authorized by local government, so that initiatives are encouraged without waiting for national legislation. This is a currency that can be "designed" to target specific special problems and specific populations. It is a currency that can be expressly fashioned to reward mutual self-help, extended family support systems, and various forms of "neighborliness" (Buhler, 1986, pp. 103, 233, 241). To the extent that societies traditionally use "moral criteria" to determine the allocation of wealth produced by the society, this currency permits citizens to redefine themselves as contributors and producers—rather than merely as worthy receivers of alms.

The insight behind the proposal is that the real wealth of a society is its people—and the time they are prepared to devote meeting their own needs by meeting the needs of others. If time is the ultimate resource, then the question becomes how to mobilize it. Could a new currency simultaneously reclaim"redundant" people and meet major social needs? By posing the question, we may at least have begun to alter our assumptions about the range of the possible.

THE MECHANICS OF THE PROGRAM

The Statutory Framework

The basic statutory scheme for a service credit program is relatively simple. The statute normally begins by directing the executive branch (either the chief executive or an appropriate department) to establish a computerized service credit system whereby persons can earn service credits providing service to others and can draw upon those credits to secure such services for themselves or their families when needed. The act defines who can earn the credits, what services are to be provided, who may receive the service, and who may draw upon (or be the beneficiary of) the credits earned. Although none of the statutes impose any means test on participation, the legislation may require some determination of actual need before a person who has earned service credits can make use of them to obtain services.

The most controversial part of the legislation is the provision that requires the government to guarantee the integrity of the credits earned. In one way or another this obligates the government to provide some kind of backup system in the event that no one is available to provide a service needed by a person who has earned credits. The rationale for the guarantee is that the government itself has benefited directly from the volunteer services rendered to persons who otherwise might have become a greater burden to the taxpayer. The guarantee is a key provision—but it has also been the primary source of concern to administrators who fear that they may face some vast contingent liability or that persons currently on waiting lists for government services will be bumped in order to give preference to persons who have earned service credits. As discussed later, there are numerous ways to provide the guarantee that prevents these problems.

There are other key provisions of the current legislation already enacted:

1. The legislation provides for an initial year of experimentation, authorizes pilot programs to be established, and mandates a report back to the legislature after a year evaluating the effectiveness of the programs and the feasibility of expansion.

2. The legislation may grant discretionary authority to experiment more broadly with the service credit program—but does not necessarily extend the government guarantee to such experiments. Thus one state expressly authorizes intergenerational programs, whereby older persons could provide tutoring or daycare to younger persons in return for service credits—and the parents or relatives would have responsibility for some kind of payback. No guarantee accompanies service credits earned in such an experimental program.

3. Funds are appropriated to cover the cost of administration, Initial appropriations have been $50,000 for the first year; normally such funds will cover the salary of one coordinator, a computer system to track the credits, and the cost of evaluation. No legislation has provided adequate funds to the local groups that actually operate the program on the community and neighborhood level.

The Legislative Process—Supporters and Opponents

Support for the program has spanned the entire ideological spectrum. Supporters include: (1) those who perceive this as a way to meet critical social needs in a time of fiscal retrenchment; (2) those who regard this as a program to reduce dependence on government, increase voluntarism, strengthen the family, and rebuild community;

and (3) those who perceive the currency as a strategy of enfranchise-
ment for people, because it converts personal time into a marketable
commodity that generates additional purchasing power.

Legislators like it because it enables them to do something for their
constituents without major expenditures. Religious groups have
often come forward spontaneously, saying that the legislation will
enable them to reward volunteers and increase their effectiveness at a
time when the movement of women into the labor market has dried
up much of the traditional volunteer pool. Some of the most moving
testimony has come from older people who feel that, for the first
time, government is saying that they have something to contribute,
that they are valuable human beings—not just a burden to the public
and a threat to the taxpayer

Opposition, either direct or indirect, has consistently been from the
executive branch, particularly the office or division charged with
providing funds for the elderly. It provides them with no substantial
funds to meet the critical needs they face; it only provides one additional staff person; considerable work is required initially in setting
up the program; they are apprehensive about what the guarantee
entails. For the most part, however, they frame their objections as
statements of concern about three matters:

1. *Quality control.* It is dangerous to let volunteers loose on the frail
elderly.
2. *The needs of nonparticipants.* Many who need the service will
never be able to earn service credits. What happens to them? In fact,
this expresses two separate concerns: (1) Will this legislation be used
as a rationale for denying additional funds that are desperately
needed? (2) What obligations are implicit in the guarantee that will
impact immediately upon waiting lists for services?
3. *Effect on voluntarism.* Will this reduce the number of volunteers
now giving so generously without any form of compensation?

This last concern is closely related to a reservation expressed by
some clergy and others who support the legislation but worry that it
may violate the true spirit of volunteer giving, which they feel should
be done without any reward. There is another objection, yet to be
voiced, which should be stated: Will service credits eliminate the
relatively unskilled jobs in the various allied health professions that
are critical entry-level positions for persons from minority and disadvantaged backgrounds?

There are answers to all of these. A partial summary of responses
would include the following:

1. Quality control must be provided through screening, training, spot checks, phone calls, and so forth.

2. Existing services must be maintained and expanded separately from service credits; there should be no "bumping" of persons on waiting lists.

3. The guarantee can be implemented by a variety of strategies that impose no additional costs on government and displace no persons on the waiting list.

4. Politically, those in need of services are in a stronger position to demand a more equitable share of public funds if they are also perceived as contributing to meeting the needs of society.

5. Service credits are intended to expand the supply of volunteer labor, both by bringing in new persons and by securing larger and more dependable commitments over extended periods of time; so far, there has been no "displacement" or substitution; there appears to be an absolute increase. But only time and research will tell.

6. Pure altruism can be facilitated by permitting a person to donate service credits earned to a charitable organization. One minister stated it this way: "One hour gives twice: once to the patient, the other to God."

7. There is nothing wrong with combining altruism with some element of self-interest. Taking care of one's own, or one's family's needs by helping others will strengthen family, neighborhood, and community.

8. Service credits may provide an avenue to entry-level jobs and a way of breaking out of the catch-22: "We are looking for employees with experience. But the only way you can get the needed experience is to be performing a job where prior experience is required."

One stance must be made clear at all times: Service credit legislation can *only* supplement available resources and basic entitlements; it must *not* be perverted into a rationale for reducing entitlements or reducing allocations to meet social needs. Service credit volunteers have two potent weapons to prevent the program from being misused by government as a pretext for cutbacks or a refusal to increase funding levels. They can stop volunteering *en masse*, and they can act in concert to spend their credits (or designate persons in dire need as beneficiaries), thus triggering a run on the bank.

Implementation—The "Nuts and Bolts"

A two-tier administrative structure is needed to implement service credits. At a minimum, the department or division charged with administering the act has to set up a bookkeeping system to keep track of credits earned and spent and to enter into agreements with local organizations and institutions to do the actual recruitment, training, and placement of volunteers. The agreement is at the core of the program; it specifies the responsibilities of each party. The state government normally develops registration and reporting forms, enters the credit hours for eligible volunteers into the computer data system, issues periodic statements of service credits earned, provides technical assistance to agencies and communities, and produces public information materials. The community organization has the tougher job: it must recruit, screen, and register the volunteers, provide adequate liability insurance, provide training and supervision, refer volunteers to persons or families needing services, and report credit hours to the state on an ongoing basis—and somehow coordinate those activities with everybody and everything.

The following variations have already been grafted on to that basic pattern:

1. In addition to using community groups, Florida is also experimenting with running one pilot program out of the state government's own regional offices.

2. In the Greater Miami Area, a group of local organizations have formed a consortium to pool resources, refer volunteers, establish operating procedures, and provide an ongoing "barter" exchange, so that service credits can be "spent" with another organization to secure different services.

3. In the District of Columbia, where a community hospital launched the program nearly six months prior to enactment of the legislation and invested large amounts of money in program development, the city government is considering contracting out the job of service credit coordination to the hospital, which would then oversee the development of pilot programs throughout the area.

Because the laws require the preparation of an evaluation report for submission to the legislature after a year of testing, evaluation is taking place focused on three concerns: cost effectiveness, impact on the supply of volunteers, and quality control.

The Guarantee

At this point, no state has yet been able to gear up in a meaningful way to implement the guarantee provision; thus responsibility for honoring credits earned realistically rests on the local operating agency. Fortunately, there has been no occasion to trigger use of the guarantee—and none appears likely in the near future. At least four mechanisms are available to the local government to honor the guarantee by creating "reserves" without incurring increased expenditures or contingent liability:

1. Organizations can secure the first services to their members (who have never had the chance to earn credits) in return for undertaking to set up a reserve corps of volunteers on standby to honor the guarantee.

2. Contractors with the local government willing to set up volunteer reserves can be awarded extra points in competitive bidding or be permitted to use such reserves to meet matching requirements.

3. Employee incentive programs can offer preferred holiday selection and rotation, flex-time scheduling, more generous carryover provision for such leave and vacation leave, or priority access to slots in training programs to induce public employees to join a standby reserve corps.

4. Preferential access to discretionary benefits could be used as inducements to develop a reserve corps available to honor the guarantee (e.g. college or vocational-technical school students could "qualify" for, or be given priority ranking in securing, low-interest loans or student housing).

The Role of Local Organizations

A volunteer paid with service credits is like an employee. Both have to be carried on payroll; they are just paid in a different currency. To a local organization, access to this new currency is like access to a grant that will enable them to put a potentially unlimited number of volunteers on "payroll." But it is a matching grant: the organization has to put up the administrative costs and, because the program is without precedent, those can be substantial at the outset.

In some instances, grants have come from foundations and from local Area Agencies on the Aging to bear some of the costs and enable the organization to secure an additional full-time professional employee to take responsibility for developing and launching the program. In another instance, a hospital has made a major investment of internal resources—both personnel and funds—to develop and launch the program. The dominant motivation was to enable the hospital to reach out and serve the community better by providing home-based care to the population served. But there were elements of self-interest that made service credits appear to be a sound long-term investment. Cost-containment efforts increase pressure for early discharge of patients who do not need the level of care provided by a hospital but who nonetheless must anticipate a period of extended convalescence. Service credits create a vehicle for a hospital to assure an appropriate level of care that is consistent with prompt discharge and that has significant fiscal implications. In the United States, a nonprofit hospital has additional reasons to become involved: community outreach provides the hospital with a "feeder system" that enables it to keep beds filled and to compete successfully with highly aggressive marketing by for-profit hospitals, which are now expanding at a phenomenal rate.

Even if foundation grants are available, service credit programs at the outset will absorb the energy of the leadership and top management to a degree never adequately compensated by grants. The organizations that have become involved do so because they are convinced that service credits will enable then to fulfill their mission in a period when fiscal constraints would otherwise force them into a holding action. In Miami, a consortium of interested community groups identified some of the critical common needs where an initial investment would be of common benefit: (1) training materials and training programs; (2) public information materials, such as brochures, slide/tape presentations, press releases, newsletters, and files of newspaper clippings; (3) management systems, including an operating manual, forms, a record keeping system, and an analysis of functions; and (4) an evaluation and research design.

Foundation and other funds have now paid for the development of:

1. A computerized management information system that tracks volunteers from initial inquiry, through training and then during all subsequent assignments, facilitates matching service providers and service users, keeps a continuing tally of credits earned and credits spent, generates monthly reports on program performance, stores data needed for evaluation purposes, and increases the effectiveness of monitoring and quality-control systems, This management information system is different from the limited credit-and-debit system that the state government has to maintain.

2. A training material library. A collection of training programs from different states and organizations provides a resource without imposing a uniform curriculum. Different organizations have different philosophies and different training needs, even when providing

identical services. The library resource was developed so that each did not have to "reinvent the wheel."

3. Public information materials. Brochures, narratives, and photos for a slide/tape show, sample press releases, and a clipping file have been assembled.

4. Two management systems have been developed: (1) an operations and procedures manual for use and adaptation by organizations initiating a service credit program; (2) a manual of strategies for delegating specific management functions to volunteers in stages so that administrative staff costs can be reduced and even eliminated over time.

5. Evaluation instruments have been designed to measure client satisfaction; other instruments have been developed to study the effect of service credits as an incentive to expand the quantity of service available, the number of volunteers, the quality and duration of the commitment, and the impact of service credit programs on traditional volunteer efforts.

In addition, other initial problems have been identified and surmounted. An IRS ruling has been obtained determining that service credits are not to be treated as taxable income; inexpensive liability insurance has been secured to insure that injury to either the volunteer or the client is compensated; application forms, request-for-service forms, record keeping systems, a code of ethics, and other materials have been developed and refined.

Coordination Issues

Tension has arisen between the government (which is primarily concerned with the guarantee, fiscal responsibility, and impact on funded programs) and the local programs, which want a considerably freer hand and much greater flexibility in responding to need and in motivating volunteers.

The most important coordination problems arise in the context of trying to operate on a metropolitanwide basis. No single community-based organization is likely to have credibility throughout a metropolitan area; none has the capacity to reach all potential volunteers or clients; and none is entitled to a local monopoly on service credits to the exclusion of other volunteer organizations. This has meant establishing a framework within in which organizations could collaborate with, reinforce, and help each other, to their mutual advantage. It is clearly to the advantage of each organization to make service credits as attractive as possible to earn. If credits earned in one program can be spent to purchase services from another organization, then the "currency" becomes more useful. Thus, for example, service credits earned providing daycare for children might be spent to purchase homemaker services for an elderly relative or spouse. Or service credits earned providing respite care for a hospice for terminally ill patients might be spent securing transportation or home repair services with another program.

Younger relatives living in one part of town might earn credits with one program that their grandparents living in another part of town might wish to use with the local organization that serves their neighborhood. This requires the establishment of some kind of centralized clearinghouse. Such a clearinghouse would refer volunteers to appropriate local organizations, keep a central data bank on all credits earned throughout the system, and match credits spent with one program against credits earned with another.

Control over that centralized "banking" and "referral" function is perceived as power both in itself and as a means of access to funding sources. Designation of the locus of those centralized functions needs to be determined collaboratively and should be subject to a policy board that represents the constituent organizations. Since there is always rivalry for organizational turf and recognition and there is frequently a history of distrust among different neighborhoods and different ethnic groups, the establishment of such a consortium requires a good deal of process and the nurturing of relationships of trust. There has been a consistent unwillingness on the part of community groups to permit a local governmental entity to discharge that coordinating function.

THEORETICAL ISSUES

The service credit currency is the equivalent of an open-ended legislative appropriation that can be used *only* for the rendering of actual service, without the need for elaborate bureaucratic machinery to enforce that restriction and monitor compliance. It is a "tied" currency—tied to service and service alone.

An increase in monetary expenditures for service will not yield the same result. It is well recognized that pumping money into a social service system will not necessarily generate more and better service.

The expenditures get diverted to institutional priorities. Top management's salaries must be increased to insure that they do not accept higher-paying positions elsewhere; top performers must be rewarded; long-delayed adjustments to the cost of living must be made to prevent staff demoralization; there are backlogs of filing and paper work that can only be dealt with by hiring a few more clerical and support staff; obsolete equipment must be replaced in order to improve efficiency; training programs must be instituted to upgrade staff skills. Only after those priorities have been met are funds likely to be allocated to meeting client needs—and then, by linear extension of past "production methods," no matter how inefficient.

Service credits thus can be a catalyst for change in service systems, because they reverse the traditional hierarchy of prestige and allocation of resources between social service providers and administrators. They provide an ongoing test of whether each function must be discharged by a full-time, qualified staff person rather than by an unlicensed, part-time, nonprofessional. While the degree to which nonprofessional service can be substituted for professional or highly skilled service is open to question, the tendency of money-driven systems is to expand professional claims to an expertise-based monopoly over more and more spheres of activity. Service credits reverse the presumption and provide a continuing test of the extent to which unskilled labor can be substituted.

Substituting purchased services at market prices for each of the functions historically performed by the family would be staggeringly expensive. And there are limits to the extent to which one can divide and contract out the functions of rearing, nurturing, valuing, supporting, choosing, consoling, and providing emotional sustenance. In the context of providing services for the elderly, for dependent children, or for the poor, nonmarket exchange systems may have a potential efficiency analogous to that of the family regarded as a multipurpose economic unit.

The Absence of Pricing: Intrinsic Versus Extrinsic Rewards

Service credits differ from money in the value necessarily assigned to the nonmonetary, or "intrinsic," reward component of the exchange. Payment in service credits does not purport to constitute full compensation as defined by the market—if only because service credits cannot be used to purchase the range of goods and services that money can. It is understood that a measure of the compensation is gained from the rewards associated with helping others.

Money is neutral with respect to intrinsic rewards. It does not
prevent considerations of intrinsic rewards from entering into market
transactions; but neither does it *require* that such considerations be
assigned any value whatsoever. Payment in money represents
"adequate compensation" defined as the full value that the market
assigns to one's labor.

Service credits, in contrast, are decidedly not neutral in promoting
the valuation of intrinsic rewards associated with helping others.
They explicitly and implicitly assign compensatory significance to the
intrinsic "praiseworthiness" of the task. When one earns a service
credit, the compensation received includes an ambiguous "noncredit" component whose worth varies from person to person. The nature
of the exchange assumes a reciprocity only partially reflected in the
quantity of currency earned. The "tax exempt" status of the service
credit recognizes and legitimates this other component—but it does
not purport to compensate it.

This still leaves open the question of whether service credits are
sufficiently attractive to induce persons to earn them. But the currency itself defines compensation in a way that necessarily incorporates
intrinsic reward. Where marginal benefit (of earning service credits)
equals or exceeds marginal cost, then even the classic "optimizer" of
economic literature will elect to earn them. The inquiry is useful
because it compels focus on the components of "utility" and on the
essential role that *intrinsic rewards* play in making service credits
viable from an economist's perspective.

We start with the traditional distinction between those rewards that
are *extrinsic* to what one does and those rewards that are *intrinsic*
because they stem from the satisfaction one gets from doing the job.
The purchasing power earned—whether in money or in service credits—is an extrinsic reward (i.e., received regardless of whether the job
is personally satisfying or not).

Extrinsic reward refers to the purchasing power of the pay received,
whether in service credits or dollars: the market value or utility of the
services that a credit buys; the immediacy and certainty with which
the service credits earned will be used by self, spouse, or another to
whom one feels a sense of duty; the enhanced security and autonomy
that accumulated savings impart.

Intrinsic reward refers to the value attached to altruism, to decreased
dependency, and to an enhanced sense of self-worth and self-esteem:
the value of being needed, the approval one gets from relevant
others, the value of social contact with clients and others associated
with the service credit program, the skills and coping competency
acquired or confirmed, the structure that scheduled obli-

gations impart to one's personal life, the welcome distraction or escape from preoccupation with one's own problems, and the extent to which dependency and vulnerability are felt to be reduced because future service is now available as a right.

Marginal Cost

In any exchange, costs as well as rewards need to be estimated. Extrinsic costs include: direct, out-of-pocket costs (transportation, meals, phone); indirect costs (clothes, grooming, cleaning, extra meal preparation); and opportunity costs—employment income or economies forgone, leisure sacrificed and obligations (with cost implications) incurred; time expended for preparation, travel, and actual provision of services; and "recovery time" needed to disengage, unwind, and reenter one's own world.

Intrinsic (psychic) costs include unpleasantness of the task, fear of the unknown, personal anxiety aroused by the nature of the work, emotional energy expended in juggling personal obligations, stress associated with deferring dealing with personal obligations or shifting them to other members of the household, stress associated with reduction in leisure time.

Since volunteers now contribute considerable time *without* earning service credits, we know that the intrinsic rewards of volunteering are an adequate inducement *for some*. The key question us whether the addition of service credits will make volunteering sufficiently more attractive to others on a scale that equals or exceeds the administrative costs of the system. Paradoxically, the primary initial contribution that service credits make may well be through enhancing the intrinsic rewards of volunteering rather than by providing an extrinsic reward of somewhat ambiguous worth. Until service credits establish a track record, their extrinsic value will be regarded with skepticism and their greatest value may stem from ways in which they operate to enhance the prestige and status associated with helping others. Service credits do this in a number of ways. Sheer quantification in our society seems to impart additional reality and status to a contribution. The legislative imprimatur of service credits and their tax exempt status confer official approval and recognition to volunteers; the monthly "statement" of credits earned provides regular reinforcement for that approval. Moreover, volunteers earning service credits are likely to be entrusted with more challenging and satisfying work: those administering the program regard service credits as a vehicle for demanding accountability and requiring satisfactory performance—something normally lacking in volunteer contexts. Working for service credits also makes volunteering virtually indistinguishable from regular, part-time employment and for some, may function to facilitate entry into the job market by providing credentialing in the form of an "employment record" complete with employer references and records on performance and absenteeism.

Finally, service credits can tap resources the monetary system does not reach because they lower opportunity costs at two levels: the level of social policy formation and the level of individual choice. Public expenditures for human services compete with other national priorities—including military requirements and national debt constraints. Money allocated to human services necessarily must be taken from some other urgent priority. Services paid for with service credits are not subject to the same competitive pressures. A locally delimited service credit program designed to meet local needs is not in competition with needs that can only be met with the dominant currency. Service credits are perceived as a "no-cost" program (except for administrative expenses). They enable human needs to be met without facing heavy competing demands at the local or national level.

On the level of individual choice, persons such as the elderly do not perceive themselves as forgoing remunerative employment in order to earn service credits. Opportunity costs are lowest for those groups with least opportunity. We tend to regard our leisure time as a "renewable resource," so that opportunity costs are perceived to be low. It "feels" costless to earn a credit, particularly when what we get is not subject to taxes or to devaluation from inflation.

An Emergent Consequence: The Dynamics of Hope

The foregoing dynamics arise as direct, first-generation consequences of the characteristics of service credits, taken one at a time. Taken together, there are emergent consequences. A dynamic of hope arises when one removes barriers to aspiration imposed by present market-bound thinking about individual needs, social justice, and human potential. The dynamic derives partly from the significance of being defined as a contributor and producer rather than a consumer and supplicant, partly from the availability of "employment" for persons who had internalized the judgment that they were "redundant," and partly from the impact of a new set of social norms generated by a synergy of altruism and self-interest. The following enumeration describes a few identifiable components of this dynamic—the dynamic of hope.

Reduced Stigma for Service Recipients

The perception of stigma by service recipients comes from within and without. They perceive themselves as powerless; but elements of condescension, insensitivity, and paternalism corroborate that sense of powerlessness. To the extent that services are *purchased* with credits earned, service recipients may perceive themselves as *consumers* rather than *donees*. As former producers of the very services they are consuming, they are likely to be unusually informed consumers. To the extent that they receive services for which a group or organization to which they belong is liable as "co-signer," they may feel able to repay that organization by being a more useful and active member. And they may feel able to turn to that organization to complain and to advocate on their behalf. That will not happen automatically —but it is a new and different possibility.

The Global-Village Effect

In an age in which moralists lament the loss of authority as destructive to the formation and reinforcement of the superego, service credits drive an information system that makes behavior highly visible and simultaneously create a relevant world of approval or disapproval. The result may be some version of McCluhan's global village, imposing expectations about what behavior is unacceptable and what behavior is socially valued. Service credits place value on activities other than material consumption and the accumulation of wealth for its own sake.

Self-Sufficiency: The Antidote to Specialization

The market system relies upon and rewards specialization and delegation. Specialization and delegation in turn produce professionalization and hierarchy. Service credits do not pay for either. They pay for relatively unspecialized labor and they pay only for the rendering of service. Specialization and delegation thrive upon crisis to justify their existence and to generate the level of dependency that will assure sustained support. Those who live by specialization and delegation need demonstrable, tangible results for which they can claim distinctive credit. Maintenance, prevention, preservation, and rehabilitation tend to lack these characteristics; they necessarily involve the beneficiary as co-producer.

Avoiding Substitution of Voluntary Service for Statutory Services

There is danger that efforts to generate an increased volume of volunteer service through creation of a service credit currency will be turned into a rationale for cutting back on entitlement expenditures or on projected increases in expenditures for services. The problem arises not only in the aggregate but also on the individual level— where access to services may be conditioned upon exhaustion of "earned" service credit benefits.

The individual problem can be avoided by appropriate legal and/or administrative strategies. The legal strategy would structure service credits as a form of supplemental insurance, with access to service credit benefits conditioned upon prior application for or exhaustion of statutory benefits. Administratively, there would appear to be room for integrating service credit services into a case management system. Under certain experiments going forward in both the United States and the United Kingdom (Challis & Davies, 1984), a "budget" is given to case managers to purchase a package of services from local "helpers" for services individually tailored to the needs of the client and subject to rapid modification to meet changing circumstances. These experiments have targeted those frail elderly persons in imminent danger of needing institutionalized care, with a view toward enabling them to retain maximum autonomy as long as possible—and with a view toward reducing public expenditures on residential and institutional care.

The major new resource, developed with the budget, has proved to be the use of local people as helpers, whether or not previously part of an elderly person's social network, to perform specified tasks for individuals, usually for relatively small payments. The actual fee paid is agreed upon by the social worker and the individual helper and may vary according to the task to be done, the characteristics of the elderly person in question, the time at which the task is done, and the circumstances of the helper. Payment is not for a given time but for the performance of the task. While the provision of human caring resources is clearly an essential requirement for most of the elderly people, it was noticeable that this extra help has been, on the whole, recruited by the teams or was already part of an elderly person's social network; it has not been provided through the private sector or voluntary agencies.

The political problem is tougher than the legal and administrative problems. Reasonable solutions would be easy if there were a consensus that the national government could be trusted to reward rather than exploit voluntarism. In the absence of trust, the issue becomes one of negotiating from strength rather than weakness. How can one increase the likelihood that service credits will result in an equitable *increase* (rather than an expedient *decrease*) in the share of national resources to which the elderly or the needy have access?

The development and implementation of a win–win strategy in which the elderly, the unemployed, and others outside the labor force can all participate to enlarge the national pie is essential if the elderly and the poor are to secure a more equitable share of that pie. Without someone taking the first step, both the citizen and the government will find themselves boxed into the position that no human being can help another human being unless he or she is paid an "appropriate" wage. That will lock all into a zero sum game in which the poor and the elderly can win only if someone else loses.

The alternative strategy will take vigilance and planning for a worst case scenario. Yet the gain seems worth the risk. The problems are vast. So are the untapped human resources. But it will require a currency that nurtures and rewards our impulse to give, to contribute, to learn, and to develop.[1]

[1]An earlier version of this Chapter appeared as Discussion Paper # 8, London School of Economics, July, 1986, London, England.

REFERENCES

Buhler, M. (1986). *Neighbours: The work of Philip Abrams* Cambridge: Cambridge University Press.

Challis, D., & Davies, B. (1984). *Home care of the frail elderly: Matching resources to needs.* Discussion Paper 329/1, Personal Social Services Research Unit, University of Kent at Canterbury, England.

Index